Felony Justice

Felony Justice

An Organizational Analysis of Criminal Courts

James Eisenstein
The Pennsylvania State University

Herbert Jacob
Northwestern University

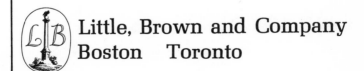 Little, Brown and Company
Boston   Toronto

Preface

Much of what the general and professional public believes to be true about criminal courts is not. The judge does not always play a dominant role. Plea bargaining is not universally prevalent; it does not lead to distinctively lighter sentences than bench or jury trials. Sentencing disparities within cities are not a fundamental problem. Blacks are not treated worse than whites; public defenders are not less effective than retained counsel; jailed defendants are not consistently convicted more often than those who win their release before trial. Defendants who escape conviction do not escape all punishment. Justice delayed is not necessarily justice denied.

Those are some of our findings about the felony disposition process in Baltimore, Chicago, and Detroit in 1972–1973. We do not know whether they apply fully in other cities and other years, although we suspect that many of them do. However, as this study repeatedly makes apparent, there are many variants of the felony disposition process. We purposely chose three cities which we knew at the outset differed, but they do not represent the total range of variation. Los Angeles has still a different system, using bench trials as slow pleas on the basis of the record at the preliminary examination.[1] Neubauer's description of a small Illinois city represents still another dimension.[2] However, we believe that our theoretical framework is applicable to those situations.

In this book we attempt to place criminal courts in a larger theoretical perspective. Although we deal only with felony dispositions in Baltimore, Chicago, and Detroit during 1972–1973, we borrow heavily from organizational theory in order to develop a more general understanding of how courtrooms do their work. Unlike many studies of trial courts or the criminal process, ours does not focus on a single participant. In our view, what judges, prosecutors, defense counsel, and others do depends heavily on how they interact with one another. None works alone. Rather they are interconnected through an intricate system of countervailing powers. Thus courtrooms are small but nevertheless complex organizations.

Our descriptions of Baltimore, Chicago, and Detroit apply in detail only to the period of our study, 1972–1973. Since then some changes have occurred in each city, so that the reader who went to a courtroom there would not find things exactly as we describe them. None of those changes, however, have been fundamental, and the reader should be able to understand them by applying the organizational framework that we develop in the following pages.

This book has been a truly joint venture. It began in 1971 when Jacob wrote Eisenstein about collaborating in a study of plea bargaining. We then jointly developed the research design and grant proposal. Eisenstein took principal responsibility for the collection of data in Detroit; Jacob was responsible for the data collection in Chicago and supervised it in Baltimore. We jointly developed the codebooks for reducing the data into machine-readable form and supervised the coding and keypunching. For those who are interested in such minutiae, Eisenstein

1. Peter W. Greenwood, et al., *Prosecution of Adult Felony Defendants in Los Angeles* (Santa Monica, Calif.: Rand Corporation, 1973), pp. 20–24, 33–46; Lynn M. Mather, "The Outsider in the Courtroom: An Alternative for the Defense," in Herbert Jacob (ed.), *The Potential for Reform of Criminal Justice* (Beverly Hills, Calif.: Sage Publications, 1974), pp. 263–289.

2. David W. Neubauer, *Criminal Justice in Middle America* (Morristown, N.J.: General Learning Press, 1974).

wrote the first drafts of chapters 4, 5, 6, 9, and 11; and Jacob wrote the first drafts of chapters 1, 2, 3, 7, 8, and 10. However, each chapter was fundamentally rewritten by the other author and then revised several times more by both. The book would not be what it is if either of us had written it alone; we think it is better for the joint effort.

We owe thanks to many. A grant from the National Science Foundation made it possible for us to collect the data and spend two years analyzing it. Jacob's year as Fellow at the Center for Advanced Study in the Behavioral Sciences made possible much of the underlying analysis. Carol Traynor provided invaluable assistance on the computer during that year. Roy M. Flemming was an indispensable research assistant in Baltimore, where he collected our data with competence and efficiency that belied his graduate student status. Lee Luskin in Detroit and Peter Nardulli in Chicago were valued research assistants; Greg Lord helped with the field research in Detroit and provided valuable assistance in the computer analysis at Penn State. The Institute for Social Research at the University of Michigan coded and keypunched much of the data. A large crew of graduate and undergraduate students assisted us, including Robert Anderson, Jean Baines, Craig Buettinger, Daniel Harris, Anne E. Hayduk, Robert Lech, Cherry J. McCall, Adolph W. Miles, Toni M. Miles, Carol Morgan, Janice Pangrazzi, Flora Pelino, Jim Reynolds, Arthur F. Roizman, Katherine Sarantos, Dan Talbot, and Marvin Weinberg. We also owe special thanks to Jeri Jensen, Barbara J. Hegenbotham, and Lucille Mayer for their assistance in preparing the manuscript.

We also want to thank the prosecutors, defense counsel, judges, and clerks who responded to our inquiries so graciously and at the very least tolerated our very long stay in their bailiwicks. Likewise a number of colleagues made extraordinarily helpful suggestions on an earlier draft. None of these persons nor the National Science Foundation is responsible for the interpretations reported here or for any errors of omission, commission, or emphasis.

Several dissertations and other papers have also resulted from this research. They include:

Herbert Jacob and James Eisenstein, "Sentences and Other

Sanctions in the Criminal Courts of Baltimore, Chicago and Detroit," *Political Science Quarterly*, December 1975, pp. 617–635.

James Eisenstein and Herbert Jacob, "Measuring Outputs of Urban Criminal Courts," *Social Science Quarterly* 54 (1974): 713–724.

Peter N. Nardulli, "The Court Organization: An Organizational Analysis of the Felony Disposition Process in Chicago," unpublished Ph.D. dissertation, Northwestern University, June 1975.

Roy M. Flemming, "Allocating Freedom and Punishment: A Study of Pretrial Release in Three Cities," Ph.D. dissertation, University of Michigan, in progress.

Janet M. Gilboy, "Perspectives and Practices of Defense Lawyers in Criminal Cases," unpublished Ph.D. dissertation, Northwestern University, June 1976.

Contents

PART I | The Theoretical Framework

The disposition of felony cases involves many persons who work in complex settings. Convicting and sentencing a criminal requires more than good police work, vigorous prosecution, or well-managed courts. Defense counsel and witnesses must also be marshalled. And all during the process the traditional rights of defendants who are legally presumed innocent until convicted must be protected so that (ideally) no innocents are punished. All this must be done in a coordinated way to produce some semblance of swift justice.

It is not done that way in the United States. In part that is because few people understand the complexity of the process or appreciate the difficulties of integrating the many elements of it into a smoothly operating whole. In these first three chapters, we shall examine the scope of the problem and present an organizational perspective that helps make sense of the complicated interactions which occur as criminal courtrooms process felony defendants.

Chapter 1 | INTRODUCTION

On the evening of January 21, 1971, John N. stepped off a CTA bus on Chicago's south side into the blustery winter wind on his way home from work. It was late and the street seemed empty. But as he passed an alley, a group of men jumped him, beat him up, and took his wallet with his week's pay. John N. fought back, and when his assailants fled, he hailed a passing squad car, hopped into it, and together with the policemen found the gang five blocks away. James P., eighteen years old, Ronnie S., twenty-one years old, and Sammy D., a twenty-four-year-old ex-con, were arrested and charged with robbery and aggravated assault.[1]

Eighteen months later, after fifteen court appearances for six of which John N. appeared to testify, all charges were dropped against James P. and Ronnie S. Sammy D., the ex-con, pleaded guilty to attempted assault and was placed on twelve months' probation.

Why this result? Was it because the victim and offenders were black? Because they were defended by a private attorney? Because they copped their plea through a plea bargain? Because of the judge assigned to the case? Would the result have been different if the incident had occurred in another city, perhaps in Detroit or Baltimore rather than in Chicago? Many Americans puzzle over such questions. On the one hand, they realize that criminal courts have extraordinary power over ordinary citizens. Few government decisions affect citizens more profoundly than those made in the criminal process, for courts decide who shall be labeled a criminal and who shall be deprived of liberty or even life. Such decisions shape the content and dynamics of public order.

At the same time, the general public has become increasingly uneasy about its safety and about the apparent ineffectiveness of the courts to deal with the crime problem. Not only has law and order been a prominent issue in presidential elections since 1964, but public opinion polls at both the local and national levels indicate that public safety is also a salient issue for many persons. The government's response has been to throw money at the problem. The federal government organized a new agency, the Law Enforcement Assistance Administration, and endowed it with hundreds of millions of dollars to combat crime. But our understanding of what causes crime, how the criminal courts work, and what can be done about convicted criminals remains much the same as before. The characteristics of the criminal justice system are as obscure as if they existed on some distant planet rather than in our own cities and towns. The number and type of criminal proceedings in American courtrooms still remain unexplored. Although we have discovered the number of jails and prisoners in them we still have no firm evidence about how decisions are made to send people to jail.[2]

This book is an attempt to reduce our ignorance of major criminal proceedings. It will also expose as false many common opinions about criminal justice. We focus on felony courts, which lie at the heart of the felony disposition process. That process encompasses all events from the moment of a person's arrest to the day when the charges against him are disposed of. Although that process also involves police and correctional facilities, felony courts play a central role.

PRECONCEPTIONS AND MISPERCEPTIONS

Public understanding of felony disposition and how felony courts make decisions remains murky despite numerous explanations. Some explanations focus on the characteristics of defendants; others emphasize the characteristics of decision-makers. Still others focus on the operation of legal procedures. The trouble is that none adequately explains the variety of outcomes that we observe in felony courtrooms. Moreover, they conflict with one another. A quick look at them will expose these weaknesses.

Characteristics of Judges as Explanations of Courtroom Actions. The judge is the most prominent person in the courtroom and appears to be the most powerful. It is natural for many descriptions of what happens in criminal courts to focus on characteristics of judges. Many observers note that sentences vary from one judge to another; but attempts to explain that variation by reference to social characteristics of judges are not very successful.[3] Judges come from a rather narrow segment of the social structure; they tend to be the same age and come from similar class backgrounds. Most of them are white; most are graduates of colleges and law schools.[4] There are some differences: Some judges are Republican, whereas others are Democrats, and still others conceal their party preference. In some states the public elects trial judges in partisan or nonpartisan elections, whereas in others they are appointed by the governor or mayor, or through some sort of merit system.[5] But partisan affiliation and mode of election do not account for most of the differences in the outcomes of cases. Republicans do not consistently judge criminals differently than Democrats; on the contrary most of their rulings are alike. Although judges who are elected on a partisan ballot appear to act differently than those chosen in a nonpartisan election,[6] the two almost never sit in the same city; therefore many other confounding factors may account for the apparent differences.

Judges may, however, vary in their attitudes toward crime and criminals. We possess no thorough examination of judges' attitudes in the United States and the relationship of those attitudes to outcomes, but a study of magistrates in Ontario, Canada indicates that their attitudes were related to the disposition of defendants in their courts.[7] However, the magistrates' attitudes were also related to their backgrounds, their legal schooling, and their religious affiliation. The work loads they faced and the characteristics of the communities in which they served were also related.[8] Consequently, one cannot confidently say, even of Canadian magistrates, that their attitudes determine how they decide criminal cases.

Characteristics of Defendants as Explanations of Courtroom Actions. Many well-publicized instances of discrimination have occurred in court treatment of persons accused of crimes. Defendants convicted of white-collar crimes seem to be sentenced to prison less often than poorer persons accused of theft.[9] Middle-class whites less frequently received the death sentence than poor blacks, when the death penalty was permitted.[10] Knowledge of these instances led to the broader accusation that criminal courts discriminate against blacks and against the poor, both by convicting them more often and by imposing more severe sentences against those convicted.[11]

Two stages of the felony disposition process are said to be particularly affected by race and income of defendants. (1) The poor and black more frequently linger in jail prior to their trial [12]; and those who fail to win pretrial release are supposedly more frequently convicted and given more severe sentences than those who are released before their trial.[13] (2) In the same way, the assignment of public defenders to indigents supposedly places poor defendants at a disadvantage, because private counsel presumably work harder and are more skilled.[14]

These assertions, however, rest on very slender empirical support.[15] Sometimes they come from studies of small numbers of cases; in most instances the studies do not attempt to hold other confounding variables constant. Most of the findings which indicate that blacks are treated worse than whites show statistically significant differences between the two, but the differences are nevertheless too small to indicate a strong relationship between race and sentence.[16]

Characteristics of the Court Process as Explanations of Court-room Actions. Still another set of proposed explanations points to the demise of the trial, especially of the jury trial, as the instrument for the dispositions that typify the criminal process today. Jury trials and adversary proceedings have allegedly declined and have been replaced by guilty pleas and plea bargaining. That is probably not true. Available evidence indicates that guilty pleas and some form of plea bargaining have been common for a hundred years in some areas.[17] Nevertheless, the "modern" tendency toward lenient penalties is said to result from plea bargaining. There are some indications that jury trials lead to harsher sentences than trials before a judge alone.[18] Thus it has been made to appear that defendants are penalized for asserting their constitutional rights to a jury trial; they seem to be induced by promises of more lenient treatment if they plead guilty and by threats of harsh sentences if they do not and are subsequently found guilty at trial. Again, although this explanation has won wide circulation, it is supported by only thin empirical evidence.

The Law and Evidence as Explanations of Courtroom Actions. Underlying all these explanations is the assumption that statutory provisions and the strength of evidence will have a strong effect on the outcome of criminal cases. The law distinguishes one crime from another and specifies different penalties for different offenses. Moreover, a complex set of rules governs the establishment of guilt in court proceedings. Those rules permit only certain kinds of evidence. Evidence must be direct rather than hearsay; no procedural flaws may tarnish it through illegal searches or seizures. If the evidence is admissable, it must show beyond a reasonable doubt that the defendant committed the crime charged. Then and only then may he be found guilty and punished according to the penalties established by the law. According to legal scholars, the ideal state exists only when the law and weight of evidence establishes guilt or innocence. All other factors ought to be irrelevant. Even researchers who deny that such strict standards actually operate give some credence to the effects of law and evidence.

Contradictions Among these Explanations. One cannot simply combine these explanations for a more comprehensive theory of dispositions in criminal courts; as they stand alone they contain stark contradictions to one another. The singular focus on the judge cannot stand comfortably with the widespread use of plea bargaining. Plea negotiations constrain judges severely. Negotiations often lead to a guilty plea to one or two of the many charges that are levelled against a defendant while all others are dismissed; those one or two limit the judges' capacity to impose a severe or lenient sentence. In other instances, plea bargaining leads to a specific sentence agreement. Further, extraordinary circumstances are required for the judge to reject a negotiated plea. In practice, guilt is determined through negotiations; the judge cannot find the defendant innocent, nor can he find him guilty of a charge other than that agreed on. Sometimes judges actively participate in plea negotiations. But even when they do not, they are an implicit party to them. In both instances, they are constrained by them. When plea negotiations occur, dispositions result from a collective activity, which at the least involves the prosecutor, defense counsel, and defendant, in addition to the judge. In such a collective process, when the judge is only one of many participants, one would not expect the judge's background or attitudes to be closely related to the disposition of charges against defendants.

The relationships between plea bargaining, bail, and the use of public defenders are also unclear. On the one hand, one might expect the public defender to take cases to trial more often than private counsel, because the extra cost does not personally concern the public defender; he does not have to make a profit. But public defenders more often represent clients who are sitting in jail while awaiting disposition; and it is commonly claimed that detained defendants are more eager to plead guilty than defendants who are out on bail.[19] On the other hand, private counsel find guilty pleas more profitable than a trial in the normal case; their clients may also be able to turn their freedom to best advantage with a guilty plea in return for probation, a bargain that may not be available after conviction at a trial.

Defendant characteristics also interact perversely with these other traits of the criminal process. Professional burglars with long prior records are likely to make bail and afford private attorneys, but their prior record makes prison sentences likely; amateur thieves are more likely to await their disposition in jail, but the absence of a long prior record may keep them out of the penitentiary.[20] Blacks may prefer jury trials in jurisdictions where many of the jurors are black, thus confounding the relationship between race, guilty pleas, and the severity of dispositions. Moreover, if guilty pleas are supposed to lead to more lenient sentences and the poor and black are supposed to plead guilty more often than middle-class or white defendants, then the presumably more severe treatment meted out to blacks either doesn't take place or is severely curtailed.

Neither defendant characteristics, nor characteristics of judges, nor features of the felony disposition process such as plea bargaining, the kind of defense counsel, or pretrial release provides us with a sufficient explanation of the felony disposition process. Nor can these variables be combined in a simple fashion. But the evidence is strong that each has some effect on the disposition of cases; moreover, they exist close to each other and visibly interact with one another. If we cannot simply sum them together, we must find more complex models which combine their effect on the final disposition of cases.

AN ALTERNATIVE VIEW

A powerful model that combines these variables together with others is the organizational paradigm. Blumberg's study of a single court system has become the standard for such analysis; his view of courts as bureaucracies in which negotiation and bargaining predominate over the adversary system has won widespread acceptance.[21] We do not agree that courts constitute a bureaucracy; they lack the hierarchy of bureaucratic organizations. Moreover, we do not think courtroom dispositions are assembly line operations. Although many cases flow through courtrooms, and most are given little time on any particular day, each receives a remarkable amount of individualized treatment. As we shall show, one could not substitute a computer for the courtroom as one can for most assembly line operations.

But though courts are not bureaucracies, they are organizations. Thinking of them as organizations directs our attention to
courtroom work as a group activity. Most persons in the courtroom perform quite specialized functions, and their activity fits
into a broader pattern and is constrained by it. Incentives and
shared goals motivate the persons in a courtroom workgroup.
Workgroup members develop relationships that are cemented
by exchanges of inducements as well as by the shared goals.
They operate in a common task environment, which provides
common resources and imposes common constraints on their
actions. The defendant does not encounter single persons or
agencies as his case is processed; rather he confronts an organized
network of relationships, in which each person who acts on his
case is reacting to or anticipating the actions of others. Individual
biases against blacks, the poor, rapists, habitual criminals — or
any other category of defendants — become operative only when
permitted to do so by the norms and actions of the collective,
the courtroom workgroup.

The courtroom workgroup rather than the court will be the
focus of this book. It is important to distinguish between the
two, because in most cities courts occupy many courtrooms and
encompass many workgroups. Each courtroom workgroup may
differ significantly from others operating in the same court.
Moreover, the term court often is understood only to mean
judges. When we speak of courtroom workgroups, we include
prosecutors, defense counsel, clerks, bailiffs, and to a limited
extent, defendants.

The interaction of these persons in common tasks determines
the outcome of criminal cases. Because persons, rather than
machines, process charges against defendants, personal characteristics of principal actors such as judges, prosecutors, and defense
counsel are significant. In addition, their perceptions of defendants are likely to be colored by their previous experiences, and
their ingrained biases, as well as by their sympathies. The techniques they use for handling cases and the manner in which they
work together — as combatants in an adversary process, as opposing parties in negotiations, or as collaborators in a common
organizational setting — provide opportunities for such personal
characteristics to affect the outcome. But those interactions also

set bounds on the scope of such biases and mute their role in the felony disposition process. In the next chapters, we will provide much fuller detail about the organizational elements that describe courtroom workgroups.

TWO FURTHER DIFFICULTIES

We must be careful to limit the sweep of our generalizations. No research on criminal courts in the United States has national scope. State trial courts work in small jurisdictions, which vary significantly. The law they administer varies from state to state; the organization of the courts often varies within states as well as between states. Police practices and the mix of cases brought to courts vary greatly from community to community. There are large differences in the way in which prosecutors, public defenders, and the defense bar are organized. Indeed, no national data exist about most of these dimensions of criminal courts.[22]

Further, courts processing criminal charges differ in terms of the seriousness of the charges and the diversity of the cases they handle. At least three types of courts may be identified. Some courts principally handle misdemeanors. Their case load is specialized and usually concerns minor charges, but it is immense. Other courts only handle felonies; they too are specialized, but the defendants face serious charges that may lead to long prison sentences. Their case load is often heavy but rarely as great as that in misdemeanor courts. Finally, some courts handle a mixture of cases, not even specializing in criminal cases, but mixing criminal and civil cases on the docket or handling both misdemeanors and felonies. The case load of such courts is typically not as heavy as those of specialized courts, but the tasks they face are more diverse and sometimes more complex.[23]

Thus, research in one locale with one kind of court does not permit generalization to all American criminal courts. The best we may do at the present is to select courts in communities that are in themselves significant (for instance, because they are large) and that appear to represent some of the distinctive characteristics existing among criminal courts. Such a strategy captures some, but not all, of the variation in felony dispositions.

The organizational perspective is also helpful in overcoming these difficulties. As a theoretical perspective, it leads us to expect variation that we do not observe in the limited set of courtrooms of a single study but that probably exists somewhere else in the United States. Moreover, the paradigm does not apply to felony courts alone. It is equally applicable to misdemeanor courts, to civil courts, and to courts that handle a mixture of cases. In each of them we find courtroom workgroups, but those groups will probably be operating under quite different conditions. They differ as a steel mill and an automobile assembly line do. Both are in factories; both are work organizations. But the speed of the auto assembly line set by management establishes the pace of each group of auto workers, whereas in a steel mill the techniques of steel smelting are more important in establishing the rhythm of the steel workers. Such differences are important in building relationships within workgroups and between them and their supervisors. It is the same with different kinds of courtroom workgroups.

THE PLAN OF THIS STUDY

In this book, most of the courtroom workgroups we will examine handle only felony charges. We studied courts in Baltimore, Chicago, and Detroit. We selected those three cities because our original interest was in plea bargaining, and we knew that those cities had quite different procedures for negotiating pleas and used plea bargaining to a varying extent.[24] Originally setting out to explain those differences, we found that explanation in the organizational context of the courtroom workgroup.

We do not imply that these three cities represent urban America; no three cities can. They do, however, reflect some of the variety of urban life that exists in the United States. Baltimore is a port city still dominated by its southern heritage. Almost half its population (46 percent) is black, but it is surrounded by largely white suburbs. The city also carries out the functions of a county government, and therefore few services are shared by the city and its suburbs. The criminal courts serve only Baltimore city. The city's political machine is no longer powerful, but its remnants remain; in general Baltimore can be counted among the "unreformed" cities of America.

Chicago is the home of the renowned Daley machine, the last vigorous urban political machine in the country. It is the largest of the three cities, and has a wide variety of neighborhoods and ethnic groups. Blacks constitute about a third of its population. The city contains about half of Chicago's metropolitan population; its suburbs are not entirely white, although they remain predominantly so. Cook County provides important services to the city, including the courts.

Detroit is America's motor city. It has a "reformed" city government with nonpartisan elections and no strong political machine, although the UAW plays a significant role in politics. While Detroit is part of Wayne County, the criminal courts serve the city alone; there is another set of courts for the remainder of the county. Like Baltimore, Detroit has a very large black population (42 percent). It is a worker's city, dominated more by a single industry — automobile manufacturing — than either Chicago or Baltimore.

Crime in these three cities, as represented by arrests, is about the same as in other large cities. Figure 1.1 (p. 14) shows the distribution of arrests for the twenty-five largest American cities.

For all twenty-five cities, violent crimes accounted for less than a quarter of all arrests; property crimes constituted almost half, and 30 percent were for narcotics offenses. The crimes that attract most public notice — murder and rape — held a small share. Most of the major crimes that come to criminal courts involve commonplace property and narcotics offenses. Not all twenty-five cities, however, have the same distribution of crimes. For instance, murder arrests in Cleveland represented 8 percent of the total rather than the average 1.9 percent; in Memphis, half of all arrests for serious crimes were for larceny, whereas in New York larceny represented only 13.9 percent of the total. In Los Angeles and San Diego, half of all arrests were for narcotics offenses; in Houston only 7.4 percent of them were for narcotics.[25] Consequently, although the data in Figure 1.1 show the average for many cities, we should remain aware that the task confronting criminal courts in some cities is distinctly different.

The three cities that we will study did not vary much from the average. Their deviations are indicated in Figure 1.2. Robbery arrests were slightly more frequent in Baltimore and Chicago; aggravated assault arrests occurred slightly *less* frequently in Chicago and Detroit; narcotics arrests were less frequent in Chicago and more frequent in Detroit. None of the deviations, however, were large. In this sense, Baltimore, Chicago, and Detroit represent well the flow of serious cases into the criminal courts of large cities in 1972.

FIGURE 1.1 Arrests for Major Offenses: Mean Distribution for the Twenty-five Largest American Cities, 1972.

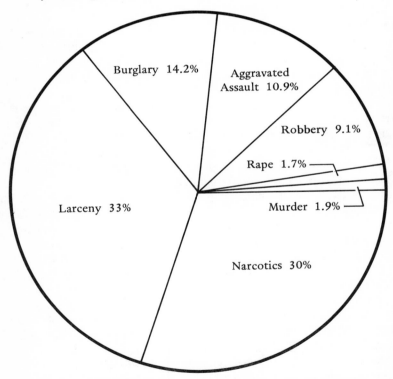

Source: Unpublished statistics supplied the authors by the Uniform Crime Reports Section of the Federal Bureau of Investigation. Those data are published in aggregate form in the annual *Uniform Crime Reports.*

Having selected Baltimore, Chicago, and Detroit, we turned to collecting information about their criminal courts. Penetrating courtroom workgroups was difficult. Little information about them exists. We could not even find reliable estimates of the number of defendants processed in each courtroom or the characteristics of their dispositions. Consequently, our first task was to collect as much information about a sample of defendants in each city as we could find in unpublished court records. In addition, we observed the activities of the courtroom workgroups for

FIGURE 1.2 Deviation from Twenty–five–City Average, Arrests by Offense for Baltimore, Chicago, and Detroit.

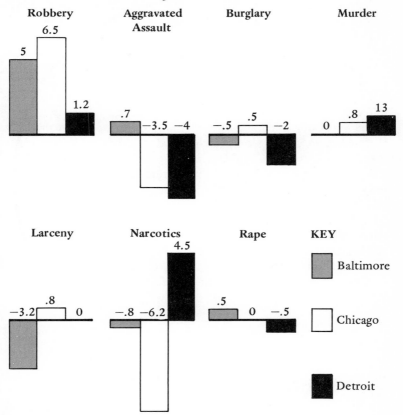

approximately one week in each courtroom. We were in the courthouse observing cases and courtroom workgroups for three months in Detroit and for five to six months in Chicago and Baltimore. We were never inconspicuous observers, because we required the permission and cooperation of courtroom partici- pants to observe and record the events that transpired. In most courtrooms we received full cooperation and were permitted to follow participants into chambers as well as to place ourselves in the courtroom where we could hear and see what was going on. In some instances our conspicuous presence may have altered behavior and interactions, but most activity appeared to occur quite naturally and without reference to our presence. Most of our analysis of courtroom workgroups is based on these extensive observations and the conversations that took place while we were in the courtrooms. Since completing our work, we have occa- sionally sent other observers into the courtrooms, and we have compared our observations with those of other researchers. We have found our observations generally supported by these inde- pendent observers. However, our observations remain subjective.

In the next two chapters, we shall outline in considerable de- tail the organizational model that provides the alternative per- spective for our understanding of the felony disposition process. We will then support that perspective in chapters 4, 5, and 6, using our observations and interviews for each of the three cities. Chapter 7 contains a detailed description of our methods of col- lecting and analyzing the data. Chapter 8 is an examination of the work of preliminary hearing courtroom workgroups, whereas Chapter 9 is an analysis of trial workgroups as they choose be- tween plea negotiations and trials. In Chapter 10 we will analyze the ways in which punishment results from invocation of the felony disposition process. Finally, in Chapter 11 we will sum- marize our findings and evaluate felony dispositions in these three cities.

NOTES

1. This and other case descriptions are fictitious, but are based on our understanding of the felony disposition process in Baltimore, Chicago, and Detroit.
2. U.S. Law Enforcement Assistance Administration and U.S. Bureau of

the Census, *Local Jails* (Washington, D.C.: Government Printing Office, 1973).

3. Edward Green, *Judicial Attitudes in Sentencing* (London: Macmillan, 1961); Henry A. Bullock, "Significance of the Racial Factor in the Length of Prison Sentences," *Journal of Criminal Law, Criminology and Police Science* 52 (1961): 411–417; and for a general summary of sentencing studies, see John Hagen, "Extra-Legal Attributes and Criminal Sentencing: An Assessment of a Sociological Viewpoint," *Law and Society Review* 8 (1974): 557–583.

4. Among the many studies, see particularly Richard W. Watson and Rondal G. Downing, *The Politics of the Bench and the Bar* (New York: Wiley, 1969); Wesley G. Skogan, "Party and Constituency in Political Recruitment: The Case of the Judiciary in Cook County, Illinois," unpublished Ph.D. dissertation, Northwestern University, 1971; Wallace S. Sayre and Herbert Kaufman, *Governing New York City* (New York: W. W. Norton, 1960), pp. 543–547; Bancroft C. Henderson and T. C. Sinclair, *The Selection of Judges in Texas* (Houston: University of Houston Public Affairs Research Center, 1965); and Beverly Blair Cook, *The Judicial Process in California* (Belmont, Calif.: Dickenson, 1967).

5. Kenneth N. Vines and Herbert Jacob, "State Courts and Public Policy" in Herbert Jacob and Kenneth N. Vines, *Politics in the American States*, 3d ed. (Boston: Little, Brown, 1976), pp. 251–53.

6. Martin Levin, "Urban Political Systems and Judicial Behavior: The Criminal Courts of Minneapolis and Pittsburgh," unpublished Ph.D. dissertation, Harvard University, 1970.

7. John Hogarth, *Sentencing as a Human Process* (Toronto: University of Toronto Press, 1971).

8. Ibid., pp. 368 ff.

9. Cf. William J. Chambliss, *Crime and the Legal Process* (New York: McGraw-Hill, 1969), pp. 365–366.

10. Marvin E. Wolfgang, "Racial Discrimination in the Death Sentence," in William J. Bowers (ed.), *Executions in America* (Lexington, Mass.: Lexington Books, 1974), pp. 71–107, 109–120.

11. Stephen R. Bing and S. Stephen Rosenfeld, *The Quality of Justice in the Lower Criminal Courts of Metropolitan Boston* (Boston: Lawyers Committee for Civil Rights Under Law, 1970), pp. 68, 86.

12. The evidence is summarized in Herbert Jacob, *Justice in America*, 2d ed. (Boston: Little, Brown, 1972), pp. 167–171.

13. Ibid.; also Stuart S. Nagel, "The Tipped Scales of American Justice" in Abraham S. Blumberg (ed.), *The Scales of Justice* (Chicago: Aldine, 1970), pp. 34–35; Jonathan D. Casper, *American Criminal Justice* (Englewood Cliffs, N.J.: Prentice-Hall, 1972), pp. 66–68.

14. Dallin H. Oaks and Warren Lehman, "Lawyers for the Poor" in Abraham S. Blumberg (ed.), *The Scales of Justice* (Chicago: Aldine, 1970), pp. 103 ff. The defendant's prospective may be reflected in Casper, *American Criminal Justice*, pp. 100–125.

15. Abraham S. Blumberg, "Lawyers with Convictions," in Blumberg (ed.), *The Scales of Justice*, pp. 51–67.

16. Hagan, "Extra-Legal Attributes."

17. Milton Heuman, "A Note on Plea Bargaining and Case Pressure," *Law & Society Review* 9 (Spring 1975): 518–527.

18. Nagel, "The Tipped Scales of American Justice," pp. 36–37; Oaks and Lehman, "Lawyers for the Poor," p. 100; Casper, *American Criminal Justice*, pp. 68–77; David W. Neubauer, *Criminal Justice in Middle America* (Morristown, N.J.: General Learning Press, 1974), p. 9.

19. Albert Alschuler, "The Defense Attorney's Role in Plea Bargaining," *Yale Law Journal* 84 (1975): 1206–1255; Oaks and Lehman, "Lawyers for the Poor," pp. 100–101.

20. Some evidence for this may be found in Harry A. Scarr, et al., *Patterns of Burglary*, 2d ed. (Washington, D.C.: Government Printing Office, 1973), pp. 77–102.

21. Abraham S. Blumberg, *Criminal Justice* (Chicago: Quadrangle Books, 1967).

22. See for instance the paucity of such data in the most comprehensive collection of criminal justice data ever published in the United States: Law Enforcement Assistance Administration, *Sourcebook of Criminal Justice Statistics, 1974* (Washington, D.C.: Government Printing Office, 1975), esp. p. 1.

23. Federal district courts are good examples. See Richard J. Richardson and Kenneth N. Vines, *The Politics of Federal Courts* (Boston: Little Brown, 1970), pp. 80–112; and Sheldon Goldman and Thomas P. Jahnige, *The Federal Courts As a Political System* (New York: Harper & Row, 1971), pp. 96–108.

24. Donald M. McIntyre and David Lippman, "Prosecuters and Early Dispositions of Felony Cases," *American Bar Association Journal* 56 (1970): 1154–1159.

25. From unpublished statistics on arrests by city supplied the authors by the Uniform Crime Reports Section of the Federal Bureau of Investigation.

Chapter 2 | TRIAL COURTROOMS AS ORGANIZED WORKGROUPS

Persons entering American courthouses expecting to witness trials usually experience swift disappointment. Naive visitors will be bewildered by the throngs in criminal courtrooms where they expected dignified decorum; they will be even more puzzled by the large number of empty courtrooms, after being told by almost everyone associated with law that courts are overwhelmed with work. In the full courtrooms, the observer will hear one case after another called and disposed of within a few seconds or minutes. Over a hundred cases may be handled in this fashion during the course of a day, with scarcely a single proceeding resembling a trial. If the observer settles onto one of the uncomfortable benches of an empty courtroom to wait and see what happens during a morning, he will see attorneys come in and out, transacting business with the court clerk and sometimes disappearing into an unmarked door, which the observer learns takes one to the judge's chambers. He may see the judge emerge for a brief ceremony when several attorneys are in the courtroom. But unless the visitor enjoys exceptionally keen hearing, he will often

19

be unable to hear what the attorneys and judges are saying. The ceremonies end as abruptly as they began, and once more judge and attorneys disappear behind closed doors or into the hallway. A kindly but curious clerk will eventually go to our visitor and ask him what he wants and then lead him to the door with the explanation that there will be no trials today.

Is the busy courtroom an assembly line? Is the empty courtroom testimony to governmental waste and inefficiency? What has happened to the classic adversarial proceedings so dramatically portrayed on stage and screen, where defense counsel and prosecutor vigorously oppose each other in a trial that takes many days? Where is the judge who is supposed to be sitting on his bench? Where is the jury? How does what we see in ordinary courtrooms fit into the exciting description of trials that can be found in almost any daily newspaper?

The answers to these questions rest in an entirely different way of looking at judicial proceedings. Courts are not an occasional assemblage of strangers who resolve a particular conflict and then dissolve, never to work together again. Courts are permanent organizations.[1] Moreover, adversarial proceedings are only one of the techniques available to disputants; trials may become so costly that few people use them. Viewing courtrooms as organized workgroups will enable us to unravel many of the mysteries of the judicial process.

THE COURTROOM WORKGROUP

Courtroom workgroups have characteristics commonly found among other organized workgroups.

1. They exhibit authority relationships.
2. They display influence relationships, which modify the authority relationships.
3. They are held together by common goals.
4. They have specialized roles.
5. They use a variety of work techniques.
6. They engage in a variety of tasks.
7. They have different degrees of stability and familiarity.

These traits establish a complex network of ongoing relationships that determines who in the courtroom does what, how, and to whom.

Courtroom Authority Patterns. The judge is the formal leader of most courtrooms.[2] In a sense, the courtroom belongs to him; he enjoys considerable formal powers to force others to conform to his desires. Most decisions the courtroom produces, including those made by others that affect the disposal of cases, usually require formal judicial approval. The judge must ratify the defendant's decision to enter a guilty plea, the prosecutor's decision to dismiss some or all charges, and an agreement on sentence. Finally, by participating in a number of decisions affecting case outcomes, judges gain influence over other courtroom organization members. Judges make preliminary decisions on bail, on motions and hearings. They rule on specific objections during courtroom proceedings and thus influence whether a compromise is reached — and if so, its content — as well as the verdict when no bargain is consummated.

Judges are universally considered the linchpins of courtroom workgroups. They are the formal leaders of the court and have the formal responsibility for making decisions that affect the flow of cases. They set dates for motions, hearings, trials, and other proceedings. The courtroom's work load is affected by their willingness to grant or deny extensions of deadlines, the time they take to render decisions on motions and in hearings, the procedures they use to empanel juries, the degree to which they cut short attorneys' examination of witnesses, and the amount of time they are willing to work. Judges also govern courtroom conduct. They are responsible for the actual behavior of attorneys, witnesses, spectators, and defendants; for example, they regulate voice level and physical movement, and decide when conversations will be allowed.

Attorneys represent interested parties to a conflict, but the judge is the neutral arbiter; even in criminal trials, he is not supposed to favor the state, even though he is a public official like the prosecutor. He represents the ideals of justice; he sits above the others, wears a robe, and requires all others to show visible respect for him by addressing him as "your honor" and by rising when he enters and leaves the courtroom. No one may openly criticize him in the courtroom; he may charge those who do with contempt of court (not contempt of the judge) and fine or imprison them on the spot. Moreover, this formal authority is often reinforced by the age and experience of the judge. He is often older and more experienced in the law than the attorneys who practice before him.

The judge, however, has less authority than many superiors in workgroups. He does not hire or fire others who work in the courtroom. Almost all of them are assigned by independent authorities — we call them sponsoring organizations — such as the state's attorney, the public defender, the clerk of courts, the sheriff (who assigns the bailiffs in many courtrooms), and the marketplace, which brings private attorneys representing individual clients to the courtroom. Each of these sponsoring agencies imposes its own requirements on the participants it sends to the courtroom workgroup. Consequently, the judge's authority is quite limited.

Judges also have few budgetary controls over the courtroom. Unlike most workgroups, courtroom workgroups typically do not have their own budget. Each participant brings his own resources to the workgroup and uses them himself or shares them with others. Neither judges nor anyone else in the courtroom workgroup can decide to install a new public address system or to hire several additional clerks; judges cannot reward hardworking prosecutors or bailiffs with a salary raise, nor can they directly withhold salary increments from malingerers. Lacking personnel and budgetary powers, judges have less authority than many workgroup supervisors.

Even on legal matters the judge's authority is not absolute. He renders decisions, of course, and they have the force of law. But they are subject to reversal by other judges. Attorneys sometimes seek to influence their content by citing statutes and appellate decisions. In addition, a judge generally can rule only when someone else raises the issue and requests a decision. Thus, his legal decisions are molded by the activities of others.

Courtroom Influence Patterns. The influence of other participants in the workgroup limits the formal authority of the judge. Their influence stems from formal authority that the law also provides them, and from superior information or control over access to the courtroom.

The law gives the state's attorney the right to determine whom to prosecute and what charges to press. In addition, the prosecutor routinely has more information about a case than anyone else in the courtroom. He possesses the police report, records of previous arrests and convictions, witness reports, laboratory tests, and the physical evidence if there is any. The prosecutor, more than anyone else, knows what the strength of a case is and when it is ready for disposition. Thus in many courtrooms, the prosecutor controls the scheduling of cases and the dispositional pattern. The judge — although possessing greater formal authority — responds to the prosecutor's actions. No experienced prosecutor will routinely overlook the judge's sentiments about how the courtroom is to be run, but many run it instead of the judge. Even where the judge maintains more control, he must take into account the prosecutor's opinion of what should be done.

Defense counsel also possess considerable influence in the work of the courtroom. They are charged with representing their client in a number of crucial proceedings. The defense attorney has a duty to insist that evidence seized illegally be thrown out of court and may ask for a hearing to accomplish that end. He can demand a hearing to determine the legality of an arrest or confession. A conscientious and skilled defense counsel may make the work of a prosecutor much more difficult and may require detailed rulings on the law from the judge.

The defendant is notably absent from most interactions of courtroom workgroups, assuming the role of a very interested spectator with a front row seat.[3] But he possesses several rights — the right to a jury trial being the most important — which cannot be waived without his formal direct participation in a ceremony. Before a defendant can waive his right to a jury trial or enter a plea of guilty, he must be questioned directly by the judge and answer in his own voice, not his attorney's. But defense attorneys may convince defendants to waive these rights and may school them in the proper responses to the judge's questions. If defense counsel is unwilling or unable to influence and control clients most of the time, the smooth operation of the workgroup is jeopardized.

Under some circumstances, clerks also possess some influence in the courtroom workgroup. In busy courtrooms where dockets are not arranged by a central computer, the clerk often determines which case will be heard next. The order in which cases are heard is important for busy lawyers who want to avoid fruitless hours of waiting for their case to be called for a two-minute ritual. Where the sequence of cases has an effect on the outcome (because one case is affected by the outcome of the case just before), the clerk's decision may also lead to more or less severe results for the defendant.

Finally, police have significant influence on the operation of criminal courts. In many cities they determine who will be sent to court by the arrests they make; at the least, they share that determination with the prosecutor. They also are the most frequent witnesses in criminal court. Their appearance or absence, their demeanor, the care with which they preserve evidence — all have a considerable effect on the work of the courtroom. Prosecutors, especially, depend on the police, but defense counsel and judges also have a considerable stake in how the police act in the courtroom.

The precise pattern of influence in courtroom workgroups varies with the degree to which each of the participants possesses these resources and how he uses them. When everything else is equal, an aggressive defense attorney will exert more influence than a reticent one. A diligent prosecutor exerts more influence than one who forgets details of the cases he is handling. An assertive judge retains more of his authority than one who sees his role solely as responding to the initiatives of others in the courtroom. Some courtrooms appear to be governed almost entirely by their judges, although that appearance almost always is an exaggeration. Other courtrooms are ruled by the prosecutor; a few are dominated by defense counsel. Many are governed by a collective decision-making process encompassing judge, prosecutor, defense attorneys, clerks, and police.

Shared Goals of Courtroom Workgroups. Courtroom workgroups have a job to do. Like most people pressed for time, their members do not often pause to philosophize about their ultimate purpose or goals. It is difficult enough just to keep going. Although they may not realize it, all courtroom workgroups share values and goals.[4] These shared perspectives undermine the apparent conflicts generated by the formal roles of workgroup members — the prosecutors' push toward convictions, the defense attorneys' quest for acquittals, and judges' inclination toward neutrality.

Four goals present in courtroom workgroups are summarized in Table 2.1. They are produced by the interaction of two dimensions: the function performed (expressive or instrumental) and the origins of the goals (external or internal to the group).[5] Expressive goals serve symbolic functions and infuse meaning into activity. Instrumental goals serve material functions and help get things done. Externally oriented goals are imposed by the workgroup's environment. Internal goals are produced by the need of the members to share perspectives that sustain the organization itself.

External goals reflect pressures on the workgroup from outside the immediate bounds of the courtroom and from the sponsoring organizations that send the major participants to the courtroom. The police, the media, governmental agencies, including the legislature and appellate courts, and ultimately the general public, all expect results from the courtroom workgroup. These "outside" groups impose both instrumental and expressive goals on courtroom organization. The most important instrumental goal is that cases should be handled expeditiously. Many people believe that expeditious disposition will deter crime. In addition, quick convictions or acquittals tie up fewer resources of the police. They also fulfill requirements imposed by appellate courts for a speedy trial and might reduce appellate business. They produce

TABLE 2.1 GOALS OF COURTROOM WORKGROUPS

Function of Goal	Origins of Goal	
	External	Internal
Expressive	Doing Justice	Maintaining Group Cohesion
Instrumental	Disposing of Case Load	Reducing Uncertainty

a steady flow of news to the media and assure the public that the courts are doing their job. Disposing of cases without attracting undue attention or criticism from outsiders is also interpreted by many as doing justice.

All members of the courtroom workgroup are interested in disposing cases, although the reason for this interest varies. Judges and prosecutors want high disposition rates in order to transmit an aura of efficiency and accomplishment. Prosecutors also prefer speedy dispositions because as cases age, memories dim and witnesses scatter, weakening the evidence and lowering the chances of conviction.

Retained attorneys face a more complicated set of incentives. Most attorneys who specialize in criminal cases depend on a high turnover of clients who can afford only modest fees. Without high volume and the investment of a modest amount of time in each case, many a private defense counsel would go broke. Yet private counsel must maintain a reputation for vigorous defense in order to attract new clients. Public defender organizations charged with representing all indigent defendants prefer quick disposition because their manpower barely suffices to handle their case load. But they also seek to establish a reputation for effective representation of defendants.

The expressive goal imposed by the external environment is to do justice. All the principal participants are attorneys, and are bound to that goal by their professional training. For that matter, nearly everyone in American society values doing justice. The specific content of the term, however, is ambiguous. For some, justice is done when criminals are caught and severely punished regardless of procedures. For others, adherence to the principles of due process and equal treatment produces justice. The ambiguity and disagreement contained in the notion of justice in society are mirrored in the varying perspectives of workgroup members. For the defense, doing justice may mean either obtaining an acquittal or a mild sentence for its clients, or forcing the prosecution to prove its case beyond a reasonable doubt. The prosecution often sees doing justice in terms of its conviction rates, because it is convinced that most defendants are in fact guilty. Judges generally see this goal as requiring impartial behavior, although their definition of impartiality often favors either the defense or the prosecution. Thus surface agreement within the courtroom organization on the goal of "doing justice" often engenders behavioral conflict.

Internally oriented goals facilitate the functioning of the courtroom workgroup. The expressive form of these goals is maintaining group cohesion.[6] Pervasive conflict is not only unpleasant; it also makes work more difficult. Cohesion produces a sense of belonging and identification that satisfies human needs. It is maintained in several ways. Courtroom workgroups shun outsiders because of their potential threat to group cohesion. The workgroup possesses a variety of adaptive techniques to minimize the effect of abrasive participants. For instance, the occasional defense attorney who violates routine cooperative norms may be punished by having to wait until the end of the day to argue his motion; he may be given less time than he wishes for a lunch break in the middle of a trial; he may be kept beyond usual court hours for bench conferences. Likewise, unusually adversarial defense or prosecuting attorneys are likely to smoothe over their formal conflicts with informal cordiality. Tigers at the bench, they become tame kittens in chambers and in the hallways, exchanging pleasantries and exuding sociability.

The instrumental expression of internal goals is reducing or controlling uncertainty.[7] The strong incentives to reduce uncertainty force courtroom members to work together, despite their different orientations toward doing justice. More than anything else, trials produce uncertainty. They require substantial investments of time and effort without any guarantee of the result. The difficulty of estimating how long they will last makes everyone's schedule very uncertain. Even bench trials require some preparation of witnesses and throw the other participants at the mercy of these witnesses, whose behavior on the witness stand is unpredictable. What witnesses say and how they say it may make the difference between conviction and acquittal. Jury trials are even worse, because attorneys must deal with the jurors as well as the witnesses. In ordinary cases very little is known about the jurors, and jury decisions are proverbially unpredictable. Even after presenting a "dead-bang" case to a jury, prosecutors suffer nervous hours while the jury deliberates. The judge is also committed to avoiding uncertainty. Most judges like to have some control over their dockets; they like to see where actions are heading and what further activity is required of them.

The desire to reduce uncertainty leads to the development of several norms designed to make behavior predictable. One is "stick by your word and never mislead deliberately." Attorneys who violate this norm find they are punished. Another is "no surprises." It is often illegal to call surprise witnesses or to introduce evidence that the opposing counsel is unaware of; it is almost always regarded as a dirty trick.

The instrumental goals we have identified are generally mutually supportive. Caseload disposition and reduction of uncertainty go hand in hand; the former is often articulated (partly because it is directed at the external environment), whereas the latter is more often an unspoken commitment by courtroom members. Expressive goals, however, are not as frequently mutually supportive. The quest for justice often threatens courtroom cohesion, and the desire to maintain a cohesive workgroup may seem to jeopardize the quest for justice. The general political culture more explicitly legitimates the externally oriented goals. There is much public discussion of the need for justice and for the clearing of dockets in criminal courts. Organizational maintenance goals are almost furtive by contrast. They are rarely articulated in public by members of the courtroom organization; they can best be deduced from private statements and courtroom behavior. Although they are not illegitimate, they have not yet been publicly legitimated.

Courtroom workgroups vary in their adherence to these goals. For instance, some workgroups value cohesion less than others because they find conflict less threatening to their survival. But in general we believe that the variation is not great. Nevertheless, it is important to identify these goals, because common adherence to them keeps the groups together.

Workgroup Specialization. Although courtroom participants have common goals, they play radically different roles. The participants rigidly adhere to the specified role differentiation. The judge maintains an air of impartiality; he responds to requests for rulings on the law and makes decisions when called on by others. He may intervene in the scheduling of cases or in questioning witnesses, but he may not take sides. The prosecutor, on the other hand, represents only the state and never the defense. Defense counsel only defend and never prosecute. There is no alternation of roles in the criminal courtroom.

However, the three leading members of the courtroom workgroup — the judge, prosecutor, and defense attorney — are all lawyers and possess the professional qualifications to do each other's work. Although role orientations are distinct and specialized, the work these three principals do is very similar. All of them manipulate information in order to reach decisions on the cases before them. They ask questions of witnesses — in private interviews or on the witness stand. They search out relevant aspects of code and case law and seek to apply them to their cases. All three are familiar with the techniques employed in adversarial proceedings; they are equally familiar with negotiations.

Little disagreement exists in the courtroom about this division of tasks and roles. It creates a situation in which everyone quickly fits into his accustomed place and in which the principals readily understand each other's work. Even novices readily fit into the work routine of a courtroom.

The other members of the courtroom workgroup engage in quite different tasks. The clerk keeps records. Although judges and lawyers may keep their own, the clerk's record is the official one. He records decisions, the dates when they occurred, and the motions and appearances that are filed with him. Together with the stenographic record of the proceedings, the clerk's file is the official record of the case and is used by everyone in the courtroom to determine what has happened in the past and what still needs to be done to complete disposition of the case. In addition, the court reporter — often a private contractor — makes a stenographic record of public proceedings. Those records, however, are not transcribed unless the defense or the state asks and pays for the transcription. Finally, bailiffs work in the courtroom to maintain decorum and guard prisoners who appear as defendants or witnesses.

Each of these members of the courtroom workgroup knows his task, role, and physical location in the courtroom. He knows it before he enters the courtroom. Little formal training or sociali-zation occurs in the workgroup. If a participant needs additional skills, he learns them informally.

The Work Techniques of Courtroom Organizations. Organiza-tions are more than stable groups of people who share goals and divide tasks in a purposive manner. Organizations also employ a technology, which in turn helps shape them.[8] The technology consists of procedures to manipulate resources into desired out-puts. For courtrooms, resources consist principally of informa-tion and the authority to make decisions that bind others. The outputs are dispositions. The courtroom organization's task is to transform information and authority into dispositions by apply-ing its work techniques.

Courtroom workgroups require an externally validated, com-prehensive, readily available, and generally accepted set of tech-niques, because the participants are sometimes unfamiliar with one another. This unfamiliarity means that they have not devel-oped common patterns of interaction. When strangers meet and interact, they fall back on commonly accepted formulas to guide their behavior. The procedures embodied in statute and case law relating to the conduct of trials and the hearing of motions provide such formulas. These techniques are not only justified because they employ norms and values relating to equal justice and due process; the very nature of courtroom workgroups also requires that some work techniques be codified and generally accepted.

Courtrooms use three sets of techniques: (1) unilateral deci-sions, (2) adversarial proceedings, and (3) negotiations. Each of them requires highly specialized knowledge and involves court-room members in intense interactions.

Any attorney member of the courtroom workgroup may make unilateral decisions that eventually turn into dispositions. The defense counsel may file a motion; the prosecutor may file a dis-missal; the judge or clerk may call up one case rather than another in his docket. In each instance, the participant uses his in-formation and authority to impose a condition on other members of the courtroom team. The extensive interdependence of work-group members, however, restricts their ability to impose unilateral decisions on the group. Consequently, unilateral decisions play a rather minor role in the courtroom's work.

Adversarial proceedings play a much more prominent role. They may be invoked by any of the three attorney members. Some of them are preparatory proceedings, such as preliminary examinations or hearings on motions; others are full-scale trials before a judge or jury. Adversarial proceedings are highly stylized interactions for revealing and sharing information that can become the basis for a disposition. During adversarial proceedings, information must be elicited in the approved manner, through oral arguments on legal points or questioning of witnesses. Neither prosecution nor defense ordinarily knows the full story a witness may tell, but the side presenting the witness generally knows more about what he might reveal than the opposing party. The judge knows almost nothing. Each side attempts to elicit the information most favorable to its cause while blocking the presentation of damaging information. This activity requires a high degree of skill in questioning and a thorough knowledge of the technical rules of evidence which guides courtroom hearings. Participants whose skills are inadequate not only jeopardize their case, but also hinder the output rate of the courtroom. It is common to see a judge take over questioning from inept prosecutors or defense counsel, or to cut them off when he thinks that sufficient evidence has been presented to reach a disposition. Similarly, counsel often advise judges about the legal basis for a decision.

Hearings require considerable coordination by the prosecutor or defense counsel rather than the judge. Witnesses must be assembled and prepared; each side must have an overview of its argument so that witnesses can be called in the most convincing sequence. Witnesses who might make an unfavorable impression or who appear fragile are often held in reserve and used only if absolutely necessary. If the hearings involve legal as well as evidentiary matters, the attorneys must read up on the law and have appropriate appellate citations at their fingertips. All of this preparation involves coordinating many people outside the ordinary ambit of the courtroom workgroup. Consequently, coordinative skills are almost as valuable as debating skills in adversarial proceedings.

Negotiation is the most commonly used technique in criminal courtrooms.[9] Plea bargaining — although most widely publicized — is only one use of negotiation. Continuances and the date of hearings are often bargained; the exchange of information is also commonly negotiated. Negotiation involves persuasion and the search for common ground. The common ground is generally based on agreement about the courtroom's goals; most members of the courtroom implicitly agree on the need to dispose cases and to reduce uncertainty. They also recognize the value of accommodating those on whom they are partially dependent. Each party to the negotiation attempts to convince the other that his solution is acceptable; in the course of negotiations, both parties are likely to move from their original positions toward a mutually acceptable outcome.

Information and the ability to make unilateral decisions that affect others significantly are the principal resources in negotiations. Courtroom participants utilize two types of information. One type is information about legal matters: the character of admissible evidence, the authorized sentence for a particular offense, the meaning of "lesser included offense," and similar matters. Most attorneys who specialize in criminal cases routinely possess this legal information. They also need to know the factual details of the case. Normally the prosecution possesses more information about the incident, on the basis of police reports and sometimes as a result of preliminary interviews with witnesses. Often there are disputes about what "really" happened, with the defense attorney attempting to put a less serious interpretation on the events than the prosecutor. At the same time, the character of the defendant is also in question. The defense attorney often claims to know more about that; he will tell of his client's family background, his employment record, his standing in the community, in addition to any disadvantages he has had to overcome. The prosecutor usually possesses only the defendant's police record. Negotiations proceed through a careful manipulation of this information. Even when both prosecutor and defense make "full disclosure," they often interpret the information at their disposal rather than simply laying it out on the table.

Information about the way in which other courtrooms handle similar incidents is also important in negotiations. What happens in other courts of the city or state is communicated principally through these negotiations. If other courtrooms readily grant continuances, that constitutes a useful argument that a continuance ought to be granted in the case under discussion. If, in an adjoining courtroom, aggravated assault seems to carry a normal sentence of two to four years, defense counsel will try hard to achieve at least as low a sentence. Because prosecutors usually work in a single courtroom, whereas private defense counsel circulate throughout several courtrooms in the city, some defense attorneys possess more of this kind of information.

Negotiations also invoke claims on workgroup cohesion. None that we witnessed did so overtly, but many were impregnated with hints that the continuing need to work together required reasonableness in negotiation. Participants joked about it; at the end of a negotiation, they often stood around and chatted about other matters as if to imply that they were still friendly partners of the same workgroup. Only when negotiations broke down did either prosecutor or defense counsel occasionally stalk out without the usual social amenities.

Clearly the techniques of presentation, the manipulation of information, and the invocation of common workgroup values are quite different in negotiations than in adversarial hearings. Not only are the negotiations much less formal, but they also depend less on the rules of evidence and other legalistic formulas that pervade so much of the adversarial performance. In negotiations much more depends on the long-run relationships between bargaining members of the workgroup. Trust, empathy, mutual understanding are important in negotiations, but matter little in adversarial proceedings. In bargaining, information is narrated; formal testimony from witnesses is the principal mode in adversarial proceedings.

Implicit threats to make unilateral decisions underlie the uses of information in all negotiations. The ability to take such actions gives weight to the efforts to control the exchange of information. Judges can render decisions that affect the outcome of specific cases and the work life of attorneys in general. The prosecutor can proceed to trial on the original charges if the defendant does not plead guilty to them. And the defense attorney can insist on a full jury trial regardless of what anyone else does, unless a complete dismissal is forthcoming. Without the existence of these threats, negotiations based on the exchange of information would carry little weight. Indeed, much of the manipulation of information is directed toward demonstrating what would happen if the case went to trial.

Courtroom Tasks. Courtrooms everywhere must complete similar tasks. These tasks flow from their fundamental responsibility in one way or another to dispose of every defendant charged. That responsibility requires maintaining physical control over defendants who may be prone to flee or to express their anger in violent outbursts. Much record-keeping is also required. A case file must be kept, containing information about all major actions taken. Then cases must be scheduled and the participants for each case assembled at the same time. All major proceedings must be recorded by a court reporter in case verbatim transcripts are required at a later stage. Finally, the law requires a variety of actions at different stages of criminal cases. Defendants must be arraigned and informed of the charges against them. Bond or release conditions must be set. In order to proceed against the defendant, a court must determine whether there is "probable cause," or a grand jury must return an indictment against him. "Discovery" — the exchange of information between prosecution and defense — must take place.

These tasks may be handled in many different ways. In some places, a single courtroom workgroup performs all of them, processing a criminal case from beginning to end. More commonly, courtroom workgroups specialize in subsets of these tasks. For instance, arraignments, bond setting, and preliminary hearings are often handled by one set of workgroups, whereas final dispositions are the domain of another workgroup. In some places, specialized workgroups process all motions; in others, all negotiations take place in a single setting. Specialized workgroups obviously operate differently than generalized ones. The more specialized the tasks of the workgroup, the more it can routinize procedures and the more familiar its members will be with the tasks they perform. On the other hand, specialized workgroups often do not see the final outcome of the case, and their decisions may hinder rather than help the work of other courtroom workgroups that later process the same case.

Workgroup Familiarity. Courtroom workgroupings almost always contain some persons who are quite familiar with one another and some who are more like strangers. The familiarity among major participants is an important characteristic of workgroups, because it has a significant effect on the manner in which they work. The more workgroup members are familiar with one another, the better they can negotiate; the more familiar, the less they need to rely on formalities and the more they can utilize informal arrangements. The more familiar courtroom members are with each other, the more likely it is that they will agree about courtroom values and goals and the less they will conflict with one another.

Workgroup familiarity depends on two factors. The first is the stability of the workgroups themselves.[10] The second is the size of the pool from which workgroup members are drawn; the smaller the number of judges, prosecutors, defense attorneys, clerks, and others working in the courthouse, the more familiar courtroom members will be with each other.

Generally the most stable assignment is that of the judge. Except during vacation or illness, a single judge ordinarily sits for a year or more in a single courtroom. However, in courtrooms hearing misdemeanors, assignments may last for as little as a month; in other courtrooms, where the judges are elected or appointed to the criminal court itself, the assignment may extend over many years. The stabilizing effect of long assignments of judges is well illustrated by what happens when one is temporarily replaced by another judge. Work routines become substantially altered. Everyone suffers from more uncertainty about what to do and how to do it, because an important stranger is in their midst. Where possible, the remaining members postpone significant proceedings until the judge returns. If action cannot be delayed, proceedings switch into an adversarial mode, because the unknown qualities of the substitute judge can best be neutralized in a jury trial.

The assignment of prosecutors and defense attorneys is much more variable. These differences have profound consequences.

The less change there is in workgroup personnel, the more interaction will occur. Frequent interactions produce familiarity with each other's intentions and probable behavior. In stable courtroom workgroups, the principal actors know each other's preferences; they have been able to develop standing accommodations with each other. They work together enough to share organizational maintenance goals; they learn to understand the pressures that each must bear from his sponsoring organization. Thus, prosecutors and defense attorneys learn what information the judge wants in routine cases; they know the sentence he will likely mete out. They know how to present a case in order to provoke the harshest response or the mildest reaction from the judge. They know what plea offers were made in the past, and can evaluate the present case in the light of that common past. The uncertainty in negotiating with each other is considerably reduced by their familiarity with one another. In addition, frequent interactions provide innumerable informal opportunities for negotiation. Prosecutor and defense counsel may talk about a case not only when it is on the docket but during the many other occasions at which they encounter each other. They can test possible compromises informally, without putting the case on the judge's desk for formal decision. By contrast, in fluid workgroups, information about each of the participants is much more sparse; members of the courtroom workgroup deal with each other more as strangers than as friends; formal roles govern them more completely. In fluid workgroups, members work in a much less certain context. They are less likely to know the judge's preferences or each other's. They do not have a great storehouse of common experiences by which to evaluate the present case. They have not had an opportunity to develop a set of shared accommodations or an understanding of each participant's work pressures.

Finally, low interaction means that no one heavily depends on the actions of any other individual to accomplish his work. Where the same individuals interact continually, however, strong patterns of mutual dependence and accompanying abilities to influence one another emerge. In addition, if interaction is high, circulation of defense counsel and prosecutors from one courtroom to another will be low. A lower circulation, in turn, facilitates the development of distinctive styles of behavior within the rather isolated courtrooms located in the same building.

Even in unstable workgroups members may be quite familiar with each other, if the pool of active participants in the courthouse is fairly small. Where there are only a handful of judges, a half-dozen prosecutors, and a dozen defense attorneys, familiarity develops as if the workgroups were the same every day. But the familiarity found in smaller cities and in rural areas can be approximated in large cities if a small group of specialized attorneys monopolizes the work.

Summary of Workgroup Characteristics. All courtroom workgroups confront the same basic task — to dispose of defendants' cases. All have the same composition — a judge, prosecutor, and defense attorney, who are familiar with each other's roles but who specialize in their own tasks. They share expressive and instrumental goals generated from within the workgroup and from the external environment. Workgroups utilize three work techniques — adversarial proceedings, negotiations, and unilateral decisions. These characteristics are found regardless of city. But workgroups also differ in several significant respects. Nowhere do judges completely dominate influence patterns within the workgroup, but the precise distribution of influence does vary. When the membership of workgroups is stable, patterns of mutual dependence develop, resulting in a more even distribution of influence. Stability also produces familiarity, but familiarity can exist even when workgroup composition is fluid, if the total number of people who form workgroups is fairly small and unchanging. When members are familiar with one another, negotiations are facilitated. When they are not, adversary proceedings are more likely.

Courtroom workgroups are like many other organizations. They are labor-intensive, are staffed by professionals, and provide services rather than products. Courtroom workgroups have an authority structure that is modified by influence relationships, but they are not hierarchies. The judge does not rule or govern; at most, he manages, and often he is managed by others.

Although workgroups dispose of many cases during a day, they are not assembly lines. Even routine decisions involve discretion. Setting bond, for instance, does not involve putting the same nuts and bolts into a piece of sheet metal (as on a typical assembly line); rather, it requires fitting a variety of factual assertions into a limited number of possible bail-bond decisions. The information required for such decisions may be communicated rapidly, and decisions may follow one another in quick succession. But it is no assembly line. On an assembly line, one worker simply relies on all the others doing their jobs; an assembly line requires few verbal or social interactions. Workgroup members must interact with one another to reach a decision.

NOTES

1. Our understanding of organizations is based primarily on the work of Herbert A. Simon, *Administrative Behavior*, 2d ed. (New York: Macmillan, 1957); Peter M. Blau and W. Richard Scott, *Formal Organizations: A Comparative Approach* (San Francisco: Chandler, 1962); Amitai Etzioni, *A Comparative Analysis of Complex Organizations* (New York: Free Press, 1961); Charles Perrow, *Organizational Analysis: A Sociological View* (London: Tavistock, 1970); and James D. Thompson, *Organizations in Action* (New York: McGraw-Hill, 1967). As will be evident to the reader familiar with organizational studies, we have been eclectic in our construction of the framework presented in the following pages.

To our knowledge, no organizational analyst has studied courts. However, several students of courts have used fragments of organizational analysis for their presentation. The most influential of these are Abraham S. Blumberg's *Criminal Justice* (Chicago: Quadrangle Books, 1967) and Herbert L. Packer's *The Limits of the Criminal Sanction* (Stanford, Calif.: Stanford University Press, 1968). Neither Blumberg nor Packer, however, lays bare the elements of an operative organizational model for courts. A more recent, but also only partial, attempt to explicate an organizational model for courts is Malcolm Feeley, "Two Models of the Criminal Justice System: An Organizational Perspective," *Law and Society Review* 7 (1973): 407–426; Feeley focuses on court systems rather than courtrooms, and again presents only a very partial model. The organizational context of the work of criminal courts is also emphasized by Lief Carter, although he focuses on the prosecutor's office rather than the courtroom in his analysis; see Lief H. Carter, *The Limits of Order* (Lexington, Mass.: Lexington Books, 1974). Exchange relationships in an organizational context are emphasized by George F. Cole, *Politics and the Administration of Justice* (Beverly Hills, Calif.: Sage Publications, 1973), esp. pp. 200–203.

2. The judge's formal role is the focus of much legal literature. It is epitomized by Bernard Botein, *The Trial Judge* (New York: Simon and Schuster, 1952).

3. Note the analysis of criminal proceedings from the defendant's perspective by Jonathan Casper, *American Criminal Justice* (Englewood Cliffs, N.J.: Prentice-Hall, 1972).

4. We are conceptualizing goals as incentive mechanisms and the goal structure as multifaceted. They help orient the calculus of decision-makers

and serve to bind organization members together. An insightful discussion of the problems associated with operationalizing goals and placing them in a theoretic scheme is Petro Georgiou, "The Goal Paradigm and Notes toward a Counter Paradigm," *Administrative Science Quarterly* 18 (1973): 291–310. Despite Georgiou's arguments, we find the concept of goals and incentive structures essential to the organizational paradigm.

5. This discussion reflects what Mohr calls transitive and reflexive goals. Lawrence B. Mohr, "The Concept of Organizational Goal," *American Political Science Review* 67 (1973): 470–481, esp. 475–476.

6. For partial evidence in support of the following see "Lawyers with Convictions," in Abraham S. Blumberg, *The Scales of Justice* (Chicago: Aldine, 1970), pp. 51–67; George F. Cole, *The American System of Criminal Justice* (North Scituate, Mass.: Duxbury Press, 1975), pp. 238–241 and 271–272; Carter, *The Limits of Order*, pp. 75–105; Jerome Skolnick, "Social Control in the Adversary System," *Journal of Conflict Resolution* 11 (1967): 51 ff; Lynn M. Mather, "The Outsiders in the Courtroom: An Alternative Role for the Defense," in Herbert Jacob (ed.), *The Potential for Reform of Criminal Justice* (Beverly Hills, Calif.: Sage Publications, 1974), pp. 268–273.

Note, however, that cohesion is not the only goal of actors and that it sometimes conflicts with others.

7. Cf. Carter, *The Limits of Order*, pp. 19–21.

8. See especially Thompson, *Organizations in Action*.

9. We have drawn from descriptions of courtroom negotiations by Blumberg, *Criminal Justice*, Casper, *American Criminal Justice;* Carter, *The Limits of Order;* Mather, "The Outsiders in the Courtroom"; and Albert W. Alschuler, "The Prosecutor's Role in Plea Bargaining," *University of Chicago Law Review* 36 (1968): 50–112.

10. Stability or cohesiveness is taken for granted by many organizational analysts. For instance, the much-cited article by D. S. Pugh, D. J. Hickson, C. R. Hinings, and C. Turner, "Dimensions of Organizational Structure," *Administrative Science Quarterly* (June 1968): 65–106 does not count stability as one of the dimensions of organizational structure.

Chapter 3

THE ECOLOGY OF COURTROOM WORKGROUPS

Courtroom workgroups decide defendants' fates. But to understand their functioning we must also examine the environment in which they operate. Workgroups are not autonomous organizations totally isolated from the outside world and impervious to its pressures. On the contrary, they are highly dependent on their environment; they depend on decisions made by others for their very existence.

In this chapter, we will examine the environments of workgroups and the effects of those environments. Courtroom environments include, first of all, the workgroups' physical surroundings. In addition, however, the workgroups' environment comprises the social networks in which they are entangled; these include relationships with sponsoring organizations, the police, legislatures, and appellate courts, and the partisan milieu in which courts operate. Finally, we shall suggest some of the behavioral implications of our perspective for understanding criminal proceedings.

COURTROOMS AND COURTHOUSES

Architecture and interior design structure interactions. Just as many supermarkets are cunningly designed to expose customers to as many goods as possible before they encounter a checkout stand, well-designed courtrooms are intended to impress and awe. In addition, their design has many unintended consequences.

The courtroom itself is usually a large public hall with assigned places for each of the participants. At the front one sees the "bench" — a platform for the judge. On one side is a small enclosed space with a single chair — the witness stand. Beneath it, one finds tables for the prosecutor and defense counsel, for the clerk, and for the court reporter. On one side of the room is a "jury box" — two rows of chairs enclosed by a railing, where juries sit during jury trials; at other times, police witnesses and other observers who want to differentiate themselves from ordinary spectators occupy the jury box. All of these assigned areas stand in front of a railing, which separates the courtroom workgroup from spectators. Behind the railing are benches for the general public. Mostly, however, these seats are used by persons who have some stake in the proceedings — such as witnesses, or relatives and friends of defendants; sometimes groups of schoolchildren fill them. The rest of the occasional spectators are mostly elderly men and women who fill their days with the free entertainment provided by courtroom activities.

The large courtrooms are designed to awe. The dais on which the judge sits focuses attention on him. But the high ceilings and large unused spaces make it almost impossible to hear proceedings; when courtrooms are full of spectators, the noise resembles an airport terminal. Although the room's design draws attention to the judge, prosecution and defense negotiations before the bench go almost unnoticed.

A series of small rooms leads off from the courtroom. The judge occupies one, which is called his chambers; it is relatively large, often carpeted and lined with books, and dominated by his desk. In addition, it usually has several arm chairs and straight chairs for visitors. Other amenities often include a water cooler and a private bathroom. Bailiffs or clerks occupy other rooms, which lead to the lockup from which imprisoned defendants are brought into court. Neither prosecutors nor defense counsel have their own offices in the courtroom suite, although both often congregate in the judge's private chambers or in one of the bailiffs' rooms. When they need to interview witnesses or clients with some degree of privacy, they must take them into the juryroom — a room in which the jury deliberates — if it is not in use. Most consultations, however, take place in the lockup, in some corner of the courtroom itself, or in the hallway.

These courtroom facilities often reside in dingy, drafty, old courthouses where marble columns stand in stark contrast to walls painted in institutional green. The buildings are often not air-conditioned; in summer, when windows are opened, the noise of city traffic constantly interrupts court proceedings. The hallways of these courthouses are often wide, as if the designers anticipated that much of the public's business would be conducted there rather than in the courtrooms. Public facilities such as cafeterias, waiting rooms, and restrooms are sometimes almost nonexistent. Finally, to enter many courthouses, one must go through a metal detector or be frisked; all weapons (including nailfiles and metal combs) and such contraband as tape recorders and radios are confiscated or checked.

These physical characteristics structure interactional patterns within the courtroom and isolate one courtroom from another. Because only the judge among key participants has his own office in the courtroom suite, he and the other participants are thrown together much more than one might expect from a reading of their formal roles. Courtroom members spend much of their free time in socializing, rather than in isolated reading or paperwork. To do paperwork or research, the prosecutor and defense counsel must retire to their offices in another part of the building or (as is typical with defense attorneys) in a separate building some distance from the courthouse. Where the clerk has no office, he spends most of his day at the courtroom table; he rarely leaves his post, because he has no locked drawers where he may secure the documents on his desk. Even when he does have a separate cubicle, he spends a large portion of his day within the courtroom, handling matters brought in by "regular" defense attorneys circulating through the courthouse.

These arrangements not only bring courtroom participants together but also isolate them from events in other courtrooms and from interaction with the personnel of other courts, although the building in which they are located may have dozens of courts operating simultaneously. One cannot look from one courtroom into another. Each has its own tempo; when one is in recess, its neighbors may be in the midst of formal proceedings. The courtrooms do not even have a common lunch schedule; regular interactions between courtroom organizations rarely occur in the lunchroom. Consequently, courtroom members are thrown together by their work space, but they are isolated from others who are doing similar work in the same building. Workgroup members have numerous daily interactions with one another — more than they have with others who perform equivalent tasks in other courtrooms. These interactions reinforce the workgroup's cohesiveness.

COURTROOM WORKGROUPS' SPONSORING ORGANIZATIONS

Courtroom workgroups depend heavily on sponsoring organizations. Such organizations determine who will be on the workgroup staff, and how long the staff members will stay. Workgroup members come from several distinct organizations. One, loosely called the court, sends judges; the state's attorneys' office sends prosecutors; the public defender's office sends defense counsel for indigents (private counsel come from the general bar); the clerk of courts sends clerks; the sheriff sends bailiffs.

Sponsoring organizations also determine the workgroup's other resources. The courtroom does not have its own budget. Rather, each member of the workgroup brings resources from his sponsoring organization; whatever is brought constitutes the total amount available to all members. For instance, the judges' organization generally supplies the space and secretarial assistance; each attorney brings his own ancilliary staff and supplies. Consequently, it is difficult to calculate the total "budget" of a courtroom in order to determine how much money is consumed in the administration of criminal justice.

Finally, sponsoring organizations attempt to regulate the behavior of their courtroom representatives. The prosecutor's office may seek to control the amount or type of courtroom plea bargaining. Judges' organizations may try to reduce the number of defendants held in jail or to speed the time between arraignment and final disposition. The efforts sponsoring organizations make to control behavior and their ability to do so vary. When sponsoring organizations institute new policies, the effects are felt immediately, even though they may not be exactly what the sponsoring agency intended. Each change generates a flurry of conferences; supervisory personnel may come to the courtroom to explain the new policy and negotiate modes of adapting to it. Such initiatives profoundly shape interactions among workgroup members.

Each type of sponsoring organization has its own power base and its own goals, which it may attempt to effectuate through the courtroom workgroup. Each also responds to its own organizational imperatives. Consequently, it is helpful to review separately the characteristics of the judges', prosecutors', and defense attorneys' sponsoring organizations.

Judges' Sponsoring Organizations. All judges belonging to a court like Cook County Circuit Court, Detroit Recorder's Court, or the Supreme Bench of the City of Baltimore form a loose organization of their own. This organization channels relations between the judges and other significant actors in their environment such as legislative bodies, the prosecutor's office, the police, the court clerk, and sheriff. Often the judges speak collectively through the chief judge, someone elected by the judges themselves or appointed from the outside. The chief judge presides over the judges' meetings, which occur at least once a month, and in which the judges discuss common concerns and make policy decisions that bind all of them. One of the most important matters the judge's organization determines is the procedures leading to the assignment of judges to particular courtrooms: how long they will serve; what sequence, if any, they will follow as they move from one kind of courtroom to another; how they may challenge or request reassignments.

Other important matters also come before the judges' sponsoring organization. The media view the judges collectively as "the Court" and hold them responsible for misdeeds of any judge and for the productivity of the courtrooms. Consequently, judges' sponsoring organizations commonly concern themselves with decorum in the courtroom and with disposition rates, backlogs, and docket management. Each of these matters impinges on the courtroom workgroup's style. Behavior that is forbidden by the judges' collective organization cannot be overtly permitted in the courtroom. When the judges collectively urge better disposition rates, courtrooms must respond. In addition, the judges' sponsoring organization acts administratively: it must coordinate vacation schedules; establish common policies for assigning counsel to indigents not represented by the public defender; handle relations with court reporters, bailiffs, and jail personnel; schedule special court sessions (for example, night arraignments); and create procedures to handle various crises, such as urban riots with mass arrests.[1] Finally, the judges' organization often expresses concern about the condition of the docket. Consensus on how long a delay in disposition is "too long" varies between jurisdictions. But criticism from the police, appellate courts, news media, and others will eventually be directed at individual judges or at the court as a whole if delays become too long.

Judges' organizations have little to do with the recruitment or dismissal of their members. Outside authorities select judges through a variety of procedures.[2] In some cities judges are elected on a partisan ballot; in others on a nonpartisan ballot. In still others, the governor or mayor appoints them; and in a few they are selected by a complex merit system combining a lawyer-citizen nominating panel, executive appointment, and a retention election. Judges may be recruited for the criminal court specifically or for a court of general jurisdiction that has criminal courtrooms. Regardless, recruitment becomes encrusted with peculiar local practices that bring at least some correspondence between judges' attitudes and local political attitudes and culture. Thus, recruitment procedures directly effect the amount of variation in judges' attitudes toward defendants, crime, and criminal justice.

Prosecutors' Sponsoring Organizations. Although the functions of the prosecutor's office are similar of those of the judges' organization (assigning personnel to courtrooms, providing resources, establishing policies, and handling external relations), its structure is quite different.[3] An elected state's attorney provides strong central leadership. He presides over a bureaucratically organized structure, has substantial clerical support, and hires and fires personnel.

The state's attorney operates in the limelight. Although most prosecutorial decisions have low visibility, there is a constant stream of occasions in which his work receives considerable public attention. The symbolic potency of the subject matter of his decisions — crime, violence, and the ability of society to cope with them — give the prosecutor's office a prominence and importance that departments of public welfare, public works, and indeed most local city agencies do not have. The political position of the office is also unusual. With the exception of the mayor, the state's attorney is the most important locally elected administrative head. The fact that his election is usually partisan increases the complexities and pressures introduced by involvement in the electoral process. Thus, party officials, voters, civic groups, and the media all find his activities salient to them and feel they have a claim on his attention and a right to evaluate his performance. In addition, like any other administrator, he must deal with the governmental bodies that appropriate funds and give him general rules and policy. Finally, his specific responsibilities bring him into contact with a unique set of organizations and individuals — judges and judicial organizations, court personnel, defendants, defense bar, and the police department.

The state's attorney must recruit assistants, clerks, investigators, and other personnel. Most state's attorneys must not only staff felony courtrooms but must also represent the state in misdemeanor courts, juvenile courts, grand jury proceedings, and appellate courts. Often they must also advise county agencies.

Thus, only a portion of his staff practices in felony courtrooms; many work elsewhere. In most American cities, assistant prosecutors' positions are viewed as temporary apprenticeships for young lawyers who wish eventually to establish private practices. Few attorneys make the prosecutor's office a career; even fewer enter the office with that intention. Because the chief of the office, the state's attorney, is an elected official, his subordinates often do not survive his tenure. They may be chosen through patronage connections or by some kind of merit examination; usually they are somewhat involved in politics. The electoral fate of their chief often concerns them at least peripherally, because they owe their job to him and they may become unemployed if he loses an election.

The state's attorney's task environment imposes expectations about his assistants' work. Their primary task is to see that substantial numbers of defendants arrested by the police are successfully prosecuted. The media judges the state's attorney's performance primarily on the basis of past experience. Roughly the same number of defendants must be convicted as in the recent past. The charges on which they are convicted must be about as near to the original charges as is customary. New developments generate additional expectations. When public concern about gun crimes rises, the number of convictions for weapons offenses must also increase. Finally, a certain number of "important" cases always surface — cases involving heinous crimes, large sums of money, or prominent members of the community — and they must be handled with visible competence.

These expectations about performance largely determine what a prosecutor requires from his assistants. His standing depends on whether the public is satisfied with his assistants' performance. Although the formal legal duty of the courtroom prosecutor is to represent the state and see that justice is done, his performance is actually judged on the number of convictions. Failure to obtain the expected number of convictions jeopardizes the career prospects of the prosecutor (including his reelection) and makes both him and his staff vulnerable to public criticism from judges, the police, the media, and segments of the general public. This is an underlying fact of life in prosecutor's offices. The primary goal for members of prosecutor's offices is to get convictions. Failing that, they prefer dismissing charges to subjecting themselves to possible criticism for "losing."

State's attorneys try not only to optimize their operation by skillful assignment of assistants to the several courtrooms, but to control their assistants' work to achieve office goals. The state's room and how they should operate. In some cities, they assign attorney must decide how many assistants to send to each court-

assistants to particular cases, and the assistant follows the case from one courtroom to another until it is decided. That method produces courtroom workgroups in which members are not very familiar with one another. An alternative policy is to assign assistants to particular courtrooms to handle whatever cases come there; when a case goes to another courtroom, it moves to another prosecutor. That policy stabilizes courtroom workgroups, but assistants know less about their cases. The state's attorney must also worry about his assistants' abilities to get along with particular judges and public defenders, and the pressures that the workgroup exerts to subvert prosecutorial policy. The state's attorney may prefer to avoid plea bargaining or to avoid charge reduction; courtroom workgroups may, however, develop their own norms. In some cities, assistants must check with supervisors on all such matters; in others, assistants are given wider discretion. A loose rein may, in part, reflect budgetary pressures, because close supervision costs more money; in part it reflects recognition of the assistants' professional competence and the difficulty of recruiting competent professionals who are willing to subject themselves to close supervision. Whichever strategy the chief prosecutor chooses, it has an immediate effect on the operation of courtroom workgroups.

Defense Sponsoring Organizations. The structure of the defense bar is more complex. Several kinds of attorneys represent defendants. Public defenders may belong to organizations like the state's attorney's office. But both privately retained and court-appointed attorneys are usually individual entrepreneurs or members of very small firms.[4] They respond to economic incentives and structural features in the environment as well as to patterns of communication, reward, and sanctions. But these forces do not operate through an organizational structure; rather, they impinge on defense attorneys through a quasi marketplace.

Traditional public defenders' offices are much like the state's attorneys'. Public defenders must recruit a staff of assistants in addition to clerks and investigators [5]; they must evolve a procedure for assigning those assistants to particular courtrooms or cases; they must decide how much to monitor and control courtroom performance. Such offices typically contain at least a dozen attorneys and ancillary staff; in large cities sometimes they are much bigger.

But there is also one very significant difference from the state's attorney's office. The public defender is often appointed rather than elected; he is usually held responsible to a governing board composed of public officials and persons appointed by public officials. These boards may be active in setting policy. Thus defender's organizations do not enjoy the independence or political stature of prosecutor's offices. They cannot forget that actions which disrupt the felony disposition process may generate opposition from the governing board and appropriating agencies. A public defender's office that demands jury trials in all of its cases is likely to experience swift budget cuts and attacks on its personnel. Public defenders become adept at modifying office policy in anticipation of possible consequences and reactions of their governing boards.

Consequently, public defenders' offices are not typically judged by the number of acquittals. Instead, they are judged by their success in avoiding a backlog. As long as the office represents most indigents without disrupting the flow of cases, it will be considered successful. Public defenders' offices are not permitted to excel by obtaining a disproportionate number of acquittals or dismissals for their clients.

Private attorneys differ in two important ways: how frequently they appear in felony courtrooms, and whether they are privately retained or are appointed and paid by the court to represent indigents. Private attorneys seek a steady income by obtaining regular work that does not require extraordinary exertion. Some attorneys appear in felony court so infrequently that what happens to their cases has little effect on their practice or income; these "occasionals" can exercise an independence that other attorneys cannot afford. A foray into felony court for the nonregulars may be an interesting diversion. Although a financially unrewarding trial or a day wasted in waiting for a case to be called is certainly annoying, it usually does not motivate such attorneys to alter their style of representation. Furthermore, many occasionals are so unfamiliar with the norms of courtroom workgroups that they do not know how to avoid such incidents. Such occasionals easily disrupt courtroom routines.

Regulars face a quite different strategic situation. Regular attorneys depend on their practice in the felony courtrooms for a significant portion of their incomes. They practice in the courthouse enough to learn what is expected of them and to realize the financial disadvantages of deviant actions. Further, the extent to which a regular depends on appointment, as opposed to private clients, structures incentives and behavior.

Every large city has a group of "regulars" who earn a substantial portion of their income from paying clients. But their income level is often marginal, and to secure it they need the cooperation of judges, clerks, and prosecutors. They must maintain a reasonable balance between the amount of money they receive from clients and the amount of time they spend on their cases. Since most felony defendants are not rich, the fees they pay are not substantial. Few defendants pay enough to compensate adequately for a trial. Thus, most defendants' cases must be disposed either by a dismissal or a guilty plea. Anything else is too costly for the defense attorney. The exigencies of making a living have another profound effect on the incentives of retained regulars. Time is money. The less time they require to process their cases, the more defendants they can handle. This interest in time does not lead to rapid disposition after initial arrest. In fact, private defense attorneys often need delays in order to permit their clients time to pay them. But they try to reduce the amount of time they spend in court. A retained regular cannot make a living if he must sit in court all morning just to get his case continued. The secret of success for these lawyers is to "get in and get out." For this reason, favors that appear trivial are in reality absolutely essential. These favors include obtaining continuances over the phone; if that is impossible, the regular tries to get his continuance as soon as he arrives in the courtroom. He also needs to be able to have his case shuffled to the top of the pile.

Collecting fees is the other major problem facing retained regulars. Once a case is completed, especially if the defendant is sent to prison, it is practically impossible to collect the fee. Hence it is important to obtain postponements until the fee is collected. Furthermore, as Abraham Blumberg points out, the retained regular needs occasions to impress clients with the quality of his courtroom representation.[6] An impressive presentation helps reconcile the defendant to a plea, encourages full payment, and helps satisfy the client that he has received his money's worth.

Similar considerations apply to the regulars who are appointed to represent indigents and are paid by the state. They respond to economic incentives just as retained attorneys do. These incentives are structured by the official payment schedules, and the details of these schedules assume great significance. When fees are based on the number of hours worked, and if courtroom time is generously compensated, the regulars will be less reluctant to go to trial. If, however, each defendant generates a flat fee, it pays to dispose of cases with as little effort as possible, obtaining dismissals or guilty pleas rather than going to trial. Such a fee schedule makes appointed regulars just as dependent on judges, clerks, and prosecutors for assistance in using time effectively as retained attorneys are. But since getting paid is not a problem, they do not need to stall final disposition until their fee is collected.

Appointed regulars face some difficulties that retained attorneys do not. Appointed attorneys have more problems with "client control" than retained counsel. They must convince the reluctant defendant to accept a plea.[7] A recalcitrant defendant, after all, can insist on a jury trial. The existence of procedures for convicted defendants to bring complaints about their attorney's representation adds impetus to these considerations. Satisfied clients are less likely to file such complaints. Furthermore, an attorney's ability to defend against such complaints rests on the quality of the record that is established in the proceedings. Here too, judge and prosecutor can help by providing occasions for the attorney to impress clients and by allowing him to build a record. Finally, appointed regulars depend on the mechanism for assigning counsel to indigents. How are appointments made? What expectations about how the case will be handled accompany such appointments? The answers to these questions affect appointed attorneys' behavior. If an attorney violates expectations or alienates those who make appointments, he will no longer receive appointments. In some jurisdictions, the incentive structures for regulars are marvelously complex, because their practice combines both paying clients and court appointments. Such attorneys may find that it pays to complete one defendant's case as quickly as possible to make time for another court-appointed client. At the same time, they jockey for delay in a private client's case until the fee is paid.

Private attorneys operate in a marketplace. To a limited degree, bar associations monitor their performance. To a larger extent, local rules about the size of fees and the number of clients they may represent at any one time regulate their availability and their activity on courtroom workgroups. The public defender competes with private attorneys for marginal clients; the more generous the definition of indigency, the fewer clients private attorneys can claim for themselves. Compared to judges, prosecutors, and public defenders, however, private attorneys are less constrained by their own task environments and enjoy more freedom from direct supervision.

Sponsoring Organizations — Conclusion. The three sponsoring organizations supply the principal staff of the courtroom workgroups. Other sponsors — the sheriff and clerk — supply ancillary staff. To the degree that the sponsors supervise their courtroom personnel effectively, the workgroups find themselves severely inhibited. Where sponsors supervise closely, workgroups are likely to exhibit little variation; where that supervision is looser, workgroups will differ considerably, even though they operate in the same courthouse and even though their personnel come from the same sponsoring organizations. Moreover, supervision also transfers to the courtrooms some of the concerns of the sponsors. Where sponsoring organizations emphasize quick disposition of cases and where supervision is close, workgroups will share that concern. Lax supervision, for instance by judges or prosecutors, may lead to long delays, as defense attorneys press for continuances. Where sponsors have specific sentencing policies and supervise courtrooms closely, the sponsors' policies may become the courtrooms' operative norms. In the absence of such policies or where supervision fails, sentences between courtrooms may vary considerably.

The quality of a workgroup depends on the actions of its sponsors. They, rather than the workgroups, decide who will be judge, who will prosecute, and who will defend in a particular courtroom. They also decide how long the personnel stay, what they are paid, and what fringe benefits they may enjoy. These powers sensitize workgroup members to the goals of sponsoring organizations. They help make the sponsoring organizations a critical element of the workgroup's environment.

OTHER ELEMENTS OF THE ENVIRONMENT

Organization analysts refer to the external forces that shape the work of organizations as the task environment.[8] For business organizations, the task environment consists of suppliers, regulators, customers, and competitors. The courtroom workgroups that staff the felony disposition process do not face serious competition. Occasionally, cases can be brought in federal court, but usually, if defendants are to be prosecuted, courtroom workgroups in the local jurisdiction must do it. The survival of courtroom workgroups is not in question in the same way that a restaurant's or manufacturer's is. On the other hand, courtroom workgroups do have suppliers, regulators, and customers, but with unusual characteristics. The sponsoring organizations just described are the principal suppliers, providing the very personnel that constitute the workgroup. They also regulate, but this function is shared with the police, legislatures, appellate courts, prison authorities, the news media, and political organizations. Each of these organizations may also consume the workgroups' output. Together, they constitute the task environment of courtroom workgroups.

The police, legislatures, appellate courts, media, and other elements of the task environment have a twofold impact on courtroom workgroups. They affect workgroups directly in ways we will describe below. In addition, they influence workgroups indirectly through their effect on sponsoring organizations. For instance, not only workgroups but the prosecutor too responds to a newspaper series on courtroom problems. Thus workgroups constantly strive to adapt to a highly complex environment.

The Police. The police supply cases to courtroom workgroups. Although they do not intervene as directly as sponsoring organizations in the internal operations of the workgroups, their effect may be nearly as great. Police arrest policies determine who will initially be charged with a felony; police work determines what evidence will be available for negotiations and trials; police supply the major witnesses for many cases.

The number of felony arrests depends on specific policies of the police. Narcotics crimes produce many arrests. Although most property crimes do not lead to an arrest, almost half of all felony arrests involve larceny or burglary. (See Figure 1.1. p. 14.) The vigor with which the police pursue the narcotics trade, their success in solving property crimes, and their policy for maintaining order (which may lead to many or few arrests for violent crimes) determine both the number and composition of cases coming to court.

The quality of police work also affects the manner in which courtroom workgroups process cases.[9] Police investigative work substantially affects the task of obtaining convictions. The police must collect evidence and identify witnesses. If they fail to do so, the prosecutor's case is usually doomed. Information and assistance that individual police officers provide to assistant prosecutors is equally important. Experienced police officers who are knowledgeable about a case give invaluable assistance to trial attorneys, whether the case is tried or negotiated. By doing a good job police officers make the prosecutor's task easier.

Police are also strategically located to criticize the prosecutor's office and courtroom workgroup. They have a better picture of overall court performance than most other organizations and can penalize prosecutors by withholding information and by dumping unwanted arrests into the courtrooms. Police detectives and commanders typically establish good contacts with reporters, making it easy to publicize their displeasure with poor performance or unpopular decisions. The police chief commands considerable standing and attention in his own right. He may use his status to bring public criticism to the media or to exert covert pressure through political allies. The militant unions formed by rank and file patrolmen also provide vigorous and visible criticism.

One result of the operation of all of these factors is that courtroom workgroups give special attention to cases that are important to the police. Assistant prosecutors commonly check with the arresting officer in charge before offering a plea bargain in such cases. Charges involving the police directly also receive special attention. Physical assaults on police officers are prosecuted vigorously. When there is a possibility than an officer will be brought before his department trial board or be the defendant in a civil action, the courtroom workgroup takes special care to obtain a conviction, because a dismissal or acquittal could injure the officer's prospects.

Legislatures and Appellate Courts.   Law-making bodies are a more distant part of the task environment. They define criminal behavior, establish standards and procedures that must be followed, define and limit the punishments imposed on the convicted, and determine the resources available.

Legislatures write the state criminal codes that label certain behavior as criminal and permit prosecution of those who engage in it. These codes not only help determine whom the police arrest, but also define the elements of offenses that prosecutors, defense counsel, and judges look for when confronted with a criminal case and the possible punishments. Penal codes are not static. Every legislative session brings changes in the law that alter the definition of some crimes, and add to or diminish the list of criminal behaviors.

State legislatures also design the structure of criminal courts, establishing courts of original and appellate jurisdiction, defining their geographical domain, and mandating the formal steps required for convictions. Thus, some legislatures require a prosecutor's approval for all formal arrest warrants that initiate prosecution. Others permit the police alone to make the determination to prosecute. Preliminary hearings can be demanded as a matter of right in some states; in others, judges can refuse a preliminary hearing. The timing of mandated stages in a criminal case may also be established by law. Finally, the character of the sponsoring organizations depends on state law. For example, legislatures decide the method of recruiting judges and prosecutors and their terms of office.

Courtroom workgroups also depend on legislative bodies for their resources. Judges often receive some or all of their pay from the state; other workgroup members are on city or county budgets. Counties generally are responsible for building and maintaining courthouses and other physical facilities. Although court budgets are usually small portions of a city or county budget, courts that desire increases must compete with claims from much more visible and popular services. Dependence on local and state appropriating authorities means that courtroom workgroups must retain some sensitivity to the demands of legislative bodies.

Appellate courts share some of these functions with lawmakers. They have little to do with making resources available, but they affect the precise definitions of criminal behavior through their interpretation of criminal statutes. Sometimes they restrict the application of sanctions. The greatest impact of appellate courts, however, rests in their power to impose standards and procedures and to reverse trial court decisions that do not meet statutory or case law requirements. This effect is continuous. Every case may be appealed, and that potential molds many of the workgroup rituals. The carefully contrived guilty plea ceremony reflects a concern over appeals. Typically, the judge asks the defendant whether any promises have been made to him, and the defendant must say no, even though, in fact, promises are the inducements for obtaining guilty pleas. Most courtroom workgroups pay close attention to what information is stenotyped "on the record" and what occurs "off the record," because appellate courts examine only the formal record. These precautions largely succeed, because few of the courtroom workgroup's decisions are appealed, and even fewer are reversed.

However, appellate courts do reverse some decisions and lay down rules that affect the work of the courtrooms. In many states, appellate courts exercise a loose supervision over trial courts and may alter their routines. Rules requiring speedy trial or regulations governing the assignment of cases to particular courtrooms may emanate from appellate court intervention as well as legislative action. When such decisions appear, courtroom workgroups have little choice but to adapt their behavior.

Prison Authorities. Executive departments run county jails and state penitentiaries. They receive the prisoners that courtrooms send them. They — or independent parole boards — ultimately determine how long prisoners stay in jail before they are conditionally released on parole. Thus, the real length of prison sentences depends on these outside authorities rather than on the courtroom. Courtroom members usually try to remain informed about parole practices so they can apply the appropriate discount to the sentences they are working with. If they know that a life sentence typically means seven years, they may try to impose a twenty-five-year sentence, which may mean ten years of imprisonment. When they negotiate, they can tell a defendant that four years really means two and a half. In addition, in some states, prisons are so overcrowded that courtrooms cannot send them any new convicts.

The Media. The media find criminal courtrooms a rich source of news. They provide many of the stories that traditionally appeal to their audience. Shocking tales of human cruelty and greed arise regularly; the odd and strange surface as well. Society's fascination with violence and its need for reassurance through the punishment of wrongdoers find expression in the recounting of crime and courtroom dramas. Furthermore, important political news sometimes emanates from courthouses. Here the activities of prominent public officials like prosecutors and judges are exposed to all.

Workgroup members and their sponsoring organizations reciprocate the media's interest. Individual workgroup members care very much about the coverage specific cases receive. For one thing, news stories can bring reward or punishment. At least some prosecutors and judges have political ambitions. They seek favorable publicity, and want to avoid criticism. Defense attorneys (and prosecutors who anticipate joining their ranks soon) believe clients will come to them if their names appear in print. Favorable mention in a spectacular case may catapult workgroup members to fame and higher public office. In addition, newspapers are the only mechanism for communicating with the general public about the members' work. Since each member depends in the long run on support and collaboration from the public, he must project a favorable image. Consequently, courtrooms accommodate and woo reporters as well as fear them. Workgroup members cultivate reporters and work hard to avoid unfavorable notice. Although reporters rarely spend much time in the courtroom, their presence is nevertheless felt almost constantly.

The principal sponsoring organizations also care very much

about media coverage of the courts. It helps structure expectations about how courtrooms and sponsoring organizations should perform. It also shows others how they actually are performing. Stories about individual cases help determine these expectations and evaluations, as do articles that describe in a general way what is happening.

Major conflicts between the police and the prosecutor's office or between the judges and the public defenders find their way into print. Sometimes prominent officials leak criticisms of others to a favored reporter; occasionally, they call a press conference or issue a news release. The papers independently evaluate performance, particularly in editorials during election time or in special reports. These articles are a major source of criticism, and they provide other decision-makers (including those who determine budgets) with crucial information. It is difficult to ignore a series of stories exposing deplorable jail conditions or inefficient administration; assertions that dangerous defendants are coddled demand some response. For those workgroup members (like the prosecutor) who must face reelection, such stories can be particularly damaging.

The media's coverage of the courts and the criminal process varies from city to city. The level of attention is by no means uniform. In some jurisdictions, articles describing the outcome of specific cases, complete with the names of the major participants, appear daily. In other places, only unusually dramatic or serious cases are covered. The ideological position of a newspaper's editors also varies, and can affect coverage. Some editors are strong law and order advocates, and critically examine conviction rates and plea bargaining practices. Others are more defendant oriented, emphasizing instances of the denial of rights or reporting on deplorable jail conditions. The behavior of all major courtroom participants responds to the specific content of the media.

The Political Environment. Like all integral parts of the political process, criminal courts respond to and reflect the basic social, economic, and partisan characteristics of their communities. Patterns of crime, the social characteristics of defendants and workgroup members, and the response of the public and media to the crime problem all condition behavior in the felony disposition process. It is difficult to demonstrate explicitly the links between social structure, political culture, and public opinion on the one hand, and the fundamental characteristics and behavior of the criminal justice system and its personnel on the other. We do not know how public opinion and local political culture are linked to court actions. Nevertheless, the generalized effect of local politics is often clear.

Political party organizations, however, no longer play the role they formerly did in American courts. Precinct captains and ward committeemen do not fix cases. In fact, partisan considerations rarely have any explicit effect on courtroom work. Their absence reflects the general decline in the power of local party organizations in American cities.

But party organizations continue to be active in recruiting personnel. In many jurisdictions, judicial aspirants must participate in political activity. The stronger the surviving political organizations, the more closely identified with these organizations judicial candidates are. The office of prosecutor is regarded as one of the most important and powerful local positions and political organizations (which are sometimes vulnerable to investigation and prosecution) want to determine who will occupy it. Political considerations tinge the recruitment of other positions, including court clerks and bailiffs, assistant prosecutors, and sometimes even public defenders. In many cities, such "courthouse patronage" is the last vestige of the spoils system. Thus, courtroom officials often have political backgrounds. Judges and assistant prosecutors often harbor political ambitions as well.

Where traditional partisan political organizations are weak, other groups seek to affect recruitment. In fact, some groups attempt to affect recruitment even in the presence of strong party organizations. Local bar associations often publish ratings and recommendations in an effort to affect the outcome of judicial elections. Other groups participate occasionally, including nonpartisan civic associations, labor unions, homeowners associations, and black groups. Thus, the kind of political groups active in a community shapes courtroom recruitment patterns. The persons who hold key posts and their attitudes reflect roughly the distribution of power and opinion in the community.

The Task Environment: Summary. Courtroom workgroups confront a complex task environment that determines their very composition, strongly influences the content and processing of their cases, and both limits and shapes their decisions. Compared to many other organizations, workgroups are unusually dependent on their task environment.

The dependence means that when elements of the task environment vary, changes will occur in courtroom workgroups. The elements of workgroups' environment discussed in this chapter do vary considerably from one city to another. Thus, even though many of the internal characteristics of workgroups remain constant from city to city, their operating procedures differ because they are adapting to different task environments. The pressures courtrooms receive from sponsoring organizations and police policies are particularly variable. However, courtroom workgroups must also adapt to pressures from legislatures, appellate courts, prisons, the media, and political authorities. These elements of the task environment interact with each other and with courtroom workgroups in intricate ways.

THE IMPACT OF WORKGROUPS AND THEIR ENVIRONMENT ON CASE DISPOSITIONS

Our principal interest is in how courtrooms dispose criminal cases. Defendants have two main concerns: whether they will be convicted; and if convicted, what their sentence will be. We want to explain other characteristics also, however. How rapidly are dispositions reached? At what stage of the case are they made? What work techniques are utilized to reach them? Finally, we want to explain differences among courtrooms within individual cities and between cities for each of these elements of the felony disposition process.

Some outcomes may appear to depend heavily on traditional factors examined in previous research — the nature of the charges, the defendant's background and characteristics, the evidence against him, and the characteristics of defense attorney and judge. But these factors exert their influence in the context of courtroom workgroups.

We have introduced a number of characteristics in the last two chapters that we believe important. The most important ones are summarized in Table 3.1. Some of them affect outcomes in obvious ways — for instance, procedural supervision of assistant prosecutors by the state's attorney's office may affect the kinds of plea bargains offered. Others are less apparent.

Workgroup characteristics heavily influence the techniques used to dispose of cases. When members are familiar with one another, many more cases will be disposed by negotiation than when they are composed of strangers. Familiarity permits workgroup members to reduce uncertainty through bargaining. They know each other well enough to predict reactions to proposals and to achieve some control over outcomes through bargaining. When workgroup members are less familiar with one another, bargaining does not substantially reduce uncertainty. It is hard to negotiate with strangers; workgroup members cannot readily anticipate their counterparts' reactions; the process is full of nasty surprises. Consequently, more dispositions will occur through adversarial proceedings, because trials under conditions of unfamiliarity are not much more uncertain than negotiations.

Workgroup characteristics also affect the time it takes to dispose of cases. Pressure for quick dispositions generally comes from the task environment — from appellate courts and sponsoring organizations. It has its greatest effect when sponsoring organizations maintain close control over the personnel they send to courtroom workgroups. Under those circumstances courtroom workgroups do not develop strong work norms. Rather, they remain responsive to pressures from their sponsoring organizations. Sponsoring organizations can most readily maintain such control over their courtroom members by establishing central supervision routines. However, if carried too far, centralized supervision can interfere with the rapid disposition of cases, for it may erode workgroup cohesion and stability, making plea bargaining more difficult.

The distribution of influence within the workgroup, itself a function of stability, also affects disposition time. If judges dominate, and if their sponsoring organization and its environment demand rapid disposition, they can coerce speedy decisions. If influence is more evenly distributed, the mix of incentives to which members respond determines disposition time. Public defenders and assigned counsel have less need to delay than the retained attorney who must collect his fee.

TABLE 3.1 CHARACTERISTICS OF WORKGROUPS AND THEIR ENVIRONMENTS WHOSE VARIABILITY ESPECIALLY AFFECTS OUTCOMES

Characteristics of workgroups

Members' familiarity with one another

Members' dependence on one another (shaping influence patterns in the group)

Workgroup stability

The relative importance of the workgroups' four goals

The degree of workgroup task specialization

Characteristics of sponsoring organizations

Recruitment and assignment procedures (affecting stability, familiarity, and attitudes of workgroup members)

The amount of control and supervision over workgroup members' behavior (affecting the effectiveness of central control)

The content of sponsoring organization policies (affecting the direction of central control)

Characteristics of the larger context

Physical layout of courthouses

Incentives and pressures produced by:
    police
    legislative bodies
    appellate courts
    prison officials
    the media
    political organizations

The severity of sentences may also reflect workgroup organization. More disparity in sentences from one courtroom to another occurs when courtrooms enjoy a high degree of autonomy from their sponsoring organizations and where they are somewhat insulated from their task environments. Where the prosecutor dominates the courtroom workgroup, sentences are likely to be more severe than where judges dominate or where the principal members reach decisions collectively.

Different task environments produce different effects on court decisions through their influence on the courtroom workgroup. A political environment that trains potential courtroom participants in political negotiation also promotes negotiation in the courtroom workgroup, because bargaining is a widely accepted political skill in such an environment. Some political environments recruit judges with a wide variety of ideological commitments and social backgrounds; others produce workgroups where judges (and prosecutors and defense counsel) have pretty much the same political values and come from similar backgrounds. Within a single court system workgroups will vary more in the first situation than in the second and will produce more variable results.

The degree to which courtroom workgroups specialize and the volume of cases they handle also affect outcomes. The more specialized the input of cases, the more routinized the workgroup's procedures and the less variation will exist in the outcome of similar cases. The less specialized the workload, the less routine the handling and the more variable the outcome is likely to be. Caseload volume puts pressure on the workgroup to streamline procedures so that uncertainty and inefficiency can be minimized. But caseload volume by itself is unlikely to result in much plea bargaining unless the other incentive to negotiate — the reduction of uncertainty — also operates.

None of these effects operates independent of characteristics of cases, of defendants, of workgroup participants, and of the legal requirements imposed on the judicial process. Rather, the workgroup combines these elements in different ways depending on its own structure.

Courtroom workgroups are not simply abstractions; they are

lively realities that may be found in every American courthouse. In the next three chapters, we shall describe in considerable detail how courtroom workgroups are structured in Baltimore, Chicago, and Detroit and how their environments affect their work.

NOTES

1. Isaac D. Balbus, *The Dialectics of Legal Repression* (New York: Russell Sage Foundation, 1973), pp. 119, 165–175, 193.

2. For a current review of these practices, see Kenneth N. Vines and Herbert Jacob, "State Courts," in Herbert Jacob and Kenneth N. Vines (eds.), *Politics in the American States* (Boston: Little, Brown, 1976), pp. 249–255.

3. The best descriptions of particular prosecutors' offices are: Lief H. Carter, *The Limits of Order* (Lexington, Mass.: Lexington Books, 1974); David Neubauer, *Criminal Justice in Middle America* (Morristown, N.J.: General Learning Press, 1974), pp. 42–65. See also the general description in George F. Cole, *Politics and the Administration of Justice* (Beverly Hills, Calif.: Sage Publications, 1973), pp. 111–155.

4. See especially Albert W. Alschuler, "The Defense Attorney's Role in Plea Bargaining," *The Yale Law Journal* 84 (1975): 1181–1206.

5. See Anthony Platt and Randi Pollock, "Channelling Lawyers: The Concern of Public Defenders" in Herbert Jacob (ed.), *The Potential for Reform of Criminal Justice* (Beverly Hills, Calif.: Sage Publications, 1974), pp. 235–262.

6. Abraham S. Blumberg, "Lawyers with Convictions," in Abraham S. Blumberg, *The Scales of Justice* (Chicago: Aldine, 1970), pp. 51–67.

7. Jonathan Casper, *American Criminal Justice* (Englewood Cliffs, N.J.: Prentice-Hall, 1972), pp. 100–125.

8. James D. Thompson, *Organizations in Action* (New York: McGraw-Hill, 1967), pp. 27–29.

9. Carter, *The Limits of Order*, pp. 76–84 gives a good account of the effect of police on prosecution.

PART II | Felony Dispositions in Baltimore, Chicago, and Detroit

What happens to defendants depends on what happens in the courtroom. The courtroom workgroups that shape outcomes share the features described in Chapter 2. But courtroom workgroups also have important differences. As suggested in Chapter 3, we believe these differences help explain case outcomes.

How can differences in workgroup characteristics between cities be explained? No one knows all of the answers, but our research suggests at least some of them. Sponsoring organizations affect their employees behavior; and those organizations have different methods of hiring, training, assigning, and supervising workgroup members. In turn, these differences can be traced to decisions of legislatures and appellate courts, the generosity of local funding agencies, and the city's political culture, structure, and traditions.

The best way to learn how a court system operates is to observe it personally over a period of time. Few readers will have an opportunity to study a felony disposition process first-hand. We did, however. Our research began when we went to the courthouse, watched, listened, felt, and began to ask questions. The chapters in Part II report what we saw and learned about felony disposition in the three cities. We describe what we observed, but not what we measured. Our analysis of defendants' case outcomes based on our measurements (which we will present in Part III) only makes sense after we describe the basic features of each city's felony disposition process.

In Part II we will examine three broad questions: How is the typical defendant's case handled from arraignment to sentencing? What are the principal characteristics of the courtroom workgroups in each city? What general features of each city, external to courtroom workgroups, affect the characteristics and behavior of those workgroups?

Chapter 4 | BALTIMORE: A CITY OF TRIALS

The aging courthouse in which most Baltimore felony cases are heard is located strategically between the downtown commercial center and "the strip," several blocks of adult book shops, strip shows, and porno movie houses. The "classical municipal" architecture of the courthouse prepares the visitor for a spacious open lobby permitting free movement. Instead, visitors are met by what resembles an airport boarding gate. All strangers (defendants and their families, victims and witnesses, college professors and students) must hand over their briefcases and packages for inspection and walk through a metal detector. Police officers, judges, clerks, prosecutors, and attorneys sidestep these security measures and accept the greetings of the guards.

The physical layout of the courthouse confuses strangers, and there is no one readily available to give directions. Five felony courtrooms lead directly from the main corridor, but they are scattered among other courtrooms and offices. The solid wooden doors leading into them are forbidding. No anteroom shields the main courtroom from the noises of the hallway. The courtrooms are old, with poor acoustics, wooden furniture, and barely adequate lighting. In Baltimore, unlike many other cities, the visitor to a courtroom frequently will find a defendant's trial in progress.

How do the defendants on trial get to court? Their presence culminates a protracted series of procedures involving organizations and individuals in several locations throughout the city. We can best describe the process by following a hypothetical defendant as he wends his way from the street to a penitentiary cell.

AN ARMED ROBBERY CASE IN BALTIMORE

A clerk in a downtown liquor store was waiting on one of his two customers one fall evening at about 11:30 P.M. Suddenly, a black male entered, pulled a .38 caliber nickel-plated revolver from his tan jacket, and announced a holdup. Tersely he ordered the two customers to lie face down on the floor, instructed the store clerk to put the contents of the cash register in a brown paper bag, and had him lie down next to the two prone customers. He then removed the wallets from the three men, warned them to lie still for three minutes, and walked briskly out the door into the night. The store clerk jumped up, raced to the back room, and returned with his own revolver. He fired two shots at the departing gunman, apparently missing. As he was about to phone the police, two officers from the central police district who were on routine patrol came running into the store to investigate the gunshots. They received a brief description of the robber — a black male, tan jacket, brown cap, about 5′ 10″, blue pants, medium build. Four minutes later, the officers noticed a twenty-three-year-old black male, Roy Brown, 5′ 8″ tall, walking rapidly about eight blocks from the liquor store. Brown was stopped and searched. No paper bag or revolver was found, but he was wearing a black cap. His wallet contained $385 and a paycheck made out to someone else (who, it turned out, was one of the victims). The officers returned to the liquor store with Brown, where the clerk identified him as the person who had robbed the store a few minutes earlier. The defendant was taken to the precinct station.

The incident and defendant are hypothetical, but the details of the crime and ensuing arrest are typical of armed robbery cases we observed in all three cities. After the defendant reaches the station house, however, important differences emerge. The Baltimore police determined the formal charges lodged against Roy Brown without consulting the state's attorney's office. They charged him with three crimes against each of his three victims: armed robbery, attempted robbery with a deadly weapon, and carrying a concealed weapon. The complaining witness (the store clerk) was not required to swear to a formal complaint, but was told he would be notified when and where to appear in court.

While the police were determining the charges against Brown, an employee of the Pretrial Release Program interviewed him. In the brief interview, the employee asked Brown about his background, employment, relatives, and similar matters. When the interview was completed, Brown was led next door to the Central District Court. A sleepy bail commissioner proceeded to arraign him, reading the charges, and informing him of his right to an attorney during interrogation and his right to remain silent. Glancing at the information gathered by the pretrial release interviewer, the bail commissioner asked Brown several questions about his family, work history, residence, and prior criminal record. Brown neglected to mention a prior robbery conviction, and the bail commissioner promptly set bail at $10,000 with surety. The requirement of a surety bail bond meant that Brown would have to hire a bail bondsman to win his release. Finally, the commissioner informed Brown that his preliminary hearing would be held in fourteen days, September 26, before the judge assigned to the Central District Court. Asked if he wanted a public defender or his own attorney, the defendant replied that he wanted to hire his own attorney.

Unable to raise the $630 premium on the $10,000 bond, Brown was taken from custody the next morning to appear before the district court judge for a review of his bail. The very brief proceeding produced no change: bail remained at $10,000. Brown stayed in jail until his preliminary examination, because his family was unable to afford the bondsman's fee. But they managed to scrape enough together to hire an attorney. Deciding to observe the attorney at work, Roy Brown's mother took a bus to the abandoned former police headquarters on the outskirts of Baltimore's downtown district that housed the Central District

Court. The police officer guarding the entrance curtly asked what she was doing in the building, had her sign in on a ledger, and ushered her up a ramp and through a metal detector. The courtroom itself was crowded, large, and noisy. The dirty walls were partially covered with peeling paint. But its most striking feature was the noise of clanging cell doors and the yells of prisoners emanating from the door at the back of the courtroom that led to the lockup. These noises punctuated the morning's proceedings as prisoners were led in and out of the lockup. Those sitting close to the lockup's door could easily smell the cellblock's various aromas. Toward the end of the morning, it was Roy Brown's turn to be led from the lockup.

The district judge who had reviewed Brown's bail presided over the preliminary hearing. Brown's attorney wanted to hold the examination, because he wished to get testimony on how the initial stop was made and what the officers said when they brought him back to the liquor store. But the judge denied the request, and the assistant state's attorney said nothing. The judge explained that he was waiving the exam because he felt there was no point to holding it; the case would go to the grand jury anyway. The proceeding ended abruptly two minutes after it began, when the judge ordered the case sent to the grand jury and Roy Brown was marched back to jail.

While Brown sat in jail, his case continued its journey. One of the two assistant state's attorneys in the grand jury section of the state's attorney's office reviewed the file quickly to determine whether the available evidence could sustain the charges. He decided to drop the charges involving the two customers and to proceed on charges of armed robbery, attempted robbery with a deadly weapon, and carrying a concealed weapon, as they related to the store clerk.

The grand jury proceedings consumed only a few minutes. One of the arresting officers summarized the case for the grand jurors, who voted for an indictment as they did in almost all cases presented to them. In legal theory, the grand jury had found probable cause that a crime had been committed and that Roy Brown had committed it. The indictment was returned October 10, two weeks after the preliminary examination and twenty-nine days after the arrest.

In his next court appearance, Brown faced another judge in another location. This time, he was brought before a judge of Baltimore's Supreme Bench in the main courthouse. The judge arraigned him on the grand jury indictment by informing him of the charges contained in it. Because Brown's attorney was not present, the judge asked if he had an attorney. After replying that he had, Brown once more returned to Baltimore City Jail, to await his first appearance in a trial courtroom.

The arraigning judge did not set the date of this appearance; it was established through negotiations between the court's Case Assignment Office, an assistant state's attorney, and Brown's defense attorney.[1] The assistant state's attorney initiated the negotiations, and after several unsuccessful attempts to contact Brown's attorney, managed to catch him in his office. The assistant state's attorney inquired about the possibility of a plea bargain, but Brown's attorney cut him short. "Look," he said, "you aren't going to be trying the case. I don't know whether the chap who will handle this in court will stick by any agreement you and I make. Besides, we don't have any idea who the judge will be." "That's OK, really," replied the assistant state's attorney. "This looks like a case that ought to go to trial anyway. Do you want a jury or bench trial?" Brown's attorney replied he'd like a bench trial. Choosing a jury trial would have resulted in a later trial date and a longer stay in jail for his client. Several possible dates for the bench trial were agreed to. After conferring with the clerk in the Case Assignment Office, the assistant settled on January 12. The clerk set the case before one of the judges who had room on his docket for that day and set in motion the procedures for notifying Brown's attorney of the official trial date and courtroom and for subpoenaing the witnesses.

On the morning of January 12, Brown, his attorney, a trial assistant from the trial team assigned to the courtroom, and the judge all met for the first time to conduct business related to the case. Brown's attorney and the courtroom assistant state's attorney had not discussed the case previously. In fact, they knew each other only slightly. The defense attorney had used the time before the trial date to prepare for a bench trial, interviewing Brown at the jail the previous week and obtaining access to the police write-up of the arrest. The prosecutor reviewed his file briefly and talked to his witnesses a few minutes before court convened. In a very brief conversation at the front of the courtroom before court convened, the two attorneys confirmed that neither wanted to plea bargain. The courtroom filled rapidly. The judge was in the midst of a jury trial begun the previous day. It was clear that it would continue at least into the late afternoon. Consequently, an employee from the clerk's office transferred the case to an empty courtroom. The entire entourage — defendant Brown, his attorney, the prosecutor, and the prosecutor's witnesses — trooped down the hall and around the corner to the new courtroom. Another bench trial was scheduled there for the morning, pushing Brown's case till after lunch.

When Brown's case was called, his attorney immediately moved to quash the arrest.* After hearing brief arguments from both attorneys, the new judge denied the motion and called on the assistant state's attorney to present his evidence. The store owner, one of the customers, and the two arresting officers testified. The judge interrupted frequently to interject questions of his own. Brown took the stand and briefly denied ever being in the liquor store. The judge, obviously in a hurry, conducted the proceedings informally to expedite their completion.

After hearing brief closing arguments, the judge found Brown guilty of armed robbery. The prosecutor moved to dismiss the two lesser charges. The entire proceeding took only fifty minutes. The judge set sentencing for January 26. On this date, Roy Brown appeared for the last time in criminal court. In a brief ceremony, the trial judge sentenced him to a minimum of seven years in the Maryland State Penitentiary. Brown learned his ultimate fate 137 days after his arrest.

THE CHARACTERISTICS OF COURTROOM WORKGROUPS IN BALTIMORE

Two distinct courtroom workgroups shared in shaping Roy Brown's fate — one in the Central District Court preliminary

---

* To quash an arrest is to declare it was illegal; if such a motion is upheld, the case must be dismissed.

hearing courtroom, and the other in the criminal court at the bench trial. In his case, the criminal court workgroup clearly had more influence over the outcome. This is not true for all defendants, however. To understand Baltimore's felony disposition process generally, we must examine both workgroups.

The preliminary hearing workgroups operated in eight districts covering the entire city. They were located in the eight police districts, and were part of a statewide district court system. In addition to conducting preliminary hearings, arraigning defendants, and reviewing bail decisions, these courts had complete jurisdiction over less serious criminal cases. In fact, most of their work consisted of handling misdemeanors. Although these courtrooms were not always as dreary, noisy, and run-down as the central district courtroom, most were inadequate and unsatisfactory places to work.

None of the principal members of preliminary hearing workgroups remained in one district court for long. Until January 1973, judges spent only a month in a district before being rotated to another. The only exception was the central district, where one judge remained for several months. District court was the first assignment for many young, inexperienced assistant state's attorneys; for reasons we will describe later, they were anxious to leave it as soon as possible. Because of high turnover in the prosecutor's office, the opportunity to leave came quickly. Consequently, most assistant state's attorneys spent only a few months in the district courts. Although there were usually two assistant state's attorneys in each district, new men did not receive much help from their slightly more experienced partner. The work load was heavy, and many of the judges tried to finish the day's work by 1:00 P.M. The assistant state's attorneys usually alternated handling cases; one prepared quickly for the next case while his partner took the one being heard. Two public defenders also worked in each district court. Like assistant state's attorneys, they were usually young and inexperienced, though their higher pay sometimes attracted more experienced attorneys. Turnover among defenders was not as rapid, and newly assigned defenders could rely more on the experience of their colleague. Private attorneys did not specialize in district court work. It was too difficult to capture enough business in a single district, and the geographical dispersion made it impractical to travel from one district to another. In fact, private attorneys appeared in district court felony proceedings only occasionally.

What were the consequences of these characteristics for district court workgroups? Most workgroup members became familiar with other members only after they had interacted with them for a time. Turnover in assistants and public defenders and the rotation of judges prevented the reunion of people who had worked together in the past and who knew each other. We do not know precisely how long particular combinations of a judge, assistant state's attorneys, and public defenders remained unchanged, but they did not remain stable for longer than a month, and probably changed more rapidly. In the one or two weeks that the same people worked together, some common understandings and expectations undoubtedly developed. Everyone in the workgroup shared the goal of disposing of the heavy case load. But the workgroups did not seem stable enough to permit substantial development of consensus on how to achieve the internally oriented goals described in Chapter 2 — maintaining group cohesion and reducing uncertainty. Furthermore, there was not enough stability for patterns of mutual dependence to develop. Hence, rather than sharing influence equally among the participants, the judge typically dominated.

Although judges stayed for only a month, they were familiar with the operations and procedures of the district courts since they usually had served elsewhere in the system. They were in a strong position to affect the outcome of felony cases, because they had the ultimate say over which procedure would be used to dispose of cases. They could simply send the case to the grand jury regardless of what the defense and prosecution wanted. (As we have said, defendants had no absolute right to a preliminary hearing in Baltimore.) Or they could hold the examination and either find probable cause, which resulted in the case's referral to the grand jury, or dismiss the case. Other dispositions required the cooperation of prosecution and defense, but the judge played a key role. He could grant or deny the defense's motion to dismiss. For some charges, he had the option of accepting a guilty plea or conducting a bench trial. Finally, he could accept the results of negotiations between prosecution and defense, and either accept a plea to a misdemeanor or hold a bench trial on a reduced charge. As a result of these prerogatives, judges tended to dominate interactions and decisions of district court workgroups.

Their domination was not complete, however. Much of the work involved misdemeanors, not felonies. Judge, prosecutor, and public defender depended more on one another to dispose of these cases. Such dependence gave prosecutors and public defenders leverage, which spilled over into the handling of felony defendants, and gave assistant state's attorneys and public defenders a share of the decision on which technique to use for dispositions. Although many defendants like Roy Brown were passed on directly to the grand jury, public defenders obtained a preliminary hearing and a dismissal in a significant proportion of cases. There was even some plea bargaining, with defendants being found guilty of lesser charges. The nature of the charges brought and the limited familiarity of workgroup members with one another, however, did not permit bargains to be struck frequently. Private defense attorneys, who appeared much less often, did not attain the influence in district court workgroups that the public defenders assigned there did. In addition, police officers — who tended to work in a particular district longer than judge, prosecutor, or defense counsel — sometimes had considerable influence, especially in such matters as bail.

Workgroups in criminal court determined outcomes for most Baltimore felony defendants. These workgroups operated in nine courtrooms located in two neighboring buildings. Most were in the main courthouse, which also housed the clerk's office, the state's attorney's office, and a number of courtrooms in which civil matters were heard. Several courtrooms, however, were in the annex, an office building a block from the main courthouse, whose top floors had been converted into courtrooms. These converted courtrooms, with their low ceilings, utilitarian furniture, and a temporary quality were clean and well-lighted, but lacked the dignity and character of some of the main courthouse's courtrooms. Ironically, the annex courtrooms had public address systems, even though the acoustics were fairly good to begin with; most of the main courthouse's courtrooms did not, despite their very poor acoustics.

Turnover in the pool of judges, defense attorneys, and prose-cutors from which trial courtroom workgroup members came was substantial, but not as rapid as at the district court level. Assistant state's attorneys who graduated from the district courts or similarly undesirable assignments typically remained at the trial courts for a year or two. The regular public defenders as-signed to criminal court were mostly experienced defense attor-neys who planned on staying for some time. Many private attorneys specialized in criminal work. The judges were assigned to criminal court for one or two years, after which they moved to another assignment.

Though the pool of people constituting trial courtroom work-groups was somewhat more stable than in district court, the composition of these workgroups was less stable. Public de-fenders were assigned to individual defendants, not to specific courtrooms. They did not appear before the same judge on all or even most cases. Privately retained attorneys, of course, also migrated throughout the courthouse. Case assignment procedures allowed few opportunities for defense attorneys to steer cases to specific courtrooms. Even if an attorney could have steered his case, it might not be heard by the judge initially assigned. The court clerk's Case Assignment Office overscheduled cases for all courtrooms on the assumption that some cases listed as bench or jury trials would result in guilty pleas. Frequently, the docket in a courtroom broke down, forcing everyone involved in the case to move to an open courtroom. This practice reduced the fre-quency with which individual assistant state's attorneys appeared before the same judge. The prosecutor's office assigned each of its trial teams to one of the courtrooms, and the team had to handle all defendants scheduled for that courtroom. But in practice, the frequent breakdown in the docket forced team members to follow cases to courtrooms scattered all over the courthouse.

The turnover of judges and assistant state's attorneys, coupled with the instability of composition in the workgroup's member-ship, often produced the situation described in the hypothetical robbery case. Workgroup members frequently did not know one another; they had seldom worked together in the past and would probably not work together again in the near future. Their lack of familiarity affected the entire disposition process. It discouraged negotiations, because workgroup members could not effectively reduce uncertainty through bargaining. Hence, few guilty pleas developed through negotiations. In addition, the judge had the most influence, because patterns of mutual dependence that evolve through frequent and sustained interaction did not develop. The formal powers of the judge became more significant when exercised in a workgroup composed of strangers.

THE JUDGES' SPONSORING ORGANIZATIONS

Each of the twenty-two district judges in Baltimore served on one of three courts — traffic, civil, and criminal.[2] Eight of them presided over the district criminal courts. A single administrative judge supervised the work of all twenty-two. A chief administrative judge based in the state capitol at Annapolis presided over the entire district court system, which extended statewide, and he frequently visited his Baltimore courtrooms.

Until the district court system was set up, the functions of these courts were performed by municipal courts, staffed by elected judges. The municipal judges' reputation for wisdom, intelligence, and industriousness was questionable, and a highly publicized traffic ticket–fixing scandal did little to enhance their standing. With the introduction of the new district court system, the recruitment method changed. The governor appointed new district judges with the consent of the legislature. In an effort to improve the district court's competence and reputation, the governor established a judicial selection commission composed of attorneys and laymen to recommend qualified appointees.

At the time of our research, problems still remained. Most district court judges were former municipal judges elected under the old system and retained as district court judges when the new system was inaugurated. District court judgeships were not prestigious; working conditions were poor; the pay was modest by the legal profession's standards. A public defender expressed a commonly held opinion when he told us that many district judges were lazy, corrupt, or incompetent. This assessment was shared by a judicial official familiar with the situation, who pointed to specific problems with the productivity, sobriety, industriousness, and propriety of some of these judges.

The district court judges rarely met as a group and had little solidarity. Even casual meetings between them were infrequent because of the geographical dispersion of their courtrooms. They worked alone and were responsible for disposing of all criminal matters that arose in their district.

The district court judges had no organizational ties to judges of the Supreme Bench, the major trial court in Baltimore. That independence and their lesser standing resulted in some resentment. District court judges felt they handled more cases and had less time for them than the Supreme Bench. They especially resented having cases remanded (sent back) from the Supreme Bench; they saw that as an attempt to dump weak cases and bad statistics on them.

Felony trials were conducted by Supreme Bench judges assigned to criminal court. Since they rotated into the criminal court for a one- or two-year stint, the group of judges hearing criminal cases changed substantially from year to year. These judges were formally elected for fifteen-year terms, but the governor appointed judges to fill vacancies. The appointees (usually members of the governor's political party) then ran in a nonpartisan election within eighteen months. Nearly all (eighteen of the twenty-one) incumbents serving fifteen-year terms gained office in this manner, though in recent years several incumbents have been defeated in the election following their gubernatorial appointment. The recruitment process produced interesting results. The remnants of Baltimore's political organizations were active in the politics surrounding judicial appointment and election. Many of the incumbent judges belonged to or were identified with one of the surviving political organizations.[3] Nearly half came from political families, and over half had held prior public office, leading one observer to conclude that for the most part, they were "people with intimate ties to local partisan politics."[4] Democratic domination of the governorship (Spiro Agnew was the one recent exception) produced eighteen Democrats and three Republicans on the Supreme Bench. One-third were Jewish; over 60 percent came from families with a high social status. Although Baltimore's population was 47 percent black, only three of the judges were black. We have no systematic measures of these judges' attitudes toward such issues as defendant's rights versus the protection of society, the purposes of bail, or other issues related to the treatment of defendants in the criminal process. Our impression, however, is that most of the judges were conservative on such issues; that would not be inconsistent with the social origins and traditional political organization ties of the judges. The most striking exception was Judge Howard, a black former assistant state's attorney who defeated an incumbent judge running for a fifteen-year term. Howard had a reputation as an aggressive liberal judge with ties to liberal black judges in other cities (including Detroit's Judge Crockett).

The judges of the Supreme Bench held weekly meetings at which the chief judge, appointed by the governor, presided. The judicial organization was not strong, and the powers of the chief judge were limited. The gubernatorial selection of the chief judge weakened his status and stirred some resentment. During our research, he presided over the weekly meetings, reserved to himself (or, as sometimes happened, his clerk) the right to authorize postponements of cases scheduled for trial (a power formerly exercised by trial judges individually), and sought to install a computerized record-keeping system. Some judges felt his assumption of jurisdiction over postponements usurped their prerogatives. Indeed, several expressed their disapproval by ignoring his refusal to grant a continuance.[5] An abortive effort by some of the judges to have him removed by the chief judge of the circuit courts in Maryland toward the end of our research dramatically expressed the internal division on the court. We also learned of splits among the judges themselves.[6] Rivalries based on antagonisms among various Baltimore political factions with which the judges were identified led to the formation of cliques. Mere joint service on the Supreme Bench did not erase these antagonisms. Consequently, interaction at the weekly meetings did not generate solidarity but rather conflict and division. The cohesion needed for strong direction from the weekly conference did not exist during our research. Evidently, however, the lack of solidarity was not a direct result of the composition and organization of the court; the previous chief judge had presided over a much more cohesive and effective group.[7]

Although the organization that encompassed the judges assigned to criminal court was rather weak and lacked cohesion, it decided several important matters. It determined the distribution of work among the various courtrooms. During part of our research, all misdemeanor jury trials were heard in a single courtroom. In a rare instance of cooperation with the district court, a district court judge was assigned to hear these cases in return for the use of the courtroom. The Supreme Bench judges routinely discussed the condition of the docket at their weekly conference. For several of the judges this discussion was an important event, for it was a source of perceived pressure to move the docket. One judge, for instance, pointed to the weekly discussions as the basis for his feeling that the evaluation of his work was based on how many cases he moved quickly. Failure to dispose of enough cases, he felt, would produce hard feelings among the other judges.[8] Notice that it was peer pressure that he perceived, not pressure from the external environment or from superiors. Finally, the judges collectively established the procedures that gave the clerk's Case Assignment Office (CAO) responsibility for assigning cases to trial courtrooms. During the initial period of our research, cases were assigned as follows [9]: An assistant state's attorney in the case preparation section would contact the defense attorney. Together they arranged three alternative trial dates. The assistant then went to the CAO, indicating whether the defense attorney wanted a bench or jury trial. The CAO clerk tried to find a date and a courtroom that could accommodate the case. In practice, this procedure offered the assistant state's attorney several possibilities for judge-shopping. First, he could try to negotiate dates that desired judges had open. His daily contact with the CAO afforded the opportunity to keep track of this information. Second, by building a relationship with the CAO clerk, he could influence the choice that the clerk made among the judges available on the three alternative dates. Only high-volume defense attorneys were likely to match the assistant prosecutor's potential for successful shopping.

In the course of our research, the state's attorney's office abolished the case preparation section. The state's attorney then had less influence on the scheduling of cases, and the CAO took greater initiative. The Case Assignment Office began automatically to set the trial date for sixty days after the defense attorney filed his appearance, unless the attorney was on its list of the "top nineteen" regulars. Because those attorneys tried many cases, the CAO found it necessary to consult them about a trial date. These regulars (who included all the public defenders) could request that the case be set for a courtroom where they had already been assigned. Thus, they had an opportunity to engage in limited judge-shopping, which occasional defense attorneys did not enjoy.

The Case Assignment Office did not assign cases to courtrooms randomly. It scheduled more cases for the judges known to be fast and eager. Case Assignment Office personnel were forbidden to reveal to what courtroom a case had been assigned. The uncertainty about who the judge would be was removed only when the attorney received his first notice of trial some twenty-eight days before the trial date. On the trial day, the clerk charged with reassigning cases from overcrowded courtrooms attempted to inhibit shopping by sending cases to open courtrooms in the order he learned of their availability. Knowledgeable attorneys, however, sometimes could engage in judge-shopping at this stage as well.

THE BALTIMORE STATE'S ATTORNEY'S OFFICE

The state's attorney for Baltimore hired and supervised assistant state's attorneys in courtroom workgroups at both the district court and criminal court levels. Thus, whereas there were two judicial sponsoring organizations, there was only one prosecutor's office. However, the internal organization of his office reflected the two-tier court system. Fifteen assistants and a supervisor handled cases in the district courts, and twenty-six worked in the criminal court courtrooms. In addition, there were several other divisions — the case preparation section of five attorneys helped set trial dates, explored the possibility of guilty pleas with defense counsel, and prepared trial briefs to assist trial team members. The grand jury unit's two attorneys reviewed all cases before they went to the grand jury. There was also a narcotics strike force, a juvenile court section, and a section handling postconviction matters, habeas corpus petitions, and nonsupport proceedings. A small corps of top administrators, including the elected state's attorney, supervised the operation.

The state's attorney was selected in a partisan election for a four-year term. In recent years, several incumbents had resigned for one reason or another (often to assume a judgeship) before the expiration of their term. Competition in the subsequent election had been intense, although the low ballot position of the office obscured its visibility to the electorate. The political clubs and factions that survived in Baltimore generally dominated the state's attorney's race.

One of the state's attorney's most important tasks was the recruitment of assistant state's attorneys. Under some previous state's attorneys, assistant prosecutors' appointments were intensely political. Each city councilman's district received its proportion of appointments. In recent years, the direct participation of local political figures in recommending appointments declined markedly. When black politicians had acquired enough influence to permit them to influence appointments, the link between district politicians and appointments was broken. This break may be part of the reason why there were few blacks in the office even though both the state's attorney and his chief assistant were black. Despite the lack of explicit links to political processes, some assistants came to the office with excellent connections and a good knowledge of the politics of the city.

The attorneys who became assistant state's attorneys rarely came from the highest ranks of prestigious law schools. The pay, the insecure tenure, and the working conditions discouraged such people. Beginning assistant state's attorneys in 1972 received $10,550; the most experienced prosecutors earned only $18,900. Pay scales were considerably below offers made to top students of graduating law classes by large firms; they were, in fact, less than the public defender's office paid at the time.

Working conditions were not attractive either. District court assistant state's attorneys mostly worked in old, decrepit, noisy, and gloomy courtrooms. Their office accommodations were no better and sometimes worse. Most of the assistant state's attorneys had offices on the second or fifth floor of the main courthouse downtown. The second-floor offices were dismal, and those on the fifth floor not much better. Both were created by installing partitions in a large room to make cubicles. The partitions, painted a cheerless barracks green, did not reach the high ceiling, forcing confidential conversations down to a whisper. The arrangement did save steps, however. It was unnecessary to get up and see if a colleague was in his cubicle. It was easier to call out his name and await the shouted reply. Dim lighting completed the charm of these offices.

Finally, the lack of a tenure system and the uncertainties introduced by electoral turnover discouraged a career orientation among assistant state's attorneys. Assistants felt no clear promotion criteria existed, further decreasing any inclinations to build a career in the office. Office traditions and local attitudes produced expectations that a career could not be built in the prosecutor's office. Many of the older attorneys and political leaders in Baltimore felt it was entirely appropriate that the office serve as a three-year training ground for the city's young lawyers. Three years became the maximum stay of a typical assistant state's attorney.

These factors produced predictable results. Not only did the brightest young attorneys avoid employment in the state's attorney's office, but attorneys who did join came primarily because they wanted several years' trial experience and exposure to potential clients and other lawyers. This experience was available only in the criminal courtrooms, not in the juvenile division, district court, or one of the other special sections in the office. The incentive of new office members assigned to district court or the juvenile division to obtain a criminal court assignment was strong. Furthermore, the pay and prestige attached to these initial assignments was low. Once an assistant state's attorney obtained a coveted trial court assignment and gained the courtroom experience he sought, there was little reason to stay, particularly if an attractive opportunity in private practice arose. In 1972, such opportunities came frequently. The office was also losing experienced personnel to the public defender's office. In fact, two assistant state's attorneys left to serve as defenders in juvenile court, a job carrying little prestige, because of the higher pay and increased opportunities to build their private practices. Consequently, during our study turnover was devastatingly high. The administrative assistant projected that if the rate continued, half his staff would have less than one year's experience. Only six of the eighty-six assistants in the office in 1973 had served for more than five years. Excluding one veteran, the average length of service was twenty-one months. A high proportion of assistant state's attorneys trying cases thus had limited trial experience.

The assistant prosecutors had strong incentives to begin to build a private practice while still in the state's attorney's office. In many jurisdictions outside employment is prohibited, but Baltimore assistant state's attorneys could handle civil matters privately, and many did so. Assistants in the district courts had more time for private work, because they were often able to leave early in the afternoon. Trial assistants found they had less time, and their inability to spend as much time as they would have liked on their private practice contributed to frustration, discontent, and the desire to leave. In addition, instead of spending late afternoons and evenings preparing for the next day's trials, assistants often worked on their private practices.

The desperate need of the office for experienced men forced its leadership to devise interim strategies to retain them. By promoting assistants to administrative positions that carried higher pay, it was possible to get some to stay. But those who had been promoted had less time available for courtroom litigation, necessitating the use of inexperienced men in courtroom assignments. As a result, the office had a severe problem with the quality of its personnel. Several of the more experienced assistants themselves recognized the incompetence of many of their colleagues in the criminal court as well as in the district courts. Administrative personnel acknowledged serious problems with the quality of the staff, though less directly.[10]

The short tenure of assistants had other implications as well. The fact that they planned on entering private practice soon frequently shaped assistants' behavior in dealing with the defense bar. Although it is difficult to document this effect precisely, field interviews suggest its validity. For example, a veteran defense attorney of some ten years' experience (including four as an assistant prosecutor) observed that when assistants start out, "They're filled with piss and vinegar." But as they get experience and anticipate going into private practice, they become increasingly concerned about avoiding bad relations with the bar. Anticipations of future private practice also reinforce their inclination to get along with the judges. The Baltimore system had an unusual feature that increased the sensitivity of assistants to judges and weakened the state's attorney's hold on them. Each year the judges reviewed the state's attorney's list of assistants whose employment he intended to renew. The judges were able to disapprove of an assistant, which resulted in his being unable to appear in court. This was not an idle threat. In the recent past an assistant who wrote a report on differential sentencing of blacks and whites in rape cases was disapproved by the judges and suspended from trying cases.[11]

Formal training of the constant influx of new assistants was haphazard. Assistants began in district court or juvenile court and then moved to trial court, to team leader, then to an administrative post. This sequence undoubtedly confronted the attorney with a variety of situations that inevitably "trained" him. Team leaders made some efforts to help new men handle their cases. One, for instance, told us he carefully went over the pleas his new assistants worked out so that the new man would not obtain a reputation as a "patsy" among the defense bar. Those judges who were accessible to assistants also helped train new men. But not all of the judges were able or willing to perform this task. None of these efforts constituted a systematic program of socialization; assistants were socialized primarily through a system of sink-or-swim.

Assistant state's attorneys in the district courts worked more or less on their own in two-man teams. Only one supervisor existed for the entire city; he could not often give on-the-spot supervision. The trial assistants were divided into teams of three or four attorneys for each courtroom; typically one or two were in court while the others were preparing the next day's cases. Each team was preoccupied with the cases on its docket and had little time or common interest in interacting with members of other teams. For example, assistant state's attorneys usually lunched with their own team. The grand jury section worked in its own cramped office and was constantly swamped with cases. It made decisions while the district court prosecutors were in court, making it nearly impossible to question them about cases sent forward from the district court. Members of the grand jury section rarely saw district court assistant state's attorneys personally, because the grand jury section operated out of the central courthouse whereas the district court teams were scattered throughout the city.

The case preparation section had too little clout to overcome these centrifugal forces to provide central control and direction. The information it obtained was not considered reliable enough by the criminal court trial teams to serve as the basis for a dismissal, trial strategy, or guilty plea. Its inability to commit trial assistants to plea bargains arranged with defense counsel was especially serious and contributed heavily to the decision to abolish it.[12]

The result was that assistant state's attorneys in workgroups at both the district court and criminal court levels were not tightly controlled by their sponsoring agency. The central office did not enforce uniform standards or policies restricting the type of plea bargains. Experienced assistants typically did not seek approval of plea bargains by a superior. Although new trial assistants often discussed their cases with their team leaders, assistant state's attorneys did not feel that supervisors or "the office" was looking over their shoulders or constraining their behavior. Contact between assistants and top administrators occurred infrequently. Even trial team leaders were not closely supervised. However, the state's attorney's office did not lack all influence over the behavior of trial assistant state's attorneys. There was a fairly strong office norm that weak cases should be plea bargained whereas strong cases should be taken to trial even if a plea bargain was possible. Assistant state's attorneys also realized that they had to move their dockets. These two norms combined to create a dilemma for assistants. They knew they had to move their docket, but if too many cases were pled, they could expect to hear about it from the front office. Thus, the sponsoring organization was concerned about both the number of dispositions and the kind of case disposed of by a plea bargain, and its concern shaped assistant state's attorneys' behavior. But it did not affect the specific content of an assistant state's attorney's plea bargains.

THE DEFENSE BAR IN BALTIMORE

Maryland employs a statewide public defender system.[13] That insulates the Baltimore office somewhat from the local pressures felt by the state's attorney's office. Most of the defenders' funds came from the state, not from the city of Baltimore, which financed the prosecutor's office.[14] The statewide public defender organization, not the electorate, chose the office's head and its top personnel. Compared to assistant state's attorneys, the public defenders were well paid. New defenders assigned to district courts received $5,000 more than assistant state's attorneys; those who practiced in criminal court received $1,000 more than the top salary in the state's attorney's office. Public defenders were also permitted to have a private practice, and many found ample time to devote to it. The legislation creating the state public defender system also required it to assign as many cases as possible to private counsel. Thus, the private defense bar received case assignments from the defender's office.

The office had an incentive to make these assignments. Each of the eight people assigned to handle cases as public defenders in criminal court rotated weekly as desk attorney. They screened all cases that came to them, keeping some for themselves and farming the rest out to attorneys included in the panel of private practitioners maintained by the office. Assigning cases to panel attorneys ameliorated possible opposition to the office from the defense bar.[15] It also reduced the work load of the staff attorneys, freeing some of their time for the pursuit of their private practices. The criteria staff attorneys used in deciding what cases to "panel out" or keep themselves varied. Defendants on bail tended to be assigned to panel attorneys. These attorneys did not like to go to the jail, and bailed defendants could come to them. The defenders, on the other hand, could conveniently send their investigators over to the jail to interview defendants confined there. Cases involving codefendants and those which looked like they would necessitate a complicated jury trial went to private attorneys with good reputations. Limits on the number of cases farmed out were imposed by the funds available to pay panel attorneys. The vouchers submitted by these attorneys for their services were higher than anticipated, even though the hourly rates were modest. Assigning too many cases to panel attorneys would have depleted the budget. Consequently, the staff attorneys found they had to take about half of the cases themselves.

Both panel attorneys and public defenders reviewed their cases earlier than the trial prosecutor, giving them more time to prepare. The public defenders also could utilize the services of a substantial number of investigators.

The office of public defender was even less centralized than the state's attorney's office. The eight criminal court staff attorneys exercised considerable discretion. At the time we conducted our field research, the office did not even bother to publish statistics on how many cases each of the eight farmed out to the panel. Some complained that everyone did not share the case burden equally, but no mechanisms for rectifying the imbalance existed. The less experienced district court defenders were geographically dispersed, limiting the possibilities for supervision. The poor techniques for passing information about cases from district court to criminal court defenders also limited supervision. Indeed, one experienced assistant felt there were really two defenders' organizations — one for each court level.

The high salaries for part-time work attracted well-established and experienced people to the public defender's office. This was especially true of the eight staff attorneys who practiced in the criminal court. But district court defenders were more experienced than their counterparts from the prosecutor's office. Although there was no formal program of socialization in the defender's office, younger staff members tended to serve in the district courts or juvenile court. As mentioned, two defenders were stationed in most of the districts, allowing new recruits to benefit from working with more experienced colleagues.

Although we did not explicitly seek to study the recruitment process for defenders, the field interviews revealed some suggestions that the statewide character of the defender system did not eliminate the value of local political contacts. Several recent appointees were identified by one respondent as relatives of money men (fund raisers) of the governor. The head of the office was the brother-in-law of an important figure in a Baltimore political organization. The father of another staff attorney was said to be active in east side politics. There were also some "merit" appointments, but political activity and connections appeared to be significant for those seeking appointments. One measure of the ties between the public defender's office and the local established political structure was the fact that to our knowledge there was not a single black public defender at the criminal court level, despite the fact that Baltimore had black attorneys and that most defendants were black.

The formation of the public defender's office had a significant impact on Baltimore's private defense bar. For one thing, some of its established members joined the office, ensuring close ties to the established private criminal bar. The office naturally reduced business for private attorneys. However, their unhappiness was tempered by the paneling out procedure, which made the office an important source of clients. Furthermore, the defense bar became more diffuse, because the public defender's panel included attorneys who formerly had not appeared in criminal court. Work became more spread out, reducing the number of high-volume attorneys. However, some concentration among regulars remained. The clerk's Case Assignment Office list of the top nineteen attorneys (in terms of case volume) included a handful of private practitioners along with all the public defenders.

The practice of paneling out cases to private attorneys produced complicated mixtures of incentives for attorneys whose appointments constituted an important part of their practice. When they were paid by the defendant, they had to handle all aspects of the case efficiently. If they consistently spent more time in preparation and courtroom appearances than the defendant could pay for, their ability to earn a good living was destroyed. Once the time spent on a case equaled the fee that could be collected, additional time was essentially free time donated to the client. Since most private clients were fairly poor, it was necessary to ration preparation time and courtroom time while keeping in mind the problem of getting paid. Thus guilty pleas and brief bench trials were strongly encouraged. However, when attorneys represented indigent defendants assigned by the public defenders, they had no problems getting paid. The defender footed the bill. There was no free time because they could bill the office of public defender twenty dollars an hour for preparation and twenty-five dollars an hour for courtroom time. Since they were paid almost as much for preparation as courtroom work, these attorneys had an incentive to spend time preparing a case. Protracted jury trials remained unattractive, although panel attorneys received at least something for their courtroom time. Guilty pleas were not much more attractive than brief bench trials, and perhaps they were less so, because guilty pleas might produce less billable preparation time.

There were other incentives shaping behavior in cases that came from the defenders. Everyone was aware that attorneys could be removed from the panel. In fact, the defender's office removed several lawyers after judges had complained about the quality of their representation and conduct. It was also important to convince the client that a good job had been done or build a paper record that would demonstrate the vigor of the attorney's defense. Unsatisfied clients could bring complaints about the quality of their representation. Appointed attorneys, whom defendants derisively called state attorneys, had difficulty controlling their clients or preventing complaints.[16] The fear of having to undergo an inquiry into their conduct, however frivolous the complaint and resounding the vindication, was real and frequently expressed. Furthermore, clients who were "out of control" were more likely to insist on a jury trial. These factors combined to enhance the value of judges' and assistant state's attorneys' ability to help a panel attorney convince his client that he had done a good job.

Several other characteristics of the private defense bar were noteworthy. First, there were few black lawyers. Second, many defense attorneys had served as assistant state's attorneys. Third, the quality of many defense attorneys was not very high. Few of our respondents had a high opinion of the defense bar. A former assistant state's attorney, now in private practice, put it this way: "The problem with the defense bar in Baltimore is that the experienced ones aren't any good and the good ones aren't experienced." One of the few black attorneys described the defense bar as ineffective, not vigorous, and not very strong advocates for their clients. Finally, defense counsel in Baltimore came to courtrooms with even less central direction than judges and prosecutors. The private defense bar is rarely cohesive anywhere, but our impression is that there was less communication among its members in Baltimore than in the other two cities. Public defenders' offices are often hierarchical organizations with some central control. In Baltimore, however, the office did not exert much influence over the behavior of its courtroom staff.

THE ENVIRONMENTAL CONTEXT

Baltimore's population was nearly half black in 1972. Almost all its judges, prosecutors, defense attorneys, and other court personnel were white. The overwhelming portion of felony defendants were black men. These stark facts dramatize the underlying importance of race in the city's politics and the operation of its criminal justice system.

Like other large urban centers, Baltimore has encountered serious difficulties. It has a highly visible and symbolically threatening crime problem. Its economy has stagnated, its population declined, its physical condition deteriorated, its welfare rolls increased. At the same time, the proportion of blacks within the declining population has increased.

A study of the politics of poverty in Baltimore written several years before our research began introduces its discussion of the ideology of race and poverty with the following words: "Until the late 1950's, Baltimore was a Southern city in the important sense that a large white majority not only controlled the political machinery but systematically reinforced an ideology of white supremacy." [17] Unlike most major urban centers in the United States, Baltimore has a conservative, Southern heritage. The conservative tradition's hold has loosened, but its effects are still felt. Blacks have not yet won as much political power in Baltimore as in cities with a comparable proportion of blacks. During our research, blacks represented constituencies on the city council and in the state legislature, but with the exception of the black state's attorney, most major elective offices were held by whites. After a flurry of activity and some political successes in the mid-1960s, the impetus in the drive for greater representation of blacks in government slowed. The reasons for this failure are complex.[18] Internal disputes among leaders of the black community, a tradition of nonvoting and apathy among the black population, and competition from surviving white political organizations provide some of the reasons. Regardless of the reasons, the defeat in 1974 of the black state's attorney who headed the office during our research provides evidence of the black community's weakness.

Despite recent reverses, black political power has undoubtedly increased in Baltimore. But the courts seem to be one of the last major areas to be penetrated by blacks. In 1972, only three Supreme Bench judges were black; there were only two black district judges. Few defense attorneys were black; no assistant state's attorneys who appeared in court were black. In fact, a study of employment practices throughout the system, conducted by a black Supreme Bench judge, found overwhelming white domination: whites held 83 percent of the 772 positions either under the direct supervision of the Supreme Bench or in the collateral support services (civil clerk's offices, office of the register of wills, the sheriff's office, the clerk of the criminal court, and state's attorney). In 1973, 77 percent of positions under the direct supervision of the Supreme Bench were occupied by whites.[19] In 1975, blacks held only 18 percent of positions in the office of the sheriff, 3 percent in the office of the state's attorney, and 18 percent in criminal court clerk's office.[20] The only aspect of the criminal justice system in which blacks were heavily represented, in fact, was in the composition of juries.

Equally striking was the absence of a substantial, pro-defendant sentiment in Baltimore. Unlike some other large cities, Baltimore had no organized group of aggressive, liberal, or radical attorneys. As noted earlier, most of the judges appeared to be moderate or conservative in their attitudes toward defendants and crime.

Finally, the dominant newspapers, the morning and evening *Sun,* generally were quite conservative on crime issues. The local Hearst paper, the afternoon *News-American,* took a consistently hard law-and-order stance. Although we have no hard evidence, it is likely that much of Baltimore's population shared these perspectives. We do know that evaluations of the seriousness of crime were fairly uniform across population groups in Baltimore.[21]

Attitudes toward the Baltimore City Jail and its problems illustrated the generally conservative attitudes expressed in Baltimore. The physical condition of the jail was bad. Its population was large, and many of its inmates were awaiting trial because they could not make bail. The *Sun* papers did not ignore the jail, but their articles focused on problems associated with the management of the institution. They criticized the warden for putting his wife on the payroll, for keeping sloppy books, for "losing" defendants. Small disturbances and a riot among the inmates attracted considerable coverage. But issues related to substantive reforms or the improvement of conditions for inmates were not raised by the *Sun* papers. Although some individuals in the system expressed concern about jail conditions, they made no effort to do anything. Nor was there much effective community pressure. People who disapproved of the jail population's size did not advocate more liberal bail policies to reduce it or new procedures to speed the disposition of jailed defendants' cases. When questioned about their inactivity, such people indicated that community pressure in general and the probable reaction of the *Sun* papers in particular made such changes impossible to implement.

The newspapers played an important role in structuring the environment of courtroom participants. Baltimore's assistant state's attorneys worried that their decisions would come back to haunt them in the press, and they modified their behavior accordingly. The papers reflected (and helped maintain) a generally unfavorable community attitude toward plea bargaining. A relatively experienced assistant for Baltimore (two years in the office) traced his reluctance to plea bargain to his aversion to the responsibility it entailed. When pressed, he revealed that this responsibility included the fear that he would read on the back page of the *Baltimore Sun* that a person recently convicted of an offense has committed another crime, and that he, as the assistant prosecutor in the first case, had recommended probation or a short sentence. "I have to protect my reputation."

The papers did more than report case dispositions in the courthouse, however. The major participants in the felony disposition process both feared them and used them for political intrigues to a degree not found in Chicago and Detroit. When the chief judge, for example, became concerned with the number of requests the state's attorney's office was making for postponements, he threatened to take the matter to the *Sun* papers. One assistant prosecutor said that he took a weak case to trial (despite office norms to the contrary) because he feared the police would complain to the papers and inspire an article that would make him look bad. This was not an unrealistic expectation, because nearly everyone could cite examples of someone having "gone to the papers." A former assistant, for example, told how he leaked the new state's attorney's decision to dismiss a case the assistant felt should have been prosecuted. The story received prominent coverage. Another assistant's report on differential sentencing of blacks and whites in rape cases that resulted in his disapproval (p. 85) came to light through a leak to the papers. The numerous stories about the outcomes of trials offer additional evidence of extensive contacts between assistants and the press. The assistants themselves frequently contacted a reporter to convey the outcome of a trial. This is consistent with our failure to observe reporters in the courtrooms despite the fact that stories about cases appeared regularly. Those stories provided ambitious young assistants with valuable publicity. Thus, the papers were both feared and courted, and were a salient factor in the calculation of strategies by both prosecutors and their adversaries.

Public attitudes and the stance of the newspapers affected the relative importance and content of courtroom workgroups' external goals. The goal of moving cases did not receive massive public support. Indeed, the jail remained overcrowded partly because cases were not rapidly disposed. At the same time, the goal of doing justice was given specific content. The principal component of justice for those charged with serious crimes was a trial disposition rather than a plea. These perspectives reflected the sentiments of the general public; the problems of the criminal courts were not portrayed from the perspective of defendants or the black community. Even the black-owned *Afro-American* did not develop an alternative perspective on the issue of crime and race. Furthermore, few among judges, prosecutors, or defense counsel adhered to a liberal or strongly pro-defendant position. And as noted previously, Baltimore's blacks were not as organized as blacks in other cities, and few effective liberal or reform oriented groups existed. Consequently, few pressures for leniency toward defendants came from the environment.

Baltimore courtroom workgroups and sponsoring organizations were not entirely removed from city politics, however. Assistant state's attorneys often had ties with political organizations. The state's attorney's office was totally funded by the city. The size of its staff, the salaries paid, and the support available depended heavily on what the City Board of Estimate did. In 1972 the city controller, who sits on the board, was known as an opponent of the office. He reportedly felt that one prosecutor per courtroom was sufficient and that the state's attorney's office was considerably overstaffed. That opinion made him reluctant to grant funds for hiring additional assistants or raising their pay to be competitive with the public defenders. In addition, the fact that the state's attorney had recently conducted an investigation of a member of the city council who was still in office was another source of friction between the office and the council.

Finally, some aspects of Baltimore's police force peculiarly affected the operation of courtroom workgroups. The state's attorney and the chief of police engaged in intense and open conflict for many months. The battle included the trading of public accusations (the state's attorney claimed the police had bugged his office) and struggles over the control of police liaison officers assigned to the state's attorney's special drug unit. Although we cannot trace with precision the effects of this conflict, it undoubtedly interfered with the effectiveness of the drug unit and deterred both parties from proposing actions that would necessitate the cooperation of the other. For example, no effective system of prosecutorial screening of cases shortly after arrest could be established without close police cooperation, since Maryland law did not require prosecutor approval of all arrest warrants. Hence, during this period, prosecutors did no screening of arrests before they came to court. Another problem concerned the police officers' association, the Fraternal Order of Police. It actively participated in public debate about the structure and performance of the criminal justice system, reinforcing the prevailing climate of opinion that emphasized the rights of the community over those of defendants.

CONCLUSION

Three major characteristics stand out in the structure of Baltimore courtroom workgroups and the environments in which they worked. First, they were not very stable, because their participants were more transient than in many other places. Judges (especially in the district courts) rotated frequently; state's attorneys and defense counsel rarely stayed in a single workgroup for several months at a time; at the trial level, they split their work day among several workgroups.

Second, the sponsoring organizations of the principal members of the workgroups exercised little supervisory control. The judges' organization was weak and decentralized. The state's attorney's office had immense difficulties in recruiting and maintaining its staff; little time or expertise remained for supervision. The public defender's office made almost no attempt to control its staff. Consequently, courtroom participants responded largely to their personal incentives and to those which were generated by the loose structure of their courtroom workgroups.

Third, the task environment specified considerable harshness toward defendants. Baltimore was a law-and-order city with few voices raised for defendants' rights. The police, the media, and the general political process combined to articulate these sentiments, which courtroom workgroups perceived in vivid terms. The career and political ambitions of many participants made them aware of these public attitudes.

One result of these characteristics was that few guilty pleas occurred in Baltimore. Instead, Baltimore was a city of trials.

NOTES

1. Until about 1970, the state's attorney's office had nearly complete control over the setting of trial dates. By the time our research concluded, it had lost most of this power to the clerk's Case Assignment Office.

2. Personal interview with district judge.

3. Joel Ish, "Trial Judges: Their Recruitment, Backgrounds and Role Perceptions," unpublished paper delivered at the 1975 Annual Meeting of the American Political Science Association.

4. Ibid., p. 10.

5. Personal observation, March 6, 1973.

y attorney's office.'s office.udge.reme Bench.e im-
pression of incompetence in the minds of district court judges. A defendant
was acting as his own attorney during a preliminary hearing. He was cross-
examining the victim of an armed robbery and rape who also happened to
be a nun. When the assistant state's attorney failed to object to the defendant's asking her if she were a virgin and how many times she had had
intercourse, the judge admonished him and cut off further questioning.

11. However, the consequences of the suspension were not too serious
in this instance; the offending prosecutor subsequently became a member
of the bench.

12. A felony complaint unit was created in its place. It was to review
cases before the preliminary hearing and make decisions on which cases
to dismiss, on which to seek preliminary hearings, and which to try to plead
out in district court. The idea was to screen junk cases quickly. We were
not able accurately to assess its effectiveness. However, the predictable
rivalry and conflict between it and district court assistant prosecutors
erupted not long after its creation.

13. This section is based on extensive personal interviews and observations between September 1972 and June 1973. Note that the following
description of the public defender's operation in Baltimore conflicts with
that provided by Paul B. Wice and Peter Suwak, "Current Realities of
Public Defender Programs: A National Survey and Analysis," *Criminal Law
Bulletin* 10 (March 1974): 161–183. The Wice and Suwak article is incorrect.

14. Some defendants represented by the public defender's office were
asked to pay partial fees if they could afford it.

15. In December 1972 there were 253 attorneys on the panel, classified
according to their ability. Personal interview with head of the public defender's office for Baltimore.

16. See Jonathan Casper, *American Criminal Justice* (Englewood Cliffs,
N.J.: Prentice-Hall, 1972), chap. 4.

17. Peter Bachrach and Morton S. Baratz, *Power and Poverty: Theory
and Practice* (New York: Oxford University Press, 1970), p. 2.

18. Ibid., pp. 74–80. The discussion that follows is based on Bachrach
and Baratz's description.

19. Joseph C. Howard, Sr., *Employment Practices in the Administration
of Justice Under the Supreme Bench of Baltimore City* (Baltimore: Center
for Urban Affairs, Morgan State University, 1975), p. 11. Howard also
reports that in 1973 (when our research ended), blacks held but five of
the eighty-eight professional positions in the state's attorney's office.

20. Ibid., table 7, p. 34.

21. Peter H. Rossi, Emily Waite, Christine E. Bose, and Richard E. Berk,
"The Seriousness of Crimes: Normative Structure and Individual Differences," *American Sociological Review* 39 (1974): 224–237.

Chapter 5

CHICAGO: WORKGROUP NEGOTIATION

The curious observer could choose between two locations to observe felony proceedings in Chicago. By far the more attractive and convenient courtrooms are in the Civic Center in the heart of downtown. Graced by a Picasso statue, the Civic Center is a modern skyscraper housing a variety of city agencies. But most defendants appeared in the courtrooms located in an aging building at Twenty-sixth and California on the city's southwest side. It is dreary, dingy, and anything but modern. It is miles from the Loop and far from commercial areas. It can be reached by bus, but not by the city's rail transit system. There are virtually no restaurants in the area. About the only building convenient to it is the equally dreary Cook County Jail. Other nearby attractions include railroad tracks, light industry, and a public housing development. No one could mistake the building's purpose on entry. Guards at the entrance not only open packages and briefcases, but also frisk strangers. The building itself contains twenty courtrooms, small and dingy offices for the assistant state's attorneys and public defenders, a waiting room for jurors, and the clerk of court's office. A stand-up snack bar the size of a two-car garage serves the entire building. The courtrooms are old, dark, sweltering in the summer, and noisy.

Thus, the felony disposition process is concentrated in a stagnant backwater, shielded from the lively controversies that mark public affairs in Chicago. Few casual observers wander into its precincts. Few notice it; even fewer can influence it.

AN ARMED ROBBERY CASE IN CHICAGO

All of the significant proceedings following arrest in most defen-dants' cases occur at Twenty-sixth and California. The principal steps in the disposition of defendants' cases will again be illustrated by following a hypothetical defendant from arrest to sentencing. We will assume the same situation presented in the previous chapter. The Chicago defendant is named Donald Charles.

The arresting officers took Charles back to the liquor store for identification and then placed him and the three victims in their squad car and drove to the police precinct station. After filling out the arrest report, the arresting officers called in a detective to help draw up the complaint. Because of the seriousness of the offense, they also obtained the watch commander's approval of the charges. The complaint charged armed robbery, robbery, and unlawful use of a weapon. Those were the formal charges on which probable cause would have to be determined.

Chicago defendants arrested after 5:00 P.M. had bail set immediately in a special bond court. However, a delay in locating Charles' prior record made it impossible to get a decision from bond court before its 2:00 A.M. closing time. So the police took him to the Cook County Jail.

The clerk in the preliminary hearing courtroom at Twenty-sixth and California called Donald Charles' case about 10:15 the following morning. He was taken from the adjoining lockup into the noisy courtroom, packed with defendants, relatives, attorneys, policemen, and witnesses. Before Charles and the bailiffs had completed their brief walk to the bench, the judge had begun reading the charges aloud. After glancing for a few seconds at the arrest report and prior record, the judge asked

Charles if he had a job, then set bond at $10,000. His next question followed immediately. "Are you ready for your hearing?" Looking bewildered, the startled defendant shook his head and muttered "no." "OK," the judge said, "continuance until October 12 by motion of the defendant. Be sure you have an attorney with you next time, or at least consult one, because these are serious charges. Next case." Without delay, two bailiffs grasped Charles firmly by the arms and led him back to the lockup.

Unlike the Baltimore defendant, Charles did not have to hire a bail bondsman to purchase his pretrial freedom. Illinois had reformed its bail system and eliminated the professional bondsman. Instead of paying a bondsman 10 percent of the bond's face value, Illinois defendants could deposit the 10 percent with the clerk of the court. Ninety percent of this sum was returned at the conclusion of the case. If Charles could raise $1,000, he would receive $900 back eventually. The total cost of bail would only be $100. Nevertheless, he needed $1,000 immediately, and like many other defendants, neither he nor his family could produce that much. So he spent the thirty days between his first and second appearance in the Cook County Jail next door to the courthouse. Remembering the judge's words, he asked his family to hire an attorney. They contacted several, but could not come up with the initial fee demanded. However, a fellow inmate gave Charles a valuable piece of information. "When the judge asks if you are ready for your hearing, just say yes."

On October 12, the bailiff once again ushered Charles into the courtroom. "Are you ready for hearing?" asked the judge. Charles replied that he was, causing the judge to turn to one of the assistant state's attorneys assigned to his courtroom. "Is the state ready? Are your witnesses here?" "No, your honor, neither the complaining witness nor the arresting officers are here." Obviously, no attempt to summon them had been made. The judge declared another thirty-day continuance by motion of the state. Noting that November 12 was a Sunday, and that both the 13th and 14th were filled, the judge continued the hearing until November 15. He announced that he was marking this date "final," signifying that if the prosecution's witnesses were not in court, he would dismiss the case.

Still without an attorney, and still a resident of Cook County

Jail, Charles walked into the preliminary hearing courtroom for the third time on November 15. The judge asked the assistant prosecutor if his witnesses were present, and when he learned they were, he asked the defendant where his attorney was. Charles replied he did not have one. The judge announced he was appointing the public defender assigned to his courtroom to represent Charles and passed the case until later that day. The defender went to the lockup to confer with his client for about ten minutes later that morning. The clerk called the case again in mid-afternoon. When Charles emerged from the lockup, his family gathered around him as he stood in front of the right side of the bench. The assistant prosecutor and his witnesses stood together on the left side. In front of them sat the court reporter. Neither side had prepared. The assistant state's attorney was surprised when the store clerk mentioned that two other customers were in the store at the time, and at the curt suggestion of the judge, obtained their names and addresses for entry into his file. The state's attorney also called one of the arresting officers. His questions focused on the identification of the defendant as the assailant and on the evidence obtained on his arrest. The public defender cross-examined all the state's witnesses but presented none of his own. Informality characterized the entire proceeding. At one point, the judge interrupted the prosecutor and began asking his own questions. The public defender began to argue for a dismissal at the conclusion of testimony, but the judge cut him off, announced he had heard enough, and informed the assembly that he was binding the defendant over to the grand jury. The proceeding consumed only ten minutes. Charles did not need to be guided by the bailiff this time. He knew the way back to the lockup, and from there to the adjoining jail.

As in Baltimore, a special section in the prosecutor's office supervised grand jury proceedings. It determined when cases went to the grand jury. The date depended largely on when the term of a case was to expire. State law required that jailed defendants had to be tried within 120 days of arrest unless a delay had been requested by the defendant. However, on September 12, when Charles mumbled he was not ready, it counted as a continuance by motion of the defendant. The 120-day term did not start running until his second appearance, on October 12. The grand jury section encountered routine problems in finding a date when the necessary witnesses were available. One of the arresting officers was on furlough. Finally, December 14, 1972 was arranged. The case's presentation was routine, as was the result — indictment on the original charges filed by the police. Ninety-four days after the arrest, the case was ready for assignment to a trial court. Charles spent all that time in the Cook County Jail.

The day following his indictment, Charles left his jail cell to go to the courtroom of the chief judge of the Criminal Division of Cook County Circuit Court. The chief judge arraigned him on the charges in the indictment and assigned his case to Judge Brown's courtroom. Later that same day, he appeared for the first time in the trial courtroom. Judge Brown asked who his attorney was. When Charles replied he had none, the judge appointed the public defender assigned to his courtroom. The assistant defender, who had worked in this courtroom for almost a year, moved for discovery * of the police write-up to permit him to read it. He also asked for a copy of the preliminary hearing transcript. The proceedings concluded when the prosecutor requested the next court appearance in two weeks, since the 120-day term was beginning to run out. The judge marked a continuance by motion of the state until December 28. Because the motion for a continuance was made by the state, the 120-day term continued to run.

On the morning of December 28, the public defender spoke with his client in the lockup adjoining the courtroom. He informed his defendant that on the basis of the police write-up, it looked as though they had grounds for a motion to quash the arrest, but that if it failed, things looked bleak. The defendant insistently asked if he could get his bail lowered. "How much money can your people raise?" Charles replied not much, maybe $100 or $150. The defender promised to see what he could do.

After this brief conference, the defender walked into the judge's chambers. Both assistant state's attorneys assigned to the

---

* Discovery is a procedure requiring the prosecutor to share with defense counsel information in his case file.

courtroom, along with the judge and two private attorneys who regularly appeared there, were engrossed in conversation when he entered. The discussion alternated between the Chicago Blackhawks' prospects and the cases docketed for the day. The defender mentioned that he had just talked with his defendant in the armed robbery case and that Charles wanted to be released on bail.

JUDGE: What sort of fellow is he?

PD: He has one prior conviction — robbery, 1967. He seems like an OK fellow, but I've just met him. I don't know if he is hooked into crime yet or not. Possibly not.

JUDGE: Once he is, there's not a damn thing can be done with him. How much can he raise?

PD: He says $100 to $150.

ASA: A $1,500 bond on an armed robbery? Come on! Let's just give him a good conduct medal.

JUDGE: I'm inclined to lower the bond. How about $2,000?

PD: I think that is reasonable. What with the motion pending and the term problem, we could probably go for a continuance by agreement if he makes bail.

The nearly empty courtroom sprang to life as the assistant state's attorneys, public defender, and private defense attorneys emerged from the judge's chambers. A few seconds later, the judge appeared and the day's proceedings began. When Charles' case was called (the third of eight the day's docket), the public defender moved for a reduction of bond to $2,000. After an objection for the record by the assistant state's attorney, the judge granted the motion. The public defender informed the judge he still had not received a copy of the preliminary hearing transcript. The judge asked the assistant state's attorney whether he could provide it within two weeks. Getting a positive response, the judge then asked whether the case could be continued for two weeks. The prosecutor replied that was fine with him if the public defender agreed. The public defender agreed, and the judge announced a continuance until January 11 "by agreement." The continuance by agreement broke the 120-day term, giving the prosecution another 120 days to bring the case to trial if Charles stayed in jail, or 160 days if he made the $2,000 bail.

On January 11, the defendant walked into the courtroom a free man, as a result of his family's successful efforts to raise the $200 deposit needed for his release. The proceedings again were brief. The defender announced that on the basis of the preliminary hearing transcript, a motion to quash the arrest was in order. The hearing on the motion was set for thirty days later, February 12. On that date, the judge conducted the hearing on the motion, hearing the testimony of the arresting officers. After denying the motion, the judge set trial with subpoenas for thirty days (March 7). "Trial with subpoenas" meant that all witnesses would be formally subpoenaed to appear on that date.

As March 7 approached, the prosecutor and public defender began to engage in a series of brief discussions about the case. Although they could not agree on the contents of a negotiated plea, both felt the possibility was worth exploring. They mentioned their feelings to the judge before court convened on the trial date. Later, in open court, the public defender asked for a conference. Courtroom regulars knew he meant a plea bargaining conference. The judge asked, "Do you gentlemen think a conference would be useful?" Their affirmative response and immediate departure for the judge's chambers left the defendant, the store owner, and the two customers puzzled. Several other attorneys were lounging in chambers when the three men entered, and they remained for the entire conference. The assistant state's attorney outlined his case briefly, stressing the defendant's prior robbery conviction and the ominous implication of his forcing the three men in the store to lie face down on the floor at gunpoint. A sentence of from eight to twelve years, he observed, was necessary. Charles' attorney noted problems the victims had in identifying his client initially and the inability of one of the customers to identify him at all. He also pointed out that his client had completed the probation imposed after his only prior offense and had stayed out of trouble. He acknowledged that some jail time would be appropriate, but that four years would be more reasonable. He added, with a hint of a smile, that it wouldn't be a bad case to try before a jury. "Besides, my man has already had a good taste of jail. He doesn't

want any more. I'm not sure he'll take anything less than probation." The assistant state's attorney sourly observed that people
who took other people's money at gunpoint, especially more
than once, deserved a long stay at Joliet prison, not probation.
The judge asked both men if the defendant was abusive or
threatening to his victims, and whether he appeared nervous or
"cool" during the robbery. The two attorneys agreed there was
no evidence of abusiveness, threats, or excessive nervousness.
"Well," observed the judge, "I'm inclined to go along with four
to eight years." The assistant state's attorney noted that armed
robbery carried a minimum four-year term. The defender suggested if his client pled to the second count of the indictment,
robbery, he could be sentenced to two to five, but added he
would not be surprised if the case had to go to a jury. The
prosecutor noted unhappily that his superiors frowned on reductions of armed robbery to simple robbery. The judge suggested
the case be continued until Friday, March 9. Everyone emerged
from chambers, and the judge announced that the case would be
continued until March 9, but that the witnesses need not appear
unless subpoenaed.

During the next two days, the case was discussed intermittently in chambers. In the final discussion on Friday morning, the
judge pointedly noted that it would be nice to get rid of the
case, especially since few cases had been concluded that week
and the calendar was getting cluttered with jury trials. The
public defender conferred briefly with his client. Charles did
not want to spend any more time in jail. But he worried about
his sentence if he were convicted by a jury. The public defender
told him about the four-year minimum and the prosecutor's
recommendation of eight to twelve years. Charles nodded,
frowned, and decided to take the plea with its four-year minimum. The defender informed him it would be closer to three
years with time off for good behavior, and counting the three
months he had been in jail awaiting indictment. They returned
from the hall outside the courtroom, and when the clerk called
the case, the defender stated his client's wish to plead guilty.
No one was in court except the prosecutor, public defender,
Charles, his family, the court reporter, and the judge. The plea
ceremony lasted only a few minutes. The judge accepted the

plea and immediately imposed sentence. Charles' family had observed the proceedings, but the victim and witnesses did not. At the end of the proceedings, Don Charles was once again taken into custody to begin serving his time. There were 179 days between his arrest and his sentencing.

COURTROOM WORKGROUPS IN CHICAGO

As in Baltimore, two sets of courtroom workgroups determined the fate of defendants in Chicago. In Baltimore, the workgroups in the district courts that conducted preliminary hearings did not make final dispositions in most cases. By contrast, preliminary hearing workgroups in Chicago disposed of almost all defendants charged with felonies. In this sense, Donald Charles' hypothetical case is atypical.

Most felony defendants in Chicago appeared in one of the five courtrooms in the aging courthouse at Twenty-sixth and California that specialized in arraignments, bail review, and preliminary hearings. Preliminary hearing courtrooms in Chicago did not hear misdemeanors as they did in Baltimore. In fact, they specialized even further. One handled homicide cases, two took drug cases, and the remaining two divided the rest of the cases according to whether the offense occurred on the north side or the south side of Chicago.

The principal members of preliminary hearing workgroups spent considerably longer in these courtrooms than their counterparts in Baltimore. The associate circuit judges assigned to them remained for a year or two. The two or three assistant prosecutors in each courtroom typically stayed at least six months. The two public defenders stationed there remained about as long. A single more experienced assistant prosecutor alternated between the north side and south side courtrooms to negotiate pleas. The volume of work and physical proximity of Chicago's preliminary hearing courtrooms permitted a few private attorneys to make a living by confining their practice to quick disposition cases there.[1] Finally, bailiffs and clerks staffing these courtrooms often had many years of service in them.

These characteristics produced stable workgroups whose members became quite familiar with each other. Several consequences flowed from this familiarity. Workgroup members depended on one another more than their counterparts did in Baltimore. Chicago's judges lacked the power to refuse to hold a preliminary hearing that Baltimore judges exercised. As a result, judges shared control over decisions more with assistant prosecutors, public defenders, and private regulars. The pressure generated by the very heavy case load reinforced tendencies toward cooperation and mutual dependance. Courtroom goals also reflected the effects of case pressure. The goals of disposing of cases and maintaining cohesion were compelling. Everyone realized that the entire felony disposition process depended on these courtrooms to screen out most defendants before they reached the trial court level.[2] Pressures applied to workgroup members by sponsoring organizations gave special importance to the goal of disposing of cases. The preliminary hearing workgroups' physical location in the same building that housed fifteen of the twenty trial courtrooms facilitated the communication of such pressure. Their low visibility to the general public (the media rarely reported their decisions) reduced the urgency of doing justice as a crucial goal.

Workgroup members exhibited considerable cooperation and mutual accommodation. Postponements were easily negotiated, particularly when they facilitated a disposition. When preliminary hearings ultimately were held, they reflected little of the conflict that adversarial proceedings are supposed to show. Rather, they were often informal.

These characteristics did not eliminate all conflict, of course. Nor did they reduce judges to mere equals of the attorneys. The formal authority of judges kept them in the position of greatest influence. Judges' unflattering opinions of some workgroup members' competence, particularly the private regulars and the young assistant state's attorneys, also limited the extent to which judges deferred to others.

Cases that survived the rigorous screening at the preliminary hearing, such as Donald Charles', went to trial court workgroups for disposition. These workgroups were even more stable than those at the preliminary hearing stage. Judges had no set term of service in the criminal division, but most spent at least a year there, and some served more than two. The state's attorney's office assigned two assistants to most judges' courtrooms. These assignments were semipermanent, although some assistants shifted periodically. Nevertheless, many remained with a judge at least a year, and most tried cases in other courtrooms only occasionally during that period. The public defender's office assigned an assistant public defender to each courtroom. Most stayed as long as assistant prosecutors did. Finally, some retained regular defense attorneys managed to concentrate many of their cases in a few courtrooms, and assumed the status of a regular workgroup member. The long courthouse experience of some of these attorneys made them familiar to judges and prosecutors even though they did not appear as often as the public defender. Once assigned to a courtroom, defendants' cases almost always remained in that courtroom. Hence, almost no last-minute shifting of courtrooms occurred as in Baltimore.

The stability of courtroom workgroups and their members' familiarity with each other produced the expected results. Mutual dependence was very high, nearly equalizing the influence of judge, prosecutor, and defense counsel, except when the defense counsel was an occasional or a maverick. Negotiation and mutual accommodation dominated workgroup interactions and facilitated guilty pleas. Stability produced standard operating procedures that simplified the work of all. Many court days began with an informal conference in the judge's chambers, which the prosecutor, public defender, and regulars attended. The participants briefed the judge on the day's docket, the likely outcome of the cases (which ones were ready for plea negotiations, which needed continuances, the likelihood of a bench or jury trial), and other matters. They often interspersed discussion of such business with social pleasantries and banter about the city's sports teams. The goals of reducing uncertainty and maintaining cohesion assumed considerable importance. When pleas could not be negotiated, workgroup members preferred the reduced uncertainty bench trials provided.

In most courtrooms, informal norms developed. Judges accommodated the work schedules of prosecutors and defense counsel. For instance, attorneys trying cases in a courtroom automatically obtained a continuance in other courtrooms where they had a matter scheduled. Both judges and prosecutors often tried to help retained regulars collect their fees. Prosecutors took care to keep judges informed about what cases were likely to go to trial and sought to build and preserve a reputation for reliability and reasonableness. Defense attorneys had perhaps the most developed set of courtroom norms, which included the following strictures: [3]

1. Never make the state's attorney answer unnecessary motions.
2. Don't mess up someone else's schedule, especially by leading him to think you are ready to proceed when you are not.
3. Disclose the nature of your case informally in chambers or hallways.
4. Don't trap the state in a bind over the 120-day rule.
5. Accommodate the prosecution wherever possible, especially with respect to scheduling.
6. Avoid trials for cases that cannot be won. [Trying cases when there *is* a chance of winning was not considered a violation of the norm.]

Although one or another of these norms could occasionally be violated with impunity, consistent violation met with sanctions from the courtroom workgroup. Violators found themselves waiting half a day for a continuance, while other attorneys were taken care of immediately. The opportunity to show off for a client would be denied, or the attorney would be scolded from the bench for petty matters that ordinarily were overlooked. In the absence of a strong defender organization that might counteract them, these norms bound many defense counsel closely to the courtroom organization.

THE JUDGES' SPONSORING ORGANIZATION

If Baltimore's judicial organization reflected its fragmented and intense politics, Chicago's reflected the machine politics of that city. Mayor Richard J. Daley's Democratic political organization brought cohesion to the operation of Chicago's and Cook

County's government in the face of decentralized and fragmented formal structures.[4]

Whereas Baltimore had two distinct judicial organizations, Chicago had a unitary court structure. The presence of a dominant political organization helped to give Chicago's court system more central control and less internal division than in Baltimore or (as we will see in the next chapter) Detroit. Both preliminary hearing and trial judges belonged to the Cook County Circuit Court. The 1964 statute that reformed the chaotic and notoriously corrupt preexisting system authorized 235 circuit and associate judges for the county, plus another 130 magistrates.[5] The associate judges for Chicago who presided over preliminary hearings gained their position by appointment. Incumbent associate judges, together with candidates selected by a committee of circuit judges, were placed on a ballot submitted to all circuit judges. The winners served four-year terms before facing reelection by the circuit judges. The circuit judges themselves had to face the electorate on a partisan ballot for their initial six-year term. However, they did not have to contest an election to win subsequent terms. Rather, they ran in a noncompetitive referendum, which asked voters whether the incumbent should be retained. A 60 percent affirmative vote sufficed for retention. Only one incumbent to date has failed retention despite bar associations' widely advertised lists of unqualified judges. Thus, once elected, circuit judges enjoyed almost certain life tenure. The crucial step in the journey to a circuit judgeship in Democratic Chicago occurred at the nominating stage. Nomination was by party primary with Mayor Daley's organization slating machine-approved candidates who usually won nomination.[6] Candidates of the party dominant in an electoral district (the Democrats in the city of Chicago and Republicans in most suburbs) almost always won election.[7] The very long judicial ballot was attached to the end of the regular November ballot on even numbered years, which included races for president, the governorship, congress, and other important offices.

These arrangements for selecting judges permitted Daley's organization to dominate recruitment. Initial access to the bench required slating by the organization. Wesley Skogan's study of the characteristics of those selected confirmed expectations about their political ties. The Democratic candidates in Chicago tended to have the same ethnic status as their electoral supporters, came from lower-status law schools, often had held party posts above the level of precinct captain, frequently held a full-time elective office before running for judge, and seldom were engaged in private practice.[8] Skogan summarized the nomination of judicial candidates from both parties as follows: "[Nominations] go to political veterans with long records of public service who grew up in service of the organization and who serve as the ethnic representatives of their constituents on the bench. Judgeships in Cook County are terminal positions to which warriors retire."[9] Judges' political ties were reflected by an experience of one of our research assistants. When he introduced himself to one of the circuit judges, the judge responded by inquiring, "What precinct are you from?"

The associate judges chosen by the circuit judges in Chicago also tended to be organization people. Support from the Daley organization counted more than approval from bar associations. Even the explicit disapproval of the city's bar usually had no effect on the selection of associate judges. But any associate judge who wanted to be retained would think hard before deliberately angering the organization.

This recruitment process produced few maverick judges. Judicial attitudes toward crime, criminals, and punishment were conventional and probably on the conservative side. Certainly, it was unlikely that anyone with outspoken or extreme views in either direction would attain a judgeship. However, judges were likely to be well acquainted with city and organizational politics, and supportive of the status quo. They also had experience in the politics of negotiation, coalition building, and accommodation that characterized the city.

Each year, the circuit judges elected a chief judge. For many years, they had regularly reelected John S. Boyle, a close associate of Mayor Daley, to the post. He wielded considerable power, including the authority to establish and staff specialized divisions of the circuit court. Dozens of courtrooms heard only minor criminal and civil matters, ranging from ordinance violations to small claims to preliminary hearings in felony cases.[10] The chief judge assigned associate judges to these courtrooms. He also determined the assignment of circuit judges to the various divisions of circuit court. Some divisions heard only marital matters; others specialized in tort and contract cases; the county division heard disputes involving the powers of officials and elections; the criminal division tried felony cases. No established procedures for rotating circuit judges among the divisions existed. Rather, Chief Judge Boyle assigned judges to divisions and courtrooms on his own.[11]

Although many judges disliked assignment to criminal courts, it was not regarded as the least desirable assignment. A few actually requested it. Many judges believed that every circuit judge had to serve in the criminal division for a time. But hints that political considerations shaped assignments were abundant. For example, one judge who won his seat on the bench by a series of accidents, and who had practically no political background or clout felt it was unlikely that he would ever serve on the politically sensitive chancery division. Evidently, the criminal division was not considered politically sensitive. In 1968, for example, 38 percent of the circuit judges assigned to it were Republicans, at a time when Republicans constituted less than 9 percent of the available judges.[12] When a Republican captured the state's attorney's position, some courthouse regulars observed that more pro-defendant judges were being shifted to the criminal division in the hope that the new state's attorney's conviction record would begin to look bad. However, aside from such fragmentary evidence, we encountered few clues as to the manner in which the chief judge exercised his assignment powers. Nor could we find any formula for deciding how long judges stayed in the criminal division. We learned only that most served from one to three years.

Any central control and direction from the judicial sponsoring organization came from Chief Judge Boyle and his appointee to head the criminal division. Informal meetings were inhibited by the geographical division between the five Civic Center and the fifteen Criminal Courts Building courtrooms. Even the judges in the Criminal Courts Building saw each other only irregularly at lunch. They all had lunch in a room at the adjoining jail, but not all the judges went for lunch at the same time. Nor did they see each other often in chambers, because their chambers were not connected and only four courtrooms were located on most floors of the Criminal Courts Building. These physical arrangements reinforced not only the autonomy of the judge but that of the entire courtroom workgroup. Furthermore, the judges assigned to the criminal division had no regular meetings or formal procedures for making group decisions.

As in Baltimore, the judicial sponsoring organization ran no formal training program for judges newly assigned to the criminal division. Some received their initiation as associate judges in the misdemeanor or preliminary hearing courtrooms, but many did not. Moreover, those who first worked in the misdemeanor or preliminary hearing courtrooms received no training at that stage. As in most jurisdictions in the United States, an attorney was expected to know how to act like a judge when he became one.

The criminal division's chief judge (Judge Power) was appointed by Judge Boyle; Power also had close ties to Mayor Daley, having been a former law partner of the mayor. His duties consisted almost entirely of circulating reports about dispositions and assigning cases to the various courtrooms. Both functions had important implications for the way in which the felony disposition process worked in Chicago but they did not involve close supervision of the courtrooms by the chief judge.

Disposition reports came out each month and indicated the number of cases disposed of by each courtroom of the criminal division. They permitted courtroom workgroups to evaluate their productivity in comparison with other courtrooms and placed subtle pressure on the laggards. Although no judges admitted hearing from Judge Power if their courtroom's production lagged, courtroom members expressed considerable interest in the reports when they appeared. Several indicated that they were doing as well as could be expected when their courtroom's productivity approached 300 dispositions by the end of the year. For judges, these reports provided some basis for hoping that their next assignment would be as desirable or at least not undesirable.

The chief judge made assignments at the arraignment on the indictment. Judge Power assigned only bailed defendants to the Civic Center. The remainder went to courtrooms at 26th and California. He also sought to equalize the work load among courtrooms. Courtrooms that disposed of many cases in any particular week were assigned a disproportionate number of new ones; those which made little progress in clearing their docket received fewer. These assignments provided significant opportunities for retained defense attorneys to shop for particular judges. It was not at all unusual for a private counsel to ask that a case be sent to a judge who was already scheduled to hear some of his other cases in order to consolidate his case load in a handful of courtrooms. Likewise, if a defense attorney objected to any particular judge, he could request that the judge not receive the case; such objections were almost always honored. This function made it important for defense attorneys to remain on the right side of the chief judge; it also increased the stability of courtroom workgroups. On the other hand, most defendants without counsel at the arraignment had no opportunity to judge-shop. Only rarely would a court-wise unrepresented defendant request a specific judge. Typically, the chief judge arbitrarily assigned unrepresented defendants.

Neither the judicial sponsoring organization nor its administrative judges supervised Chicago judges closely. Each courtroom managed its own docket; unlike Baltimore's chief judge, the chief judge in Chicago sought no control over the granting of postponements. Nor did we find evidence of extensive or frequent direct pressure on the handling of specific cases. Nevertheless, Cook County judges worked for a unified judicial organization that made its presence known in many subtle ways. The sensitivity of the judges to such pressures was enhanced by their political background. It is important to note that the judges who staffed the preliminary hearing courtrooms were part of the same judicial organization. In stark contrast to the Baltimore situation, those judges depended on the circuit judges for their jobs and worked in the same building as most of the criminal division judges. One would expect much more collaboration and much less conflict between the two kinds of courtrooms in Chicago than in Baltimore, and that indeed was the situation.

THE CHICAGO STATE'S ATTORNEY'S OFFICE

The Cook County state's attorney headed an office of 190 attorneys. The office staffed misdemeanor courts, provided legal advice for the county, investigated white-collar crime, ran the grand jury, and assigned attorneys to its criminal division. Fifty-seven assistant state's attorneys worked for the criminal division. Beginning salaries were $12,700 and ranged up to $28,000 for experienced men in supervisory positions.[13] The offices of assistants who worked at Twenty-sixth and California were almost as dingy and unappealing as Baltimore prosecutors' offices.

Every four years, the voters of Cook County choose the state's attorney in a partisan election. Although Democrats have dominated county politics in recent decades, the state's attorney's office has been one of the few posts Republicans have captured from time to time. At the beginning of our research, the incumbent was Edward Hanrahan, a Democrat chosen by the Daley machine. Hanrahan thrived on controversy and conflict, and was best known for the notorious Black Panther raid during which his agents killed the head of the Black Panther Party in Illinois. He lost his bid for reelection in November 1972 to a Republican, Barnard Carey, after the Daley machine had unsuccessfully sought to dump him from the Democratic ticket in the primary.

The state's attorney's party affiliation made little difference in the day-to-day operation of the felony disposition process. But it did affect the recruitment of assistant prosecutors who staffed the courtrooms. When Democrats had held the office in the past, party clearance was required of most applicants for assistant prosecutor's jobs. The importance of party clearance depended on the party's hold on city, county, state, and national offices. When Democrats controlled all, party clearance was less important because of the abundance of patronage positions; when the party occupied only some of those offices, party clearance was more important. When Republicans captured the state's attorney's office, clearance from party committeemen was less important, reflecting the weaker condition of the party. The Republican elected in 1972 built a coalition of Republicans and Independents at a time of great weakness for the Cook County Republican Party; consequently, he did not rely on party clearance very much.[14]

Nearly everyone regarded assistants' positions as patronage posts. Most assistants did not expect to continue in their jobs when the opposite party won the office. In November 1972, in the midst of our research, the Democratic incumbent was defeated. By the following February, thirty-seven assistants had decided to leave. A core of career assistants in middle management posts remained from one administration to another. However, the expectation that one could build a career in the office was not established firmly.

Most assistants did not seek a career in the office anyway. Like their Baltimore counterparts, they wanted to gain trail experience and contacts that would be useful later when they entered private practice. Typically, they began in juvenile, misdemeanor, or preliminary hearing courtrooms before promotion to a criminal trial courtroom. When they gained the experience they sought, usually after about a year in trial court, they left voluntarily. In general, turnover in 1972 was less rapid in Chicago than in Baltimore. The office had a number of men with three to five years' experience, and a small core of career men provided long-range continuity and experience. Nevertheless, most trial assistants were rather young and inexperienced. They often graduated from the less prestigious local law schools and presented political credentials that at least rivaled their academic record. We heard complaints about their competence, particularly from preliminary hearing judges who found the least experienced assistants shoved into their courtrooms.

The office ran no formal training program for new assistants. All assistants attended a meeting one Saturday morning each month to discuss common problems and learn about the content and implementation of office policies from supervisors. The office's leadership did attempt to supervise the work of assistant prosecutors. The chief and deputy chief of the criminal division spent much of their time at Twenty-sixth and California, answering queries from assistants and maintaining some semblance of uniformity among courtrooms. In addition, two supervisors oversaw the work of assistants assigned to preliminary hearing courtrooms. The state's attorney established explicit policies in several areas.[15] He also required assistants to fill out forms reporting all plea bargains offered, all sentences imposed, and the outcome of jury trials. Supervisors thus had information about the decisions assistants made and could detect deviations from office policy. Assistants who violated office policy could expect to be called in and be grilled, particularly under Hanrahan. Consequently, they usually checked with their supervisors before taking nonroutine actions.

Despite these provisions, trial assistants enjoyed a large measure of discretion. Sentence recommendations that did not involve an offer of probation or a reduction of charges did not require a supervisor's approval. Each trial team exercised primary responsibility for the 150 or so cases on their courtroom's docket, giving them little time to interact either with peers in other courtrooms or with supervisors. Irregular schedules and the lack of a lunchroom prevented informal encounters at midday. Hence, there was little peer supervision.

A few office norms developed. Most assistants offered increasingly less attractive plea bargains as cases approached trial. Assistants felt that the more work put into a case, the longer the prison sentence resulting from a plea bargain ought to be. To ensure this result, offers made at the preliminary hearing were written in the state's file. When the defense insisted on a hearing for a motion, assistants often felt it voided any previous offers and jeopardized the prospects for any agreement.

Despite the lack of close supervision, assistants felt the presence of supervisors more than their Baltimore counterparts. Under the Republican Carey, assistants felt they had more leeway than under his predecessor, Hanrahan, but in both cases courtroom attorneys exercised considerable discretion. The difference was more of style than policy, with Carey's office being relaxed and Hanrahan's tense. Assistants under Hanrahan felt they were watched more, and to some extent they were. For instance, we learned from one supervisor that close tabs were kept on prosecutors' conviction rates in jury trials.

THE DEFENSE BAR IN CHICAGO

Public defenders set the tone of defense attorney activity in Chicago courtroom workgroups. They represented many preliminary hearing defendants, and half of the defendants who reached the trial courts. Furthermore, assignment procedures guaranteed that individual defenders spent most of their time in a single workgroup. The public defender's organization adopted a "zone defense." Each courtroom had its own defender (or in exceptional cases, a pair) who represented any eligible defendant who entered the courtroom.[16]

These defenders worked for the Cook County public defender's office, which handled the defense of indigents in minor as well as serious criminal matters. The responsibility to defend all indigents imposed a heavy case load on individual defenders.[17] The task of running the office fell to the defender, a man who had served for many years and owed his appointment to the chief judge of the circuit court. The public defender's office was consequently more closely tied to the court organization than in Baltimore.

What kind of people became assistant public defenders? In most respects, they resembled public defenders everywhere: young attorneys (primarily men), typically just out of law school, and looking for trial experience. Certainly, they did not seek the job for the money. They earned somewhat less than assistant state's attorneys. Like assistant prosecutors, they left the office after gaining the trial experience they sought. Consequently, they stayed about as long as prosecutors. Few made careers in the office and few could be called seasoned veterans. Assistant public defenders depended less on patronage connections to get their job than prosecutors, although such connections were not useless. In general, defenders were less politicized; fewer harbored political ambitions.

The public defender's office supervised its assistants still less than the state's attorney's office. Even inexperienced defenders sent to the preliminary hearing courtrooms for training received little supervision. Despite their inexperience, almost the only time the office intervened was when other members of the workgroup complained to superiors. As long as a defender's action met the approval of other workgroup members, especially the judge, he heard little from his front office. Trial courtroom defenders also experienced little supervision. They did not attend regular meetings of defenders, because none were called; informal contact occurred infrequently, because most defenders worked alone in their courtroom and spent most of their time there. The defender established few explicit policies; rather, policies were largely implicit. Assistants filled out reports on dispositions once a month, but such reports contained too little information to provide supervisors with effective control mechanisms. In general, assistant public defenders scarcely felt the hand of their supervisors.

Of the several thousand attorneys in private practice in Chicago, most never appeared in the criminal courts at all. Several hundred represented a few defendants each year. These occasionals handled enough cases to spread the case load handled by retained attorneys among a fairly large group. Finally about fifty attorneys handled enough defendants to constitute an identifiable group of regulars who helped set the tone of defense-prosecutorial relationships in workgroups.

The preliminary hearing workgroup regulars formed the most distinctive group of retained regulars. Held in low esteem by practically everyone, these men earned their living by turning over a large number of cases for rather modest fees. They depended on bailiffs to recommend their services to prisoners in the lockup or prowled the hallways soliciting business from worried defendants and their families. Several hours before court began, these "operators" or "hustlers" (as other courthouse regulars called them) set out to obtain their day's quota of clients. They sold their availability and knowledge of the court's personnel, not their minimal legal abilities. If they could not obtain a rapid disposition through a dismissal or guilty plea, they dropped out of the case and referred their client to a trial attorney. Hence, they almost never ventured beyond the familiar confines of the preliminary hearing courtroom.[18]

Although trial courtroom regulars sometimes appeared in preliminary hearing courts (especially when representing a relatively wealthy client), they concentrated their practice at the trial level. Many of them can best be described as "clubhouse regulars." Many were former assistant prosecutors. Most had political connections. They often expressed antidefendant sentiments in chambers, though never in open court. They relied primarily on obtaining "efficient" dispositions — handling large numbers of clients without wasting time — through the cooperation of prosecutors, judges, clerks, and bailiffs. These attorneys, along with the public defenders, subscribed to the informal norms facilitating cohesion and uncertainty reduction described earlier. A unique feature of Chicago's bail system encouraged their adherence to these norms. An amendment to Illinois' 10 percent bail provision permitted defendants to assign the rebate (90 percent of the sum deposited with the court) to their attorney. This provision provided a marvellous solution to one of the most serious problems faced by retained attorneys — getting paid. But unless the defendant actually made bail, it was irrelevant. Hence, retained regulars very much wanted bail set at a level their clients could make. In turn, obtaining a makable bail level often required a reduction in bond that depended on the cooperation of the judge and prosecutor. A clubhouse regular who had just obtained reduced bond for his two clients could not suppress a smile as he approached our courtroom observer. "Well, that's $1,000 of my fee. I couldn't get it from the relatives any other way."

Not all regular defense attorneys subscribed to the informal norms that facilitated internal cohesion and reduced uncertainty. These non–clubhouse regulars took a more adversarial stance, and their relations with other workgroup members were tenser and more conflictual. They did not expect and did not obtain the cooperation in lowering bail or scheduling of cases that clubhouse regulars did. An incident we observed illustrated the difference between them well. An attorney who refused to negotiate what was thought to be a "bad" case was forced to spend three consecutive days in the courtroom. His case was always one of the last to be called and was sandwiched in between other proceedings. Much to his chagrin, a clubhouse regular walked in and his case was called immediately.

Clubhouse regulars further facilitated the handling of their cases by passing small sums of money to clerks and bailiffs. These attorneys carried a large wad of small bills as part of their standard equipment. Attorneys who specialized in the preliminary hearing courts relied on bailiffs as "runners" to steer clients to them. Insertion of five to ten dollars into the file when it was handed to a clerk improved the chances of an early call of the case. And bailiffs could grant attorneys access to their clients confined in the lockup. We witnessed an overt request for payment from a bailiff who had let an attorney into the back room of a trial courtroom to interview a client. "Don't forget the bailiff for letting you see your client. Drop it [that is, drop a few dollars]," he suggested.

THE ENVIRONMENTAL CONTEXT

Chicago, the nation's second largest city and third largest metropolitan area, experienced its full share of the problems found in Baltimore, Detroit, and other large American cities. But it was known more for its politics than its problems. Since the middle fifties, Mayor Richard J. Daley and the political organization he built dominated city and county politics. Even the explosive growth of the suburbs during the 1960s and a substantial increase in the city's black population did not erode the Daley organization's strength.

The courts, like all other major components of city and county government, reflected the Democratic organization's dominance. We have already seen how partisan political considerations shaped the recruitment of associate and circuit judges and members of the state's attorney's office. This influence extended to clerks and bailiffs. Both were sent to courtrooms by sponsoring organizations headed by elected officials — the clerk of courts and the county sheriff. Both were known as patronage preserves. As noted, Chief Judge Boyle of the circuit court had close ties to Mayor Daley.

The Cook County Board of Supervisors, presided over by another protégé of Mayor Daley's, exercised general authority over the entire operation, including the provision of budgetary support. Consequently, although individual case outcomes were not perceptibly influenced by partisan politics, patronage appointments, electoral politics, and budgetary controls firmly anchored the criminal process in the politics of the city and county.

The role played by blacks in the felony disposition process corresponded to their participation in the city's politics generally. Although black members of the Daley organization controlled ward organizations in predominantly black areas and sent blacks to local, state, and federal legislative bodies, they did not hold many of the higher posts in the organization of government.

That was true of the courts as well. In fact, as in Baltimore, blacks occupied fewer important positions in the felony disposition process than in most other areas of political life in the community. Other city departments employed many blacks. But almost no assistant prosecutors were black. Only two criminal division judges and several assistant public defenders were black. Blacks filled few of the less important positions as well. Only a few were bailiffs; none of the clerks were. Not even many private attorneys practicing in the criminal courts were black. Yet blacks constituted one-third of the city's population at the time. Thus, a wave of black defendants swept into an essentially white lake every morning.

The strong hold of the Democratic organization insulated courtrooms and sponsoring organizations from the influence of outside organizations. Several organizations in Chicago held intense opinions about the courts' operations. These included militant black organizations, civil libertarian groups, and other groups that held pro-defendant views. It is significant that black politicians in the Daley organization did not push vigorously for black-related causes.[19] In addition, the plethora of Chicago's good government groups and its collection of bar associations (one purporting to represent the whole bar, one made up of young turks, one composed of black attorneys) sought to influence the courts' recruitment of personnel and policies. None of these groups, however, exerted effective influence despite their efforts. When any of these groups made recommendations or issued reports, they were met with silence. Whatever the challenge, it was simply never accepted. When bar associations publicly labeled certain associate judges incompetent, the circuit judges nevertheless proceeded to reelect them. The chief judge sometimes met with groups issuing reports on the courts but rarely responded to their recommendations. Most of these groups operated not only outside the regular Democratic organization but in opposition to it. They did not have the power to impose their views on courtroom participants or sponsoring organizations.

The media played an ambiguous role. They gave publicity to groups seeking to influence the recruitment of judges, and they exposed problems in the courts. But they did not support the goals of pro-defendant reformers. In fact, their general stance on crime fit the typical conservative, law-and-order mold fairly well. Occasionally, the papers devoted substantial resources to special in-depth studies of the criminal court's operation. In fact, one conducted its own empirical analysis of criminal cases' outcomes.[20] The media, however, covered the day-to-day operation of the courts less intensively than in Baltimore. The electronic media assigned no regular reporters to the courthouse beat. Each of the city's two newspaper organizations (the *Tribune* and the *Sun-Times/Daily News*) plus the City News Bureau stationed a single reporter at the Criminal Courts Building to cover the fifteen courtrooms operating there; coverage of the courtrooms in the Civic Center was still more sporadic. Reporters concentrated on spectacular cases that had high audience appeal. Typically, they would come into each courtroom once a day and ask the clerk or assistant prosecutor whether anything interesting had occurred or was about to take place. These officials easily steered them to jury trials of spectacular crimes or cases involving prominent individuals. Normal dispositions commonly reported in Baltimore simply did not appear in Chicago's newspapers. Nor did individual participants invite press coverage for themselves, because notoriety was clearly more dangerous for their career than anonymity. For instance, when a story was run that one of the criminal division judges had hired his wife as personal bailiff and she packed a pistol to court for their protection, he was quietly reassigned to another division and his wife dismissed. Likewise, a public defender featured in a *Newsweek* story about the operation of the office quickly became a private attorney.

CONCLUSION

Despite the long delays in disposing of Chicago defendants' cases, courtroom workgroups and their sponsoring organizations felt no intense external pressures to dispose of cases. The elements of the community concerned about delays and the jail population did not receive strong support in the media. The goal of disposing cases received some emphasis in courtroom workgroups, but the impetus for it stemmed primarily from the judge's organization and the state's attorney's office. As in Baltimore, the goal of doing justice, tinged with an element of harshness toward defendants, received more public emphasis. However, the workgroups' context encouraged greater stress on the internally generated goals of reducing uncertainty and maintaining cohesion than in Baltimore. The tendency toward plea bargaining produced by stable workgroups was reinforced by their compatibility with the traditional way of doing things in Chicago politics. Almost all major participants had been socialized into a culture that emphasized negotiation and accommodation.

The intensity of the conflicts that sometimes arise between courtroom workgroup members over the importance of the various goals increased somewhat during our research, because the election of the state's attorney occurred as our data was being gathered. The incumbent, Hanrahan, long a rising star in the Daley organization and a possible heir to Daley himself, became a liability in the aftermath of the raid on the Black Panther headquarters and his subsequent indictment for obstruction of justice in the case. Daley sought to deny Hanrahan the Democratic nomination, but Hanrahan defeated the organization's challenger. Hanrahan projected an image of a no-nonsense, hard-nosed, conservative crime fighter. Faced with a strong challenge from his Republican opponent in the general election, he sought to make sure that his assistants' courtroom behavior conformed to his public image. Office policies tightened, and everyone perceived that assistant prosecutors had to "hang tough" in negotiations. Consequently, doing justice, in the form of producing convictions and prison sentences at the trial level, assumed increased importance for assistants. Naturally, this goal interfered somewhat with workgroup cohesion.

Nevertheless, workgroup negotiation remained the dominant operating mode for the Chicago courts. Their stability and mutual dependence encouraged negotiation as the effective means for reducing uncertainty and producing a steady flow of dispositions. Case assignment procedures and the assignment policies of the state's attorney and public defender contributed substantially to the stability of courtroom workgroups. In addition, the political background of many workgroup members encouraged acceptance of negotiation as a legitimate means for disposing cases.

NOTES

1. This practice and the phenomenon of "sequential representation" is described by Janet A. Gilboy, "Perspectives and Practices of Defense Lawyers in Criminal Cases," unpublished Ph.D. dissertation, Northwestern University, 1976, pp. 36–43, 110–133.

2. For a description of the screening functions performed by Chicago's preliminary hearing courts prior to our research, see Donald J. McIntyre, "A Study of Judicial Dominance of the Charging Process," *Journal of Criminal Law, Criminology, and Police Science* 59 (1968): 481.

3. Based on interviews and observations in sixteen trial courtrooms between January and April 1973.

4. For a description and analysis of Chicago's politics and government that supports this view, see Edward C. Banfield and James Q. Wilson, *City Politics* (Cambridge, Mass.: Harvard University Press, 1963), pp. 104–107.

5. This discussion is based on Wesley G. Skogan, "The Politics of Judicial Reform: Cook County, Illinois," *The Justice System* 1 (1975): 15 and passim.

6. Wesley G. Skogan, "Party and Constituency in Political Recruitment: The Case of the Judiciary in Cook County, Illinois," unpublished Ph.D. dissertation, Northwestern University, 1971, pp. 43–53.

7. Skogan, "The Politics of Judicial Reform," p. 22.

8. Ibid., pp. 18–19.

9. Ibid., p. 20.

10. The structure of the courts is described by the Chicago Bar Association's Commission on Administration of Criminal Justice in Cook County, *Program of Action* (Chicago: Chicago Bar Association, 1975), pp. 30–37.

11. Personal interviews with judges in the Criminal Division of the Cook County Circuit Court between January and April 1973.

12. Skogan, "The Politics of Judicial Reform," p. 22.

13. These data were supplied the authors by the state's attorney's office.

14. Based on interviews with ward committeemen and personnel officers of the incumbent and several preceding state's attorneys.

15. For instance, under Hanrahan reductions in armed robbery cases were prohibited; dismissals required a supervisor's approval as did plea bargains involving probation.

16. At preliminary hearing, anyone who did not have an attorney and claimed indigency received a public defender; at the trial court, a rule of thumb used by judges was, if the defendant makes bail, he must get his own attorney.

17. In 1975 there were 171 staff attorneys and 27 investigators in the office. Chicago Bar Association, *Program of Action*, p. 149. In 1972 there were considerably fewer attorneys, with only one assigned to most courtrooms.

18. Gilboy, "Perspectives and Practices."

19. Banfield and Wilson, *City Politics*, pp. 304–305.

20. *Chicago Sun Times*, September 16, 17, 18, 19, 20, 21, 24, 27, 1973.

Chapter 6

DETROIT: BUREAUCRATIZED PLEA BARGAINING

The modern, twelve-story Frank Murphy Hall of Justice that houses Detroit Recorder's Court rises above a hospital, the Wayne County Jail, the abandoned old Recorder's Court Building, and Detroit police headquarters. Downtown Detroit is clearly visible from its upper stories. It is not as centrally located as Chicago's Civic Center courtrooms or the Supreme Bench of Baltimore, but it is not as isolated as Chicago's courthouse at Twenty-sixth and California. All major formal proceedings in felony cases, from arraignment to sentencing, are conducted within it. Attorneys, defendants, witnesses, and visitors come and go freely without passing through a metal detector, having packages and brief cases searched, or being frisked. Strangers are aware immediately, however, that this is no ordinary municipal building. Uniformed police, with their revolvers conspicuously lodged in their holsters, are everywhere.

AN ARMED ROBBERY CASE IN DETROIT

This time, we will call our hypothetical armed robbery defendant James Dent. The facts leading up to the arrest are again identical, but what happened from then on differs from what happened in both Baltimore and Chicago.

The arresting officers took Dent from the police precinct station to the Wayne County Jail adjoining Recorder's Court. As part of the routine arrest procedure, they filled out a report of the incident and arrest on a Preliminary Complaint Report (PCR) form. An officer assigned to the police department's court section used the PCR to fill out another form known as a Request for Warrant Recommendation (RWR). It contained a few basic facts about the defendant, the crime, the arrest, and the evidence (including the names of witnesses). Nowhere on this form was there any indication about charges the police booked Dent on or what the police felt the formal charges ought to be. Instead, the form served as a formal request by the police to the prosecutor for authorization of a formal warrant for the defendant's arrest. The police left blank the bottom of the form where the formal charges would be entered. In Michigan, defendants cannot be arraigned on felony charges until a judge approves a formal request for a warrant from a prosecutor. Before James Dent had to answer formal charges, both a prosecutor and a judge had to give their approval. Thus, it was up to the prosecutor to fill in the blank that indicated what the charge was.

The next morning, while Dent was in Wayne County Jail, one of the arresting officers, the store clerk (who had been interviewed by the court officer earlier that morning), and the court section officer who prepared the RWR form arrived at the warrant section of the prosecutor's office of the eleventh floor. The receptionist sent them back to the office of a career assistant prosecutor assigned to the warrant section. With a grunted greeting, the court officer handed the prosecutor the RWR form and sat down. After reading it quickly, the assistant prosecuting attorney turned to the store clerk.

PROS.: Did you get a good look at this guy before he made you lay down on the floor?

CLERK: Yeah. He came up to me and asked for a pint of Old Crow. Then he pulled the gun. I seen the guy there before.

PROS.: You know the guy?

CLERK: Well, I seen him. He bought from me before.

PROS.: How was he dressed?

CLERK: He had on a dark jacket, tan cap, trousers. About my size.

PROS.: Did he have the tan hat when the officers brought him back?

CLERK: Well — maybe it wasn't tan. But it was the same guy, I know.

PROS.: You sure?

CLERK: Yeah.

PROS.: How much did he get?

CLERK: I don't know for sure — at least $150, maybe $250.

PROS.: You willing to testify?

CLERK: I'll testify.

PROS.: OK. Wait outside for the officers, so you can go before the judge to swear out a complaint. Then you can go home. [*To the arresting officer*] Why did you stop the defendant?

ARR. OFF.: Well, he resembled the description we got; he was in the area, walking fast; and he didn't look too pleased when he saw us cruise by.

PROS.: What happened to the gun and the bag?

ARR. OFF.: He must've ditched them somewhere. We're looking for the gun.

PROS.: What about the wallets?

ARR. OFF.: I guess he pitched them too. He got about $350 in all. He had the paycheck of one of the customers, you know.

PROS.: Yeah. I read. It would be real good if you could find the wallets or the gun. How about the ID of the customers?

CT. OFF.: We haven't talked to them. Evidently they identified him when he was brought back to the store.

ARR. OFF.: Well, one of them did. The other wasn't sure.

PROS.: We might have problems with the initial stop. I think the identification will hold up OK. The clerk makes a pretty good witness. This guy have a record?

CT. OFF.: Yeah — robbery unarmed about five years ago.
PROS.: I'll authorize on a robbery armed.

The assistant prosecuting attorney filled in the blank space, authorizing a charge of armed robbery and signed the form. The court officer took the form to a typist a few feet away who prepared a multipurpose form that included the complaint and an arrest warrant. An automatic typewriter permitted the clerk to finish in a few minutes. The court officer took the forms and accompanied the store clerk, who was acting as the official complaining witness, to the basement courtroom of the presiding judge. As the court officer and complaining witness approached the side of the bench, the judge got up, told the store clerk to raise his right hand, and affixed his signature to the form without reading it. The procedure took fifteen seconds and did not interrupt the arraignment that was occurring simultaneously. The prosecutor's office had determined the precise charge to be lodged against Dent, and the judge had just authorized his formal arrest.

At 2:30 that same day, James Dent was brought over from the jail to the presiding judge's courtroom to be arraigned on the warrant approved and signed a few hours earlier in the same courtroom. The arraignment took just sixty seconds. The judge informed Dent that he was charged with armed robbery of the liquor store the previous evening, and asked him if he had ever been arrested before. Dent admitted his arrest for robbery several years before. The judge set bail at $2,000 with sureties and asked Dent whether he could afford an attorney. Dent replied that he could not, whereupon the judge instructed him to sign an affidavit of indigency. He told Dent that an attorney would be appointed for him and that his preliminary examination would be held in eight days, on September 19.

Like Roy Brown's family in Baltimore, Dent's people had to hire a bail bondsman to secure his release, because the judge had imposed a surety bond rather than a personal bond. However, since the face amount of the bond was only $2,000, Dent's family was able to scrape together the $220.00 (11 percent of the bond) charged by the bondsman. The bond was posted the day after arraignment, and Dent walked out of jail less than two days after his arrest.

At 8:30 on the morning of the scheduled preliminary examination, James Dent arrived at Recorder's Court and was directed to the fourth floor by the police officer sitting at the desk in the lobby. He found his name posted on a list outside courtroom 401 and with some uncertainty entered and sat down. He had heard nothing from anyone (including his attorney) since his arraignment. Shortly after 9:00 A.M., he heard his name called out by a forty-year-old white man in a suit. This was his court-appointed attorney, a private regular. The attorney escorted Dent into the hall for a ten-minute conference. The attorney listened to Dent's story, including how the arrest was made, and decided to hold, rather than waive, the preliminary examination.

After checking briefly with the clerk, Dent's attorney left the room. Dent sat on the hard wooden benches all morning, returning after lunch. About 2:00 P.M. his attorney reappeared, and at 2:30 his case was called. The proceedings were formal. The courtroom was quiet, and Dent's family and the witnesses remained in the spectator's section rather than gathering around him as in Chicago. The arresting officer and the store clerk both testified. Dent's attorney cross-examined the arresting officer about the circumstances of the arrest and the store clerk about the certainty of his identification of Dent as the robber. Both direct examination and cross-examination took about ten minutes. In a routine manner the prosecutor moved that the defendant be bound over for trial on the charges contained in the complaint and warrant. The defense argued that the charges be dismissed, since there was no probable cause for apprehending the defendant in the first place, and since the identification of him in the store was tainted. The judge responded that all he was required to do was find probable cause, and that these issues could be appropriately raised later. He bound over the defendant for trial, set October 19 as the date for the pretrial conference, tore off a slip of paper from a pad containing a randomly generated list of names of all the trial judges, and informed Dent that his trial judge would be Judge Singleton.

Michigan does not require a grand jury indictment as do Illinois and Maryland. Prosecutors proceed by issuing an information after the judge has determined probable cause at a preliminary hearing. An information is the equivalent of an indictment but is issued by a prosecutor rather than voted by a grand jury. The judge's finding of probable cause and the issuance of the information in Dent's case came just nine days after his arrest. The information had been prepared as part of the multipurpose form typed in the warrant section.

On the morning of October 19, Dent went to the pretrial conference division of the prosecutor's office on the courthouse's eleventh floor. The clerk instructed him to take a seat. About 10 o'clock his attorney, whom he had not seen since the preliminary hearing, walked into the waiting room. He told Dent to wait for him outside and disappeared into the inner office of the pretrial conference division. Once inside, Dent's attorney picked up the prosecutor's case file and waited his turn to see one of the assistant prosecutors assigned to the division. The pretrial conference, required in every case for which probable cause has been established, was designed to explore the possibility of a plea bargain. The assistant prosecuting attorney, obviously pressed for time, reached for the case file, scanned it briefly, and looked up at Dent's attorney.

DEF. COUNSEL: How ya doing, Ron?

PROS.: Not bad. What have you got?

DEF. COUSEL: It's another RA. The guy doesn't have much of a record, but it's for robbery unarmed. That was in 1967. My guess is it was reduced from robbery armed, but I'm not sure. He has stayed out of trouble since then, I'll say that.

PROS.: Are you retained?

DEF. COUNSEL: No, appointed. I think there may be a problem both with the initial arrest and the identification. The cops brought my man back to the store and asked if this wasn't the man who robbed them. I've got a pretty good basis for a motion.

PROS.: Oh, I don't know. I think that it will hold up all right. Who's the judge?

DEF. COUNSEL: Singleton. That's the problem with the motion.

PROS.: Well, you know the office policy on robbery. We can't give anything less than assault with intent to rob while being armed. It's still a life maximum, but at least he has a chance for probation.

DEF. COUNSEL: Fat chance. I guess attempted armed robbery is out?

PROS.: We can't give that. I'm not sure I'd want to in this case anyway. I could go no reduced plea and we could try it on the armed robbery. (Looks at the write-up of the case in the prosecutor's file — the RWR.) What the hell, he's been clean since '67. Do you think he'll take the plea?

DEF. COUNSEL: I've no idea. I'll try the motion first. If it fails, I'd like to take it. I'll see what he says.

Following this brief exchange, which consumed about three minutes, the attorney conferred briefly with Dent in the hall about the outcome of the pretrial conference. His lawyer told him that if he pleaded guilty to the assault with intent to rob while armed, it would leave open the possibility of probation. Conviction on robbery armed carried a mandatory prison term. But, he added, he didn't know if the judge would give probation even if he did plead. As they entered the elevator, Dent's attorney informed him he would file a motion to quash the arrest and see what happened. The clerk in Judge Singleton's courtroom nodded as the attorney and Dent entered several minutes later. In a few minutes, the clerk called the case and the judge immediately asked about the outcome of the pretrial conference. "This will be a motion to quash the arrest, your honor." Judge Singleton set the hearing on the motion for thirty days later, November 20. The defense attorney then moved for a copy of the preliminary hearing transcript, and the judge granted it routinely. The assistant prosecuting attorney assigned to Judge Singleton's courtroom stepped out for a moment as the case was called, and learned from the clerk on his return that a hearing on the motion was coming up. The entire proceeding lasted only several minutes.

On November 20, the judge, Dent's attorney, and the assistant prosecuting attorney conducted the hearing on the motion. Both arresting officers recounted the circumstances of the arrest. After a fairly vigorous cross-examination, both sides summarized their arguments briefly. The judge barely hesitated before denying the motion. Dent's attorney requested a brief recess to confer with his client. They moved to the hall outside the courtroom, sat on the hard wooden benches, and discussed the options.

DEF. COUNSEL: Well, now that the motion has failed, we've got a problem. It looks like the prosecutor has a pretty good case — there are the people in the store and the customer's paycheck found in your wallet. Judge Singleton will probably find you guilty if we go without a jury. Of course, nobody ever knows what a jury will do, but my feeling is they'll probably convict in a case like this.

DENT: One of those dudes can't say for sure it was me robbed the place.

DEF. COUNSEL: I know. I know. Look, the other two can. And you were in the neighborhood and had that paycheck. What do *you* think a jury will do?

DENT: Well, what can I do?

DEF. COUNSEL: I'll give it to you straight. If we go to trial, it will be on the armed robbery. You'll probably be convicted, and the law says the judge has got to give you some time. Knowing Singleton, if the jury convicts you, he won't hesitate to give you time either. You can plead guilty to the other charge — assault with intent to rob while being armed.

DENT: What would I get then?

DEF. COUNSEL: Well, if you plead, it will be a conviction. You *could* get probation, but you might still get time. I don't really know what he'll give you.

DENT: Damn! What should I do, man?

DEF. COUNSEL: Look, I'm just your attorney. You have to decide. I guess if I were in your shoes, I'd take the plea.

DENT: Yeah. Yeah. OK.

Dent's attorney then told him the questions the judge would ask in taking the plea and listened carefully to the replies the client said he would give. They returned to the courtroom after about ten minutes. When the clerk called the case again, the attorney announced that at this time his client would like to enter a plea to assault with intent to rob while being armed, the plea offered at the pretrial conference. The judge asked a series of questions to ascertain that Dent understood his right to a jury trial, to call witnesses, and to refrain from testifying. Judge Singleton informed him that his plea would be the same as a conviction and that he could be sentenced to as much as life in prison. Dent's answers satisfied the judge. The entire ritual, conducted by the judge in a legalistic and stilted fashion, took only four minutes. After accepting his plea, the judge set sentencing for December 30. He expressed some concern about Dent's being free on bail, but his attorney interjected that he had always appeared up to now and seemed to be responsible. Judge Singleton continued bond at $2,000.

James Dent appeared in Recorder's Court for the final time a few days after Christmas. In a brief ceremony, Judge Singleton sentenced him to three to five years in the Southern Michigan State Prison at Jackson. As the prosecutor shuffled his file and Dent's attorney mumbled a few words to his client, the bailiffs who had taken a position behind Dent during the sentencing ceremony came forward, grasping his arms, and led him to the lockup. It had taken exactly 100 days to reach this moment since his arrest.

THE CHARACTERISTICS
OF COURTROOM WORKGROUPS IN DETROIT

Nearly every defendant formally charged with a felony went to one of the two preliminary hearing courtrooms on the courthouse's fourth floor. These courtrooms heard only preliminary hearings, and unlike analogous courtrooms in the other two cities, did not specialize in cases according to the charges or location of the offense. At the time of our research, only assistant prosecutors among workgroup members appeared regularly in them. Two experienced career prosecutors oversaw the office's work in these courtrooms, handled the more difficult or serious cases, and even took some routine cases. Newly hired attorneys typically began here as well. They stayed anywhere from a few weeks to a few months depending on how quickly other positions in the office opened. No defense attorneys specialized in preliminary hearings. Defendants obtained counsel or had a lawyer appointed to represent them before the preliminary examination, and the same attorney usually stayed with the case until disposition. Courthouse regulars, however, appeared often enough to become thoroughly familiar with the procedures, clerks and bailiffs, and the career prosecutors assigned there. Frequently, both prosecution and defense encountered a judge whom no one knew. During 1972, visiting judges from Detroit's suburbs staffed the preliminary hearing courtrooms. They stayed less than a month. At the beginning of the visiting judges' stints in a courtroom almost no one knew anything about them.

These arrangements produced preliminary hearing workgroups with unstable membership. Only the bailiffs, clerks, and career prosecutors (who handled only part of the case load) provided continuity. The appearance of many regular defense attorneys meant that the defendant's counsel often knew the courtroom staff and career prosecutors even though they handled only several preliminary hearings each week. But many occasionals represented defendants too. And just when the regulars in these courtrooms became familiar with a visiting judge, he left to be replaced by another stranger.

Not surprisingly, these unstable groups did not develop distinctive working styles or clearly articulated goals. The visiting judges, who had even less interest in case outcomes at the trial level than Baltimore's district judges, were not eager to eliminate weak cases by finding no probable cause or reducing charges. They had some interest in processing cases rapidly, however. The state supreme court had sent them to Detroit to help reduce the case backlog. Furthermore, the permanent courtroom staff consistently expressed their interest in finishing the day's business by early afternoon. The visiting judges probably emphasized the goal of doing justice even more than disposing of cases, however. Many people we encountered in our research felt these judges expressed their generally conservative, suburban, law-and-order orientation toward Detroit's crime and its accused criminals in their courtroom behavior. The assistant prosecutors and some defense attorneys shared this interest in doing justice, though their beliefs about what constituted justice clashed sharply. The prosecutor also demonstrated interest in disposing of cases, a trait shared with a group of defense lawyers (primarily regulars) who wanted to complete their defendant's preliminary hearings quickly. Together, these factors resulted in some pressure to dispose cases quickly. Before our research began, this pressure manifested itself in the practice of some visiting judges who raised the bond of defendants insisting on holding rather than waiving the exam. Although this practice halted after the presiding judge intervened, subtle pressures were exerted on attorneys known for their propensity to hold the exam. They reportedly had to wait until later in the day for their cases to be called. Those who took too long cross-examining witnesses found the judges interrupting them, curtly asking them to finish with the witness, or dozing.

Preliminary hearing workgroups in Detroit had fewer important discretionary decisions to make, diminishing the importance of reducing uncertainty and maintaining cohesion. The prosecutor's office had already eliminated many of the weak or unimportant cases before they got to court. Workgroup members requested fewer continuances than in Chicago. Most defendants either asked for a preliminary hearing on the scheduled day or waived their right to one. In practice, the visiting judges usually resolved any doubts in favor of the prosecution. They almost never changed the nature of the charges or accepted guilty pleas. Judges retained control over two important decisions: whether to reduce bond, and whether to dismiss charges because probable cause had not been proved. But most defendants did not request a lower bail, and probable cause was clear in many cases. Defense attorneys and their clients decided whether the preliminary hearing would be held at all. Prosecutors affected the speed of the day's proceedings through decisions on how many witnesses to put on the stand and how long to question them.

In Detroit preliminary hearing workgroups, then, influence was distributed fairly equally. But this equality did not emanate from mutual dependence, because the workgroups lacked the stability that produces interdependence. Nor did it stem from a common emphasis on maintaining cohesion and reducing uncertainty. In fact, the goals of disposing of cases and doing justice received more emphasis. Rather it resulted from a structured environment that restricted the decisions made and from the options available to each member in arriving at those decisions.

Twelve trial courtroom workgroups disposed of charges against defendants bound over from the preliminary hearing courtrooms.[1] A regular Recorder's Court judge presided in each of the twelve courtrooms, and all were located in the Frank Murphy Hall of Justice. We found the hard wooden benches in these courtrooms as uncomfortable as in Chicago and Baltimore, but in most other respects these courtrooms were more attractive and functional than the other cities. An outer door opened into a short hall with another door that guarded the courtroom proper. This double-door arrangement cut down the hallway noise that filtered in whenever anyone entered or left. The courtroom's design allowed spectators to hear and see the proceedings more easily. The rooms had ten sides of unequal length, and the wooden benches placed in front of several of them partially surrounded the central area occupied by the raised judge's dias, the clerk's and court reporter's desks, and the attorneys' tables. Unless workgroup members deliberately tried to speak confidentially, it was easy to hear the proceedings, especially because microphones were routinely used.[2]

Since Recorder's Court heard only criminal matters,[3] judges did not rotate to another assignment after a year or two. In fact, unless death or resignation intruded, they spent years in the same courtroom. At the time we began our research, the prosecuting attorney's office assigned one or two assistant prosecutors to each of the courtrooms. They handled all cases sent to the courtroom by a random number assignment procedure instituted in September 1972. Although shifts in assignments were occasionally necessary, the trial assistants usually remained in a single courtroom. By contrast, defense attorneys appeared everywhere. It made no difference whether a defendant hired an attorney or had one assigned to him. The attorney followed the defendant to whatever courtroom came up in the blind draw. Even Baltimore defense attorneys had more opportunities to control where their defendant's case went than their counterparts in Detroit.

The stability of trial courtroom workgroups in Detroit fell between Chicago's and Baltimore's. Two of the central participants, judge and assistant prosecutor, worked together routinely. But a parade of defense attorneys joined them every day, and it was unusual to see the same defense lawyer on more than one or two cases during the week. However, the other workgroup members knew the regular defense attorneys well. The judges, of course, served for years on Recorder's Court. In addition, Detroit had the largest group of career prosecutors of the three cities. Even though a veteran judge and career prosecutor might interact with a regular defense attorney only once every few weeks, years of previous experience made them both known and predictable. Thus, familiarity was significantly greater than in Baltimore and rivaled Chicago's. Occasionals or new defense attorneys sometimes became workgroup members in Detroit and presented the others with uncertainty, but the same thing happened in Chicago as well.

The story of James Dent's armed robbery case described his attorney's meeting after the preliminary hearing with an assistant prosecuting attorney in the pretrial conference division of the prosecutor's office. Every defendant's attorney participated in a conference (referred to merely as "pretrial" by courthouse regulars). The prosecutor's office permanently assigned three experienced assistants to the pretrial conference division. They already knew the veteran regular defense attorneys and soon came to know every attorney who had any significant number of cases in Recorder's Court. Consequently, many pretrial conferences involved attorneys who were familiar with one another.

The forces that motivated Detroit's workgroups were complex. The structure of courtroom workgroups did not encourage cohesion as a goal. We will describe later the pressure to dispose of cases that existed throughout the system. Courtroom workgroups felt this pressure too. External pressures also produced considerable concern about doing justice, and conflicting views of what this entailed resulted in a considerable degree of adversariness. The goal of reducing uncertainty did not assume overwhelming importance, in part because there was little uncertainty in many cases. Workgroup members, as mentioned, often knew each other fairly well. In addition, decisions about the disposition of many cases were made at the pretrial conference and merely ratified in the courtroom. Unlike their Baltimore counterparts, defense attorneys in Detroit faced no uncertainty about who the judge would be, because the trial judge was assigned seconds after the preliminary hearing finished. Finally, prosecution and defense more readily shared information than in either Baltimore or Chicago. Material in the prosecutor's file, which could be obtained only after the defense filed formal motions for discovery in the other two cities, was routinely given informally to the defense in Detroit.[4]

Influence patterns among workgroup members also fell between those found in the other cities. Judges did not dominate as much as they did in Baltimore, but neither did they share influence as much as their brethren in Chicago's close-knit and stable workgroups. Although we have no hard evidence, our impression was that the relative influence of workgroup members varied considerably from courtroom to courtroom in Detroit.

THE JUDGES' SPONSORING ORGANIZATION

Detroit had a unitary judicial organization whose formal structure was even more centralized than Chicago's. Detroit Recorder's Court had complete jurisdiction over all crimes committed in the city. Unlike Chicago's courts, it had nothing to do with crimes committed elsewhere in the county. Wayne County Circuit Court heard those cases. Unlike Baltimore's Supreme Bench, Recorder's Court handled all criminal proceedings, both misdemeanors and felonies. It staffed the misdemeanor court, arraigned defendants on the arrest warrant, conducted preliminary hearings, and disposed of cases bound over for trial.

Normally, Recorder's Court assigned one of its regular judges to the misdemeanor court and two to conduct preliminary examinations. However, in 1972 visiting judges were assigned to Recorder's Court in the state supreme court's "crash program" to reduce the case backlog and were used to staff these courtrooms during our research. As indicated, these judges came primarily from the lower courts of suburban communities surrounding Detroit, although several were residents of Detroit. Most of these visiting judges found the cases regarded as routine by Detroiters to be extremely serious. Their response reflected the conservative bias of their communities toward crime. These judges were not formally part of Recorder's Court, did not participate in the monthly judges' conference, and did not stay long enough to develop a sense of responsibility for the performance of the court. Thus, most visiting judges had neither the inclination nor the incentive to dismiss cases for lack of probable cause, even when the evidence was weak. Questionable cases could painlessly be sent on their way for the regular judges to handle. In the interim, they would go back to their home jurisdiction never to return. Despite the more centralized formal structure, these judges' actual relationship to the trial court resembled the relationship of Baltimore district judges to the Supreme Bench. The judges resembled Baltimore district judges in another important respect: many were men of undistinguished reputation and questionable legal ability. Courthouse regulars spent many enjoyable moments recounting stories about the incredible decisions and comments that came from the visiting judges.

Although the visiting judges created problems, the thirteen regular Recorder's Court judges tolerated them because they knew they would soon be gone. Detroit's voters had approved an increase in the size of the court to twenty judges. The new judges, elected in the midst of our research in the fall of 1972, were to take office in January 1973, obviating the need for outside manpower.

Detroit elected Recorder's Court judges in nonpartisan elections for six-year terms. As in most elective courts, many incumbent judges had come to the bench by appointment to a vacancy and ran for the remainder of their predecessor's term with the advantages incumbents have. The 1972 election demonstrated these advantages. Six incumbents sought reelection. Two faced no opposition. The other four ran against six challengers in the primary to determine which eight candidates would contest the four positions to be filled in November. All four incumbents won reelection despite vigorous opposition to two of them.

The reelection of six incumbents and seven new judges provided an excellent opportunity to observe the recruitment process. It contrasted sharply with both Baltimore's and Chicago's. Many attorneys found the position attractive. Recorder's Court judges received $39,000 annual salaries, equal to what circuit court judges elsewhere in Michigan earned. Recorder's Court had also managed to shed its lingering reputation as a lower court.

Its judges had a status equal to that of circuit court judges and even had representation at the Michigan Supreme Court's conferences of circuit judges. Competition was stiff and wide open. Forty-three hopefuls vied in the primary for the fourteen ballot positions in the race for the seven new judgeships. Detroit's strong tradition of nonpartisanship in city elections had stunted the growth of city-based political organizations. Nothing resembling the central control over nominations exercised by Chicago's Democratic Party organization existed. No political organizations or factions like Baltimore's were active either. In fact, political parties played less of a covert role than they do elsewhere in nonpartisan elections. Nevertheless, intense politics surrounded Recorder's Court elections. The races attracted considerable newspaper attention despite their coincidence with the presidential and congressional election.[5] Many of the groups and interests that make up party coalitions were active in Recorder's Court campaigns. The United Auto Workers Union, civil rights groups, and other liberal organizations endorsed and worked for certain candidates. Homeowners associations were also active. In addition, several citizen groups and bar associations rated and endorsed candidates. Although the nonpartisan character of the election blurred lines of cleavage somewhat, the election process reflected many of the basic divisions in the political life of the city — labor versus business, black versus white, liberal versus conservative. According to a newspaper report, one candidate told a white homeowners group, "It's them against us." "Them" included the UAW, super-liberals, and those who wanted more black judges.[6]

The election's outcome suggested that no group dominated the selection process in 1972. Two of the successful incumbents, judges Maher and Poindexter, had reputations as conservative, law-and-order advocates. Many people questioned their legal acumen, and both major newspapers, despite their conservative to moderate outlook, recommended their defeat.[7] But both received strong support from conservative, white homeowners' groups such as the Greater Detroit Homeowners' Council. In fact, one of the conservative incumbents was a founder of this group. White liberals and blacks failed to defeat either of them.

On the other hand, three of the seven new judges were black, and two of the whites were outspokenly liberal. Included among them were Justin Ravitz, an avowed Marxist radical, and Susan Borman, who served with the Legal Aid and Defender's Association immediately prior to her election. Only one of the winners (a black) came from the prosecutor's office, though about half of the incumbent judges had served there. In all, three of the seven winners had prior experience in Recorder's Court, and a fourth had served as a common pleas judge.

Recorder's Court operated with a stronger central organization than the judicial sponsoring organization in either Baltimore or Chicago. The thirteen regular judges met monthly in conference and made many important decisions.[8] Because their jurisdiction extended only to criminal matters, they could focus exclusively on the problems of the criminal case load. All had a sustained interest in the court's functioning because, unlike their Baltimore and Chicago colleagues, their assignments did not alternate between civil and criminal courtrooms. Their power to coordinate their work benefited from their control over the clerk's office. The judges selected the clerk and had the power to fire him. Finally, the monthly conference (not a political organization or the governor) selected the presiding judge for a one-year term.

In addition to selecting the presiding judge and the clerk, the monthly conference established general policies for administrative matters affecting the entire operation of the court; the method of assigning defendants to trial courtrooms is a good example. Before September 1972, a central assignment procedure was used. The presiding judge or a clerk under his formal supervision would docket the case for an open courtroom shortly before trial. After September 1, cases were assigned by a strictly random blind draw immediately following a finding of probable cause at the preliminary examination. The implications of this change were profound. It drastically limited opportunities for defense attorneys to shop for judges.[9]

Some attorneys were friends of judges and actively helped in organizing and contributing to the judge's reelection efforts. Others had strained relations with certain judges. The new assignment procedure severely limited the ability of attorneys to capitalize on these relationships and on their knowledge of judges' value preferences. The change also increased the pressure on judges to dispose cases. Since each judge received an equal number of cases over the year, his productivity could easily be measured and publicized.

The judges' decision to require that every defendant's attorney meet with the assistant prosecutors in the pretrial conference division was probably an even more important procedural innovation. None of the problems encountered by the Baltimore state's attorney's office in getting cooperation from defense attorneys arose in Detroit. Technically, Detroit attorneys who refused to appear for the pretrial conference opened themselves up to the possibility of formal contempt proceedings. The unspoken threat to deny them future appointments to represent indigents, however, won their cooperation just as effectively.

The monthly conference also decided how to staff the misdemeanor and preliminary hearing courtrooms. As we have said, the conference delegated these tasks to visiting judges. The presiding judge handled all arraignments. Finally, the judges jointly established procedures for assigning legal counsel to indigents. This was a particularly sensitive decision, and the disputes that surrounded it revealed much about the powers of the monthly conference, the norms of the court, and the constraints on its behavior coming from its task environment.

In early 1972, the monthly conference decided to change from a weekly rotation of the responsibility for assigning counsel to a monthly rotation. The six sitting judges up for reelection were the first six to receive the opportunity to appoint. This change helped the incumbents to encourage private attorneys to contribute to their reelection campaigns. The impending primary and general election increased the incentive to appoint private attorneys (who were likely to make contributions) rather than the defenders. This incentive, coupled with the fact that many incumbents were hostile to the defenders, led to a significant decline in the proportion of appointments the defender received and threatened the survival of the defender's organization until the state supreme court intervened by requiring a quarter of all indigent appointments to go to the defender.

Even after the supreme court's intervention, controversy over the appointment of counsel for indigents continued. This controversy brought to the surface the dominant norms governing the conflict between the Recorder's Court judges acting collectively and individual judges making decisions autonomously. When it was proposed that no judge be allowed to appoint any lawyer to more than five cases a year, the presiding judge of the Recorder's Court responded as follows:

For more than a century now, the laws of Michigan have authorized the presiding judge of multimember courts to assign counsel for indigents (poor people). More than 50 years ago the judges of Recorder's Court correctly determined that such extensive power of assignment should not be lodged in one person. We have provided a court rule for rotating that power.

It may occasionally appear that one or more of our fellow judges may not have properly exercised their responsibility in the selection of counsel for indigents, but that — like the setting of bond or the imposition of sentence — is an individual judicial decision to be made by that judge, and his discretion in this respect is not subject to control by his fellow judges.[10]

Clearly the powers of the conference were limited not only by the supreme court's intervention but also by the norm of individual autonomy for judges.

These norms of autonomy also restricted the role played by the presiding judge. His influence depended on the combination of the resources available to the position, his personality, and his political skill. The formally established resources of the presiding judge were limited. He was elected by his colleagues, and the one-year term coupled with a prohibition against a second consecutive term restricted his ability to complete long-range projects. He did not control assignments of judges and did not assign cases to courtrooms. His formal controls over his colleagues, thus, were almost nonexistent. But he did have some resources. For one thing, he could call on whatever qualities he possessed that had caused his colleagues to choose him for the post. He presided over the monthly conferences. He spoke for other judges in handling mutual problems with the prosecutor's office, the police, the Michigan Supreme Court, and local governmental bodies. He could also command media coverage by virtue of his position. Finally, he was responsible for handling day-to-day administrative problems. This responsibility was particularly important during the period when there were ten visiting judges assigned to the court. He was called on to handle the problems created by these unassimilated and sometimes troublesome individuals.[11]

Perhaps the presiding judge's most significant ability was to initiate changes. He could impose few changes on his own initiative, but he was in a good position to propose reforms to his colleagues and, if he was particularly skillful, obtain their voluntary cooperation in matters normally within the prerogative of individual judges. For instance, Judge Evans, when he became presiding judge in 1971, and responding to external pressure, became quite concerned about the size of the jail population. He convinced his colleagues to shorten the period between the preliminary examination and pretrial from thirty days to ten days, much to the unhappiness of the prosecutor's office.

Detroit judges displayed less internal conflict and dissention than Baltimore's Supreme Bench judges, but lacked the cohesion and uniformity found in Chicago. No counterpart to Chicago's strong political organization existed to moderate conflict. But neither were political factions strong enough to be reflected in cliques as among judges in Baltimore. Although some Recorder's Court judges intensely disliked each other, the level of interpersonal animosity did not equal that found in Baltimore. Most of the judges got along with each other fairly well. Cohesion was high enough to permit their organization to administer the court effectively. However, on such matters as the utility of long prison sentences, the credibility of the police, and the value of legal arguments favoring defendants as opposed to practical arguments based on ensuring public safety, Detroit's judges held widely divergent opinions. This disparity reflected the diversity and conflict in the city proper. In this sense, Detroit differed markedly from the other two cities, where the judges by and large held similar conservative views on these questions.

THE DETROIT PROSECUTING ATTORNEY'S OFFICE

As in Chicago, Detroit's voters elected the prosecuting attorney in a county-wide, partisan election. Similarly, the heavily Democratic vote in the city overwhelmed Republican-oriented votes in the out-county areas. The most significant battles for the office consequently were fought in the Democratic primary. Detroit's Democratic Party was fragmented and weak. It possessed none of the centralized power of Mayor Daley's organization. In the past, this weakness frequently had led to intense competition for the Democratic nomination. The prosecuting attorney's term expired in 1972 as in Chicago, but the election exhibited none of the conflict or drama found in Chicago. In fact, competition in the Democratic primary did not even materialize, and the incumbent won renomination in an uncontested race. He easily beat his Republican challenger in the November general election.

In 1972 the Wayne County prosecutor's office had an authorized strength of eighty-nine attorneys. The criminal division had six attorneys assigned to the warrant section, four charged with conducting preliminary exams, three assigned to the pretrial division (including the head who was on a leave while running for a judgeship), and forty attorneys authorized for the trial division. However, a hiring freeze imposed by the County Board of Commissioners cut the trial division's manpower to only twenty-eight, forcing a change in the technique for staffing courtrooms. At the start of 1972, the office assigned cases to one of six trial teams. Each team was headed by a veteran prosecutor and had five members. The team prosecuted cases assigned to it regardless of which judge heard the case. At the end of the summer, declining manpower forced adoption of the zone system: two attorneys (and in some cases only one) handled all cases assigned to a particular judge's courtroom.

As in many prosecutor's offices, no individual was responsible for a case throughout its journey in the courts. But the structure of the Detroit prosecutor's office heightened the potential for conflict between those handling a case at different stages. It was not the police but the prosecutor's warrant section that determined whether a defendant would be charged with a felony. It was only natural for assistant prosecutors in preliminary exams or in pretrial or trial courtrooms to criticize the warrant section for authorizing bad cases. Similarly, attorneys in the pretrial and trial divisions criticized the preliminary exam attorneys for failing to dismiss poor cases. Office policies and procedures at times exacerbated such tensions. The regular warrant prosecutors did not normally work on weekends, one of the busiest times for the section. All attorneys in the office (including those assigned to the Wayne County Circuit Court Division) rotated weekend warrant assignments. Many questionable warrant decisions turned out to be the product of a weekend substitute. The attempt to establish a "pure trial docket" made trial attorneys particularly vulnerable to problems created by earlier decisions. The policy dictated that no pleas would be accepted on the day of trial. Thus, when a weak case survived to this stage, the trial prosecutor either had to violate office policy by taking a plea or go to trial and lose. A somewhat milder form of the pure trial docket policy prohibited trial attorneys from agreeing to accept any plea lower than that offered at the pretrial conference. Trial attorneys resented this infringement on their discretion. On the other hand, at one point the trial teams were given authority to go below the pretrial attorney's offer in a temporary effort to reduce the backlog. The pretrial attorneys then became frustrated, because they felt they had been undercut by the trial attorneys.

Although the tensions just described were real, they did not appear to disrupt seriously the office's performance. Some of the tension was released through friendly joshing and rivalry. In some instances, the long-standing friendship of the individuals involved moderated the conflicts. Office morale was generally high.

The composition of the staff contributed in large part to high morale. Unlike Baltimore and Chicago, Detroit had a substantial group of veteran prosecutors who had been with the office for years; some made a career in the office. In addition, there were a number of older men who came to the office after retiring from the police department or leaving private practice. One man, for example, had worked for eight years for an insurance company defending auto accident claims, spent four years as a plaintiff's attorney, and then came to the prosecutor's office. Another was in general practice for several years before joining the office in his late forties. The office's reputation, the expectation that assistants could remain even if the prosecuting attorney was replaced, and a moderately good salary coupled with financial security, retirement benefits, and a manageable work load attracted many such men. Competition for the jobs held by younger men who came for the experience and then left was fairly intense. In 1972, starting salaries were $13,200. According to the chief of the criminal division, over 80 percent of the staff earned more than $20,000 in 1972. Although it is difficult to compare the competence of assistant prosecutors from city to city, our impression was that Detroit's exhibited greater competence, experience, and expertise than Chicago's or Baltimore's.

Pleasant working conditions also contributed to high morale. Each assistant prosecuting attorney had an individual and conveniently located office. A number of decent restaurants were located several short blocks away. If time was short, the ninth-floor cafeteria was available. Compared to conditions in both Baltimore and Chicago, working conditions for Detroit prosecutors were modern, spacious, convenient, and pleasant.

The office had no formal training program for new prosecutors, and the experience new assistants brought with them varied greatly. Usually some ad hoc arrangements were made. Often they involved assigning the newcomer to a more experienced colleague who was told to "break him in." The sequence of assignments also followed a pattern, with the first experiences in less complicated and less important situations (misdemeanors and preliminary exams) which took place in high-volume courtrooms where adversarial norms learned in law school would be washed away. Rapidly the newcomer received less supervision in these situations; eventually, he was given more challenging assignments. The following description by a young assistant of his socialization conveys the informal nature of the training:

INTERVIEWER: I wonder if you could tell me a little bit about how you learned the ropes?

RESPONDENT: It's a frightening kind of position to be in. Let me tell you what happened. . . . I came into the job a couple of days before the primary election. Everybody was very busy with the election, and consequently that left very little time for me. I thought that was OK because it would be over shortly. There was no formalized program. It's in somebody's head what they like to see the newer people do. But it isn't institutionalized in any way. . . . First, I spent one day in warrants . . . just watching. After that they put me in preliminary exams. That's a very variable situation. Some people spend weeks.

INTERVIEWER: Did you get to watch some first?

RESPONDENT: Just watching. I watched for a day. . . . By about the sixth day on the job I was sent into an examining courtroom, in with Tom. I started handling some of the CCW [carrying concealed weapon] cases; they were less complicated factually. . . . I spent three weeks in exams, and shortly after maybe about three or four days in exams, the fellow I was there with would step out for coffee or something and I would be there alone. And then it would be longer gaps that he would be out. And then I would be there alone.

All of the attorneys in both the warrant and pretrial sections were experienced trial prosecutors. The new assistants assigned to the trial division were most affected by informal socialization. When assigned to preliminary examinations or misdemeanors, they spent much of their time in the courtroom. But when they moved to a trial division post, they received substantial informal socialization. Suddenly they had a good deal of spare time during the day and could interact with more experienced attorneys in the twelfth-floor coffee lounge. Neither Baltimore nor Chicago had an equally convenient or central gathering place for assistants. The lounge was the gossip center and gathering place for staff attorneys. Several people could be found there at almost any time. Sometimes the number grew to ten or more. The informal discussions covered a number of topics bearing on prosecution: gossip about the predilections, personal affairs, and decisional tendencies of the various judges; evaluation of police witnesses; the abilities and faults of the various regular defense attorneys; the details of the progress of current trials from the perspective of the trial attorney; substantive points of law; bantering and joshing about trial tactics (especially when cases were lost); and general philosophy toward criminals, the defense bar, judges, juries, and the entire criminal justice system. Exchanges were sometimes sharp and the clash of strong-willed individuals not infrequent. The younger attorneys normally listened, occasionally asked questions, and often received brief lectures of advice.

Although sharp disagreement existed on specific issues, there was a fairly broad consensus on a number of topics — which may be called the office view. It included the following: nobody cares about victims; defense attorneys are often devious, sometimes make ridiculous arguments, and occasionally are dishonest; many judges are too lenient; appellate judges are naive and render ridiculously pro-defendant decisions; many defendants deserve to go to jail — more than are actually sent and for longer than they are sent; prosecutors are about the only ones who represent the interests of the public. Although somewhat amorphous in content, the view was shared by nearly all experienced attorneys, and its effect on the attitudes of newer attorneys was substantial.

In many ways the Detroit prosecutor's office was more "professional" than Baltimore's or Chicago's. A management-oriented administrative staff directed the work of experienced career prosecutors. The prosecuting attorney, William Cahalan, demonstrated his interest in administrative innovation in an article appearing in the journal of the National District Attorney's Association describing his office's innovations for reducing delays between arrest and trial. The head of the criminal division made frequent trips to other jurisdictions and was conversant with the major operating characteristics of criminal justice systems in Baltimore, Chicago, Houston, Los Angeles, and Washington, D.C., among others. The staff devoted constant attention to the details of administrative management. During our field research, the accounting firm of Arthur Anderson conducted a study for the office to determine the cost of prosecuting misdemeanors as opposed to felonies. The staff gathered internal statistics on almost every phase of the office's operation. A case evaluation procedure devised in Washington, D.C. to help that office allocate its very limited manpower to the most serious cases was adopted in Detroit (though its usefulness was seriously questioned by most of the staff attorneys). The concern with efficiency was real and serious. For example, every case dismissed at the preliminary examination was returned to the warrant section for review to provide the section with feedback on the quality of its warrant decisions.

The office gained a national reputation for its efforts to improve its efficiency and management procedures. Visitors from other jurisdictions came to observe the work of the warrant and pretrial sections. Several men were sent to the Cook County state's attorney's office to advise it on organization. The Baltimore state's attorney's office openly acknowledged its efforts to transplant several features of the Detroit system (most notably warrant screening and pretrial) to Baltimore. Also, the top administrative staff seemed to have a sophisticated understanding of the system's operation.

Consistent with its managerial-professional orientation, the Detroit prosecutor's office made vigorous efforts to establish and enforce office-wide policies. The most significant of these policies during our field research established guidelines for plea bargaining in three major crime categories. Office policy forbade offering a defendant anything less than a charge of attempted carrying a concealed weapon in exchange for carrying concealed weapon charges, assault with intent to rob while being armed in exchange for armed robbery charges, and attempted breaking and entering an occupied dwelling in exchange for charges of breaking and entering an occupied dwelling. The centralization of plea bargaining in the pretrial conference division enhanced the office's ability to implement such policies. Indeed, the desire to control plea bargaining was part of the motivation underlying its establishment, though Detroit already had a tradition of centralized bargaining.[12] The veteran prosecutors assigned to the pretrial division shared the office view. Assignments to that division were reviewed periodically by the prosecuting attorney. In addition, prosecutors prepared summaries of all decisions at the request of the central office ("upstairs"), and these readily provided information on whether the policies were being followed. Thus, the centrally established policies on plea bargaining were mostly followed in pretrial.

The supervisory staff realized that pretrial's adherence to the policies did not guarantee their ultimate implementation. The trial prosecutors also had to conform, especially by refraining from undermining bargains offered at pretrial. This need reflected the central office's concern about consistency of the bargains agreed to from courtroom to courtroom. A top administrator expressed this concern in an interview:

One other advantage [of having a pretrial division], even though the plea may be taken at the day of trial, there is a consistency there.

We would much rather have Laster, McConnell, and Bartholomew pretrial the case even though it [the plea] may not be taken at the time they take it. [At trial] they have any one of thirty-six assistants, some of whom have no experience at all attempting a pretrial, even though they may have a better insight in some respects. Because their experience . . . we get too wide a variance in what they are going to do. Some of them are afraid to try one; some are buffaloed by defense counsel; some of them are too nice; some of them don't really know what's involved in a case; some are too tough or too careful or too worried. And for no other reason, one of the advantages is I wouldn't have my phone hassled away for thirty-six different assistants saying this is what I'm going to do, what do you think?

These considerations led to the attempt to implement two policies: (1) no trial prosecutor could agree to a lesser plea bargain than was offered at pretrial without obtaining the pretrial man's approval; (2) no prosecutor could accept a plea on the day of trial that had been turned down by the defense when they appeared before the judge on the day of pretrial. Both policies, and particularly the second, were intended to lead to a pure trial docket. With a pure trial docket, the effectiveness of pretrial would be enhanced by the defense's knowledge that their only opportunity to bargain was at pretrial, and that if they did not accept pretrial's offer on the day of pretrial, they would be forced to try the case on the existing charges. To work, the policy needed the complete cooperation of the judges. The idea was that if judges had the courage to force a few defense attorneys to trial by refusing to accept a plea that the defense had spurned earlier, word would soon get around the defense community that it was "take it or leave it" on pretrial day. The office's inability to convince enough judges to follow this practice in 1972 was the major factor frustrating the establishment of a pure trial docket.

The willingness of judges to accept a plea bargain a defendant had rejected thirty days earlier created obvious pressures on the assistant prosecutors assigned to their courtrooms. Judicial pressure produced a strong incentive for trial attorneys to undercut office policies.[13] The administrative staff was fully aware of these pressures and sought to counteract them. The following exchange with a top administrator reveals this recognition and the optimism of his assumptions about their ability to control trial prosecutors. He had just described his intention to assign two men permanently to each courtroom when a new set of judges took office in January 1973.

> INTERVIEWER: Isn't there a danger they will be co-opted by the judges?
> RESPONDENT: Yes, there is. It is a danger that we are not unaware of. You will maintain your professional separation. We don't want to see them going out to lunch with the judge or socializing with him. If that happens they will get changed.
> INTERVIEWER: They can get co-opted without socializing. . . .
> RESPONDENT: And if he does, and he does not object on the record [to a plea on trial day], he is coming out. We will find out about it. . . . We are also keeping records. A sheet will be handed in from each courtroom each day.

The office succeeded fairly well in getting its staff attorneys to adhere to policies. But adherence was by no means complete, and the optimism of the supervisor just quoted was not entirely justified. It was particularly difficult to tell experienced career prosecutors what to do. Like the judges, these men did not want to be told how to handle their cases. Their status and force of personality guaranteed them a certain immunity from close supervision unless they blatantly and consistently subverted policy. It was particularly unlikely that experienced trial prosecutors would willingly try sure losers in order to maintain the principle of a pure trial docket. Speculating on the prospect, one such man observed that if he were stuck trying bad cases, "they will have to straighten up upstairs. There are supposed to be forty prosecutors in the courtroom, and if all of them are screaming and hollering, you will have to change." Even newer assistant prosecutors could avoid complete adherence to mandated policies. A man with only eighteen months' experience in the office expressed the belief that one of the pretrial prosecutors was unrealistically severe in offering pleas. When he had a case pretried by this prosecutor, he went ahead and accepted a lower plea without checking back to obtain approval even though he knew he was supposed to check. We also observed several instances in which pretrial prosecutors themselves violated the supposedly inviolable policy about pleas on breaking and entering and gun cases.

Two other characteristics of the prosecutor's office are relevant to understanding courtroom behavior. First, as in the other two cities, trial prosecutors faced pressures that motivated them to avoid losing cases. They were especially sensitive about losing jury trials. The coffee lounge culture guaranteed that many office members knew about each trial and were able to follow its progress through the reports of the attorney trying it. Second, the general attitude toward plea bargaining was more favorable than in Chicago and especially Baltimore. No one hesitated before trying serious cases involving violent crimes. Many prosecutors preferred to try them. At the same time, most of them acknowledged the legitimacy of accepting reasonable pleas in such cases. Few adhered to the belief that there was something reprehensible about pleas, a belief fairly prevalent in Baltimore. The concern for efficiency and the backlog, coupled with a strong tradition of bargaining, also contributed to the acceptance of bargained pleas.

Courtroom prosecutors thus worked under much closer supervision in Detroit than in the other two cities. They also felt they were part of a team rather than autonomous courtroom participants. Decisions made at later stages were systematically fed back to those responsible for earlier decisions; information collected early in the process became important resources for later decision-making. The career perspectives of the staff were much longer than in the other two cities. Thus, staff members were more vulnerable to office supervision and at the same time needed less of it, because experience provided a degree of socialization to office norms that was not matched elsewhere. To a greater extent than in the other two cities, the prosecutor's office was a cohesive organization that did more than send prosecutors to courtrooms; it gave substantial direction and content to their behavior in the workgroup.

THE DEFENSE BAR IN DETROIT

The most notable feature of the defense bar practicing in Recorder's Court was its dependence on appointments. Attorneys appointed by the judges represented over half of the defendants in our sample. More than a quarter of the appointed attorneys worked for the Legal Aid and Defenders Association.

Although they are called public defenders, Legal Aid and Defenders Association attorneys differed in important respects from assistant public defenders in most cities. Their office was not public in the formal sense, as the absence of that word in its name implies. An independent board with no formal connection to government chose the office's head and set general policy. The fees paid to the office for representation of defendants by its twelve staff attorneys provided most of the office's financing. When the judge responsible for appointing counsel for indigents designated the defenders, one of its attorneys handled the case. The attorney submitted a voucher to the clerk of the court for his services, as did any other attorney so appointed, and the clerk calculated the fee on the same scale. These fees went into the general fund of the defender's office and were used to pay office expenses and salaries. Unlike the public defender's office in Chicago, the Detroit defenders did not face the problem of disposing a massive case load with a fixed budget. The more work assigned to them, the more fees generated. The incentive to turn over cases rapidly that retained attorneys have carried little weight with the assistant defenders. They received a salary; and as long as the office met expenses, they could devote as much time as they wished to each case.

The twelve defenders enjoyed several advantages that most of their counterparts in private practice did not. In addition to good clerical support they had the services of investigators who interviewed defendants before the preliminary examination and wrote a report for the staff attorney. If an attorney had a conflict of schedules, he could usually get another member of the office to make the appearance.

Despite the fact that assistant defenders received lower salaries than assistant prosecutors (salaries ranged from $11,500 to

$23,000), the director of the office reported no trouble in getting good applicants. In fact, he felt that he got the best applicants and that the leftovers went to the prosecutor. The director, his deputy, and many of the staff attorneys were black. The white staff attorneys were ideologically committed to the defendant's perspective. One newly hired attorney had obtained his first legal experience working in a legal aid program for migrant workers in his second year of law school. The Law Students' Civil Rights Committee had placed him as an intern in a local firm of radical lawyers his next summer. He then worked as a clerk for the defenders until he passed the bar exam. A colleague had a similar background, working in a free legal aid clinic while in law school and then spending several years at Neighborhood Legal Services before joining the defenders. Thus, the office staff contained more committed, defendant-oriented, liberal-to-radical attorneys than in either Chicago or Baltimore.[14]

Like the Detroit prosecutors, the defenders also developed an office view. High office morale was an important component of the common view. The office exercised little formal supervision over staff attorneys. Rather, assistant defenders consulted with each other extensively. Morale was also boosted by the belief that the office was doing a good job under difficult circumstances. Another important component of the defenders' view was that the prosecutors, many judges, their clerks, the police, and even most private defense attorneys were hostile to them. The belief that many black defendants were ill-treated by society in general and the legal process in particular, however, formed the core of the office view. The defenders felt the police all too often committed perjury, the prosecution overlooked such perjury and sought overly harsh disposition, and many judges let their anti-defendant and antiblack biases color their decisions and deny defendants due process. Underlying most components of the defenders' viewpoint was the belief that widespread and deep-seated racial prejudice shaped much of what happened. They suspected that many people in the court community did not like them because those people objected to the provision of vigorous representation for blacks. Finally, they felt the appropriate response to this situation was to offer their clients just such a vigorous, adversarial defense.

We encountered considerable impressionistic evidence that many key participants did harbor hostility toward the defender's office. Prosecutors, judges' clerks, the judges themselves, and many private attorneys freely attacked them. The most frequent criticism was that the defenders held too many exams, unnecessarily prolonged the examination of witnesses during exams, filed too many motions, and in general were "nitpickers." There was a measure of truth to the chief defender's public observation: "A lot of judges still don't like us. They want to move their cases, see each individual case disposed of quickly. They like lawyers who waive exams and don't file motions, and we were created to offset these practices." [15]

The ideological cast of the office also produced hostility. An experienced black private regular observed with some passion, "The militants or Marxists have made a difference. You can put the defenders in any category you want."

Finally, resentment toward the defenders was possibly generated by the perception that they in fact did a good job. The best evidence came not from the office itself, though it was not reluctant to make such claims on its own behalf,[16] but from its detractors. The black regular just quoted revealed a grudging respect for them. "The defenders have caused more exams. There is better quality. Everyone works harder to be competitive." The result, he observed, was that the whole process had moved to more of a balance between a legalistic and a pragmatic approach to litigation. Everyone, including himself, now did a better job. His contention that the defenders had caused more exams to be held was repeated by several other respondents. There is quantitative evidence for the decrease in the proportion of preliminary examinations waived. In 1970, 55 percent were waived; in 1971 it dropped to 47 percent, and in 1972, it was only 36 percent.[17] One mechanism by which the defenders' practice of holding exams might have forced other attorneys to hold them was described by another respondent. As defendants and their families crowded into the preliminary hearing courtrooms and witnessed the defenders holding exams and vigorously cross-examining police witnesses, they began asking their private attorneys why they weren't getting the same treatment.

The distinction between regulars and occasionals applied to

private attorneys in Detroit as in the other cities. Most of the regulars obtained clients through both appointment and the marketplace. Consequently, they did not encounter the same problem of getting paid when representing an indigent that they had when a defendant retained them. But the fee structure had quite a different effect on appointed attorneys than on the defenders who were also paid by these fees. The defenders were on salary and usually earned less than private attorneys; their organization buffered the effect of the fee structure by obtaining additional funding from outside sources. Private attorneys sought to earn more and depended entirely on the fees they received. Attorneys obtained $50 whether they held the preliminary exam or waived it, providing an incentive to waive. Similarly, most attorneys found it more profitable to obtain a guilty plea than to conduct a trial. Attorneys who argued a motion received an additional, though modest sum. The average fee paid in 1972, just over $180,[18] was low enough to encourage most attorneys to opt for a quick disposition.

The appointment system, which provided many attorneys with a substantial number of clients, had a significant effect on the structure of the defense bar. The widespread impression that attorneys who contributed to judges' reelection campaigns got appointments in return was undoubtedly partially correct. But the process worked the other way too. A young private attorney told us that he contributed to the campaigns of judges who had given him appointments and treated him decently. In his case, appointments preceded contributions. He felt it only natural to contribute to those who had treated him well. He felt no pressure to give to those who had not.

The system also could exert strong pressures on attorneys to conform to specific norms regarding handling cases. The threat of withholding appointments from an attorney who violated norms was powerful, and did more than elicit campaign contributions. It kept defense counsel in line in the courtroom. However, it did not produce a single preferred set of norms and expectations about how to handle cases, because appointments were made by all of the judges on a rotating basis. The diversity of the bench was reflected in the styles of the men they appointed. Although an attorney might jeopardize his chances of getting future appointments if his handling of cases antagonized those who appointed him, it is also true that what antagonized some judges pleased others.

Individual attorneys, however, may have found themselves locked into a particular style. Once they had established a reputation for one style of practice, it was difficult to get appointments from judges disposed to a different style. Consequently, someone whose behavior began to alienate judges who already gave him appointments could find that other judges were unwilling to give him appointments even when his style changed. Although such incentives to conform are difficult to document, we encountered indications of their presence. For instance, when one attorney was asked why he did not simply refuse to waive the formal arraignment on the information in order to obtain a transcript of the preliminary examination before he went to the pretrial conference, he replied that the presiding judge would not permit it. "But why can't you refuse to arraign your defendant without the transcript as you are entitled to do," he was asked. "You can't do that," he replied. When asked why, he began to fidget, mumbled something about "hidden pressures," and elaborated no further.

The assignment system thus produced a segmented defense bar, each element having its own style of handling cases and its own set of appointing judges. Although the lines were vague, there were at least two distinct groups, and possibly three: the old-time regulars, referred to as the Clinton Street Bar; the new regulars; and the new adversaries. The old-time regulars adhered to many of the same norms as the clubhouse regulars in Chicago. They liked to waive exams and plead their clients, relying on heavy turnover. The new regulars, like the man described in the preceding paragraph, were younger, somewhat less dependent on an exclusive practice in Recorder's Court, and somewhat more adversarial. The new adversaries included the defenders plus a group of young attorneys who were strongly pro-defendant, critical of the court as a whole, and committed to vigorous defense of their clients.

The ideological stance of defense attorneys and the norms informally enforced by the group of judges who appointed them modified the effect of the fee structure on the handling of cases.

Many attorneys responded to fee incentives and avoided time-consuming adversarial dispositions. Others, including the defenders, did not.

There were several other noteworthy features of the defense bar in Detroit. Widespread consensus on the dangers of sentence bargaining shaped the pattern of plea bargaining. Even the most established and successful members of the Clinton Street Bar, who regularly pleaded out almost all of their clients, expressed strong reservations about practices that were accepted routinely by almost everyone in Chicago. There was considerable camaraderie and communication within the defense bar, even among attorneys with different styles of practice. This communication network passed information about the predilections of the various judges, significant new decisions, changes in the personnel and policies of the prosecutor's office, and the quality and characteristics of various police witnesses.[19] Finally, the possibility of a convicted client's bringing charges against them before the state bar grievance committee concerned most appointed attorneys and may help account for the increase in the frequency of holding preliminary exams. It also may have reduced the extent to which attorneys pressured clients to accept a plea.

Thus the defense bar in Detroit had a substantially different structure than in the other two cities. The defenders handled fewer cases than the more traditional public defenders in Baltimore and Chicago, and their effect on the operation of the courts moved them toward a more adversarial posture. Private attorneys appointed by judges represented defendants who would have been clients of the public defender in Chicago. The distinct ideological and stylistic divisions among defense attorneys in Detroit were absent in the other cities. In general, Detroit's defense bar had a more vigorous and adversarial style. And finally, defense attorneys faced a more unified prosecutor's office.

THE ENVIRONMENTAL CONTEXT

The question of race dominated Detroit in the early 1970s.[20] The 1967 riot and its aftermath renewed the city's history of racial violence and increased racial tensions and their salience and intensity. Two other developments converged to shape the environmental context. First, the city's problems stemming from unemployment, a shrinking tax base, poverty, and decay were exacerbated by a particularly virulent crime problem. The high rate of narcotics addiction not only generated a rash of addict crime, but also produced a series of bloody conflicts between rival drug-supplying organizations. The widespread ownership of handguns, which increased markedly in the "arms race" that followed the 1967 riots, contributed to high rates of murder, assault, and armed robbery. Second, the growth of black political power did not lag far behind the increase in the black population. The 1970 census found that just under 44 percent of the population was black; and by 1973 it approached 50 percent. In Detroit, unlike Baltimore, numerical strength translated into political power. Nearly everyone, for instance, assumed the next mayor would be black, a prediction that subsequent events confirmed.

As in the other two cities, nearly all defendants were black. This racial imbalance produced a complex set of conflicting pressures and sentiments. On the one hand, most segments of the community (including blacks) worried about crime. But at the same time, politically significant and articulate groups expressed concern about the practices of the police department and the treatment black defendants received. This concern struck a responsive chord in significant components of the felony disposition process, especially among blacks and white liberals.

In Detroit, blacks had managed to occupy several important positions, which they had not done in the other cities. Five of the thirteen regular Recorder's Court judges were black. With the addition of the seven new judges (three of whom were black) the proportion rose to eight of twenty (40 percent). The defense bar contained a significant and growing number of black attorneys.[21] A few were old-time regulars; most were new regulars; a few formed the nucleus of the new adversaries — aggressive, vigorous, and willing to challenge prevailing practices. Some of the adversaries worked for the Legal Aid and Defender's Association, which, as we have said, contained many blacks. In addition, the composition of juries had recently changed to better reflect the city's population, partly as the result of a successful law suit challenging discriminatory practices in jury selection.

Everyone familiar with Recorder's Court noticed the growing difficulty of obtaining guilty verdicts, particularly in cases that hinged on the jury's willingness to accept the testimony of white police officers. Even the police department was in a state of flux. Many of the old-time officers from the era of white domination were retiring. Some had hastened their departure because of their unhappiness with the rising number of young black officers. A black man headed the Wayne County Sheriff's Department, which ran the jail. Only the prosecutor's office was largely unaffected by these trends at the time of our research. There were few black attorneys in the office.

White liberal and moderate elements of the community shared the concerns of most blacks. Several of the incumbent white judges held moderate-to-liberal views, and their numbers increased with the election of the new judges. Thus, polarization was not complete. Many whites expressed conservative views and supported conservative judicial candidates, but white liberals prevented the formation of a monolithic white bloc. Similarly, segments of the black community supported a strong law-and-order position though few gave whole-hearted approval to the police department. The judge with the reputation as the harshest sentencer was black and generally was well liked by militant prosecutors.

The policies pursued by various components of the criminal justice system reflected the complex mix of community attitudes. The police and prosecutor's office announced a "get tough" policy on guns. The police department gave priority to gun arrests, and the offense of carrying a concealed weapon (CCW) became the most frequently prosecuted felony. The prosecutor's policy of offering no lesser offense than "attempted carrying a concealed weapon" in plea bargaining in CCW cases reflected this concern. In fact, a common justification given by pretrial conference division assistant prosecutors for stingy plea bargain offers was the "general crime situation" in the city. The media, especially the dominant *Detroit News*, emphasized the seriousness of the crime problem. For years, the *News* ran a "Crime in Detroit" column daily, which recounted the more serious crimes reported to the police, complete with the racial designation of alleged perpetrators.

But unlike either Baltimore or Chicago, significant pro-defendant sentiment was expressed in Detroit. Attitudes toward jail conditions are a good example. In 1971, several liberal and radical attorneys jointly sued Wayne County Board of Commissioners over jail conditions. A decision ordering the board of commissioners to increase the jail's staff and upgrade conditions resulted. Since most of the jail's inmates were Recorder's Court defendants awaiting trial, pressure was brought on the judges to reduce the jail population. As a result, they reduced the time between the preliminary hearing and the pretrial conference, reversed their policy of taking bailed defendants' cases first, and increased the number of defendants released at arraignment on personal bond (no-cost bail). Michigan, unlike Illinois, had no provision for the "10 percent bail" that eliminated bondsmen and returned 90 percent of the cost of bail to defendants. It had no statutory bail reform equivalent to Maryland's establishment of bail commissioners. Yet, largely as the result of the lawsuit and the community sentiment that supported it, the proportion of defendants released on personal bond increased within a year from 34.1 percent (1971) to 48.2 percent.[22] By the end of 1972, only 389 jail prisoners were awaiting trial, the lowest figure since the mid-1960s.[23]

The pressure to keep the jail population down and dispose cases quickly continued into 1972. Nearly all major participants in Detroit's criminal justice system adhered to the goal of disposing cases more strongly than their counterparts in the other cities. The Michigan Supreme Court's "crash program" to reduce the backlog by assigning additional judges to Recorder's Court kept everyone aware of the docket problem. The media reinforced these tendencies by publicizing jail conditions. The homosexual rape and fatal beating of a man unable to post a $50 bond received substantial publicity. At the end of October 1972, the *Detroit Free Press* devoted its entire editorial page to the jail, including a long editorial, interviews with the sheriff and a county commissioner, and a firsthand account of the rape of an eighteen-year-old during his three-day stay in the jail.[24] Editorials and stories about the jail appeared frequently. Even the electronic media covered the jail story. One of the local television stations ran a special documentary on the jail in 1971 entitled "The Cage."

The papers also reported on the "efficiency" of the judges. A prominently placed story in the *Detroit News* nicely summarized performance in 1973. Emphasizing the overall efficiency of the court, the article noted, "Nevertheless, there is a large disparity between the work output of the . . . judges. Some work harder and faster than others and that shows up in the statistics." The article went on to name the most productive and presumably hardest-working judges as well as those who were "at the bottom of the list." [25]

If conditions and opinions in the community elicited almost everyone's support for disposing of cases, they also generated support for the goal of doing justice. We have already described briefly the conflicting views of what doing justice meant to various workgroup members, but these differences revealed significant splits in the community that deserve reemphasis. Differences in the ideological positions of the judges reflected disparate views most clearly. Detroit judges disagreed more sharply on questions of crime, due process, protection of the community, and related issues than the judges in either Baltimore or Chicago. But differences also emerged in the attitudes and behavior of the defense bar.

The cross pressures resulting from the concern with expeditious disposition of cases and with doing justice produced somewhat paradoxical outcomes. The concern with moving cases united law-and-order advocates who wanted swift justice with pro-defendant interests desiring reduced jail stays and adherence to due process. It also facilitated the bureaucratized plea bargaining that occurred at the pretrial conference. But when cases were not plea bargained there, formal adversarial work techniques were often employed. Thus Detroit's felony disposition process reflected the city's politics. However, the other links with the political process took a different form than in Chicago or even Baltimore. Partisan politics, which provided an important link in both of the other cities, had little effect in Detroit. Voters chose judges in nonpartisan elections. Although the prosecuting attorney gained office in a partisan contest, the office itself had an established tradition of nonpartisanship that permitted career attorneys to remain regardless of election outcomes. The defenders, at least somewhat tied to partisan politics in both the other two cities, avoided any such link in Detroit.

Of course, the felony disposition process depended on support from other political bodies, but partisan politics rarely affected how it was provided. The Wayne County Board of Commissioners contributed three-fourths of the annual $10 million budget for Recorder's Court; the Detroit Common Council (itself a nonpartisan body) appropriated the rest. About $2 million went to pay attorneys appointed to represent indigents. There was little the county could do to control these costs, though the chairman of the board of commissioners was quoted in the *Detroit News* as expressing concern about the lack of care in Recorder's Court in determining the eligibility of defendants for appointed counsel.[26] We have no evidence that these bodies influenced court actions, but they stood as a significant background factor, available to disgruntled parties when the occasion arose. The implications of budgetary decisions for the operation of the prosecuting attorney's office, however, were clearly evident in 1972, when the Wayne County Board of Commissioners instituted a hiring freeze on all county positions. The freeze applied to the prosecutor's office, and attrition rapidly produced a shortage of twelve attorneys. As described earlier, the manpower squeeze had a significant effect. The office was forced to staff the courtrooms of the temporary judges. It became impossible to continue the trial team form of organization, and the office had to assign one or two assistant prosecutors to each courtroom. As manpower declined, case preparation suffered, and the defense attorneys' incentives to reject pretrial conference plea offers in hope of obtaining better offers from unprepared trial prosecutors became more powerful. These developments eroded the effectiveness of pretrial. Thus the hiring freeze initiated a sequence of events that had important implications for the entire system.[27]

The police department, whose chief was appointed by the mayor (also elected in a nonpartisan contest), was another important link between the felony disposition process and other components of the political system. The Detroit police were embroiled in controversy, and it inevitably spilled over into Recorder's Court. We cannot explore its ramifications here, except to note that the hostility between the black community and many white officers found expression frequently in disputes about the veracity of police testimony. As more blacks served on juries, challenges to such testimony before juries were more successful. As everywhere, the quality of the evidence prosecutors had to work with depended on the police. Several changes made in police department procedures considerably hindered the prosecution's task.[28]

Finally, in sharp contrast to the other two cities, state appellate courts had a significant effect on Recorder's Court. It went considerably beyond the effect nearly all appellate courts have through their rulings on appeals. The Michigan Supreme Court involved itself in important details of the court's operation. It forced Recorder's Court judges to use the Legal Aid and Defender's Association attorneys for one-quarter of all poor defendants who received appointed counsel. Its assignment of visiting judges had a profound effect on the manner in which preliminary examinations were conducted. When Recorder's Court adopted a random assignment of cases to judges, it was reportedly in response to concern by the supreme court that most pleas were being taken by two judges who therefore had half of all dispositions of the court. The Supreme Court even concerned itself with such details as whether judges wore robes and displayed the American flag in the courtroom. Finally, in July 1972, the supreme court significantly restricted the sentencing power of judges, by ruling that minimum sentences could not exceed two-thirds of the statutory maximum. This ruling ended the practice of some judges who imposed minimums of nine and a half years for offenses carrying a ten-year maximum.

We have already described the media's role in Recorder's Court elections and in reflecting concern with the larger issues of crime and defendants' treatment. Individual stories on the outcome of trials, complete with the prosecutor's name, which were common in Baltimore's *Sun* papers, seldom appeared in Detroit. Assistant prosecutors did not convey the outcome of cases to reporters and rarely received the favorable publicity that assistants in Baltimore did. But most assistant prosecutors feared unfavorable publicity, especially in stories that might make them appear to be too lenient. Avoiding leniency, of course, fit the office's prevailing view of what should happen to most defendants. But extra impetus to taking a tough line came from the recognized possibility of adverse publicity if a case "blew up" – that is if a defendant who received lenient treatment because of their decision went on to commit a serious, well-publicized crime. Everyone connected with the court recognized this fear implicitly but few articulated it. A prosecutor with several years' experience proved to be an exception. When questioned closely about his concern that too lenient pleas might get "kicked back," he admitted that he had the possibility of newspaper publicity in mind. When asked what difference it would make, his answer revealed an interesting combination of motives.

First, it's an elective office. Second, it's a public office. Appropriations come from the board of supervisors. You are always conscious [that] it's a public office. Also, it's a matter of prestige. You don't like to see shit printed about yourself in the paper. So it's pride and self-interest.

A young public defender also was able to describe the pressures present.

The prosecutors in pretrial face a lot of pressure from the public and the supervisors. . . . If someone is in on a gun charge and gets offered a plea to failure to present [a ninety-day misdemeanor] and [then] he commits a murder, there is a high likelihood it will make the papers, especially the *Detroit News*. It's a definite reality. The prosecutor is aware of it and is very conscious of it.

Although routine trials were not covered in the same detail as in Baltimore, each paper had a reporter who regularly reported on the operation of Recorder's Court. The more conservative *News* was somewhat more favorably disposed to the incumbent prosecutor than the rival *Free Press*, but its law-and-order inclinations encouraged the publication of critical articles. The *Free Press*, clearly more defendant-oriented, openly criticized the incumbent prosecutor and his staff.[29] Hence, the concern about possible adverse publicity was entirely rational.

CONCLUSION

The strength of Detroit's sponsoring organizations was the most distinctive element of Detroit's felony disposition process. The prosecuting attorney's office exercised more control over court-room assistants than its counterparts in the other two cities. That control came not only from a centralized structure and self-consciously applied supervision but also from staffing with more experienced and career-oriented professional prosecutors than were available in Baltimore or Chicago. At the same time, public defenders and judges were also more coherently organized. The interaction of representatives from these strong sponsoring organizations in courtrooms produced workgroups in which influence was evenly divided and in which adversarial techniques were widely used when the occasion presented itself. It also produced workgroups whose members were almost as familiar with each other as in Chicago.

But bureaucratic plea bargaining severely restricted opportunities for holding trials. Joint action by the judges and prosecuting attorney's office promoted plea bargaining in every case in the pretrial division. Those negotiations settled many cases in which little doubt about guilt existed or where the defendant was unwilling to risk trial, and set the stage for more adversarial processing of the remainder.

The organizational structure of the workgroups allows us to understand why bureaucratized plea bargaining worked in Detroit — as we shall see in Chapter 9 — and what the effect of outsiders like the visiting judges proved to be. In addition, it allows us to take into account the wide attitudinal variations of Detroit judges within the context of organizational cohesion.

Finally, Detroit felony courts operated in a different political context than those in Baltimore and Chicago. They were more insulated from partisan politics, although the media placed them in the limelight at least as much as it did in the other two cities. Detroit's courtroom workgroups operated in a fragmented political environment that gave them room to maneuver.

NOTES

1. The visiting judges also accounted for some dispositions at the trial level during our research. Because visiting judges assigned to hear cases at the trial level disposed of so few cases each day, it proved impractical to

place an observer in their courtrooms. The description that follows applies to the courtrooms of the twelve regular judges.

2. The courtrooms used for preliminary hearings were identical to the trial courtrooms.

3. Recorder's Court also exercised jurisdiction over land condemnation proceedings brought in the city, but these cases accounted for only a minor portion of the work load. Only 131 judge days were spent on condemnation cases in all of 1972. See the "Annual Report: The Recorder's Court of the City of Detroit, Michigan," 1972, p. 11.

4. In fact, defense attorneys routinely were allowed to examine the prosecutor's case file at the preliminary hearing. They carried the case file to the assistant prosecutor at the pretrial conference, and often had a second opportunity to read it before beginning the conference.

5. An incomplete clipping file contained the following: "Detroit Needs New Judges with Intelligence, Ability," *Detroit Free Press*, August 4, 1972; "Voters Have a Good Chance to Better Recorder's Court," *Detroit Free Press*, October 24, 1972; "7 Court Candidates Compete for Voters," *Detroit News*, October 17, 1972; "Challengers Plan to Oust 2 Judges," *Detroit News*, October 24, 1972; "7 New Judges to Boost Recorder's Court," *Detroit News*, October 27, 1972 (a full page with pictures and brief biographies of all candidates); "Time for Changes in Recorder's Court," *Detroit News*, October 25, 1972 (editorial).

6. See "7 Court Candidates Compete for Votes," *Detroit News*, October 27, 1972.

7. There was little attempt to soft-pedal the editor's judgments. Said the *Detroit News*, "Thomas L. Poindexter had demonstrated little judicial ability and should be defeated. Joseph E. Maher was suspended for misconduct as a lawyer several years ago. George W. Crockett . . . looks upon himself as an advocate of causes rather than as a detached judge of the law, hence we cannot support him." Editorial "Time for Changes in Recorder's Court," *Detroit Free Press*, October 25, 1972.

8. The duties, responsibilities, and powers of the monthly conference are not entirely clear. For years it operated with an effective norm of secrecy. Furthermore, the Michigan Supreme Court has broad supervisory powers over lower courts, which creates complex patterns of influence around decisions about procedural and administrative aspects of the court's functioning. The picture is further complicated by the lack of clarity in the presiding judge's official powers and role. It is difficult to find authoritative descriptions of what his formal powers are. In addition, his role varies considerably depending on who he is.

9. It was impossible to eliminate maneuvering by the defense and prosecution entirely. Judges got sick and went on vacation, and some arrangements had to be made to cover for them. By influencing the time cases were ready for disposition, it was sometimes possible to avoid a particular judge. In addition, several judges designated another as an alternate. Thus, defendants assigned to Judge F_____ (a notoriously harsh sentencer) were permitted to plead guilty (but not go to trial) before Judge E_____.

10. Quoted in the *Detroit News*, "Crockett Shifts Sides on Assigning Lawyers," March 26, 1974.

11. One visiting judge with an antidefendant law-and-order bias began raising the bond of defendants who held preliminary exams, especially when their crimes were violent. The presiding judge ordered him to make no bail decisions at all. Another visitor was so prosecution-minded when he presided over misdemeanor court that it caused a furor. Defense attorneys complained vociferously to several of the regular judges. The presiding judge then removed the visitor from misdemeanor court. See "Judge is Transferred After Complaints," *Detroit Free Press*, June 24, 1972.

12. Personal interview.

13. The judges' organization had a significant effect on the prosecuting attorney's office in another area. It forced the office to schedule all pretrial conferences in the morning. This made hearing the results of pretrial conferences more convenient for the judges. But it created an imbalance in the pretrial conference division's work load. In the morning they were incredibly rushed. In the afternoon, they had virtually nothing to do.

14. The Detroit public defender's office is the only one that approaches that described by Anthony Platt and Randi Pollock, "Channeling Lawyers: The Careers of Public Defenders," in Herbert Jacob (ed.), *The Potential Reform of Criminal Justice* (Beverly Hills, Calif.: Sage Publications, 1974), pp. 235–262.

15. The chief defender's remarks were quoted in "Legal Aid Lawyers Given High Marks," *Detroit News*, March 29, 1974.

16. Ibid. The head of the office told us, "We set the standard for the whole court."

17. "Annual Report: The Recorder's Court," 1970–1972.

18. Ibid., 1972, p. 13.

19. The physical arrangement of the courtroom and the procedures established by the court facilitated the operation of the communication network. Many attorneys gathered in the presiding judge's arraignment courtroom and in the two preliminary hearing courtrooms. Defense attorneys were permitted to sit together inside the railing during proceedings, and they gathered there before sessions began. It was an ideal place to exchange gossip.

20. Cf. Joel D. Aberbach and Jack L. Walker, *Race in the City* (Boston: Little, Brown, 1973).

21. Black attorneys represented about 30 percent of the defendants we observed at the preliminary exam.

22. "Annual Report: The Recorder's Court," 1972, p. 13.

23. On January 1, 1967, more than 5,000 defendants were awaiting trial. Over 1,000 of them were in the Wayne County Jail. See the *Detroit News*, January 4, 1973.

24. See the *Detroit Free Press*, October 30, 1972, p. 6A.

25. "Recorder's Court — A Model of Efficiency," *Detroit News*, January 17, 1974.

26. "Stricter Rules on 'Free' Lawyers Urged," March 1, 1973. The chair-

man complained that defendants were only asked cursory questions about their ability to pay a lawyer. Our field research repeatedly confirmed the accuracy of his charge. In 1972, defendants were typically asked only "Can you afford an attorney?"

27. The cuts in staff led Prosecutor Cahalan to threaten in interviews with reporters from both major newspapers that prosecutions would have to be curtailed. The *Detroit News* quoted him as saying, "If we don't get help pretty soon, we may have to engage in selective prosecution." According to the article, Cahalan admitted he was making the threat public in an effort to pressure the Board of Commissioners to provide help. "Cahalan Threatens Cut In Prosecutions Unless He Gets Aid," *Detroit News,* July 7, 1972.

28. The most significant change came after the police department, as the result of an efficiency study by an outside consulting firm, established a "court section," which handled the prosecution of cases after arrest. The rationale was to free the arresting officers from time-consuming court appearances and to delegate their court functions to a section staffed by officers who would specialize in this area. The plan saved the department a substantial number of work hours. From the prosecutor's standpoint however, it created very serious problems. The quality of case preparation declined considerably. Investigations were less thorough because the arresting officers knew they would not be responsible for assisting in prosecution. The court officers were regarded by most prosecutors as being less motivated than the arresting officers who formerly handled their own cases. Finally, the court officers knew little about the cases. The advantages that came from the continuity provided when a single officer followed a case from arrest to trial was lost. As a result, cases were much weaker. Next to the lack of time for prosecutors to prepare cases, this was probably the factor that most hindered effective prosecution in Detroit.

29. An example of the *Detroit Free Press'* willingness to criticize the Wayne County prosecutor can be found in an editorial titled "The Case Against Cahalan," June 2, 1972. The editorial said, "Prosecutor Cahalan has apparently demonstrated that he is unfit to be entrusted with such an important institution as the citizen's grand jury."

PART III | Stages of the Felony Disposition Process

The police arrest hundreds of armed robbers every day in the United States. They bring thousands of other defendants to court. What happens to these defendants? How long is it before they are back on the street? Are they freed only until convicted, or are they released unconditionally? What difference does it make whether the defendant is black or white, on welfare or working? Do jailed defendants face different fates than those released before trial? Does police work in bringing in good evidence make conviction more likely? Does the crime the offender allegedly committed make any difference? What is the effect of the courtroom workgroup on the disposition of felony charges?

There is considerable uncertainty about how much punishment the courts mete out and on whom they inflict it. Casual observers perceive thousands of dismissed defendants leaving the courtroom apparently unpunished. Many are troubled by charges of racial and class discrimination in sentencing; more lenient sentences are allegedly given to whites and the not-poor than to blacks and the poor. Judges are often charged with responsibility for such disparities. Other disparities are alleged to exist between different jurisdictions; the same crime is said to draw a light penalty in one city and a harsh one in another.

Our study permits us to address these problems with more precise data than is available from published reports. We shall examine these questions and others, not only by using statistical analyses of data from case files but also by examining the activity of courtroom workgroups based on our observations and interviews.

Chapter 7

INTRODUCTION TO THE QUANTITATIVE ANALYSIS

Observations provide a partial view of the felony disposition process, but the observer cannot be everywhere at the same time. To assess the relationships among courtroom traits, defendant and case characteristics, one must examine a very large number of cases. Such quantitative tests, however, require explicit methods for counting cases, for measuring important variables, and for conducting the analysis.[1] In each instance, however, in confronting the intricate reality of criminal proceedings one must compromise textbook methods.

SAMPLING CASES

The three cities processed too many cases to examine each case occurring during a reasonable time period. Nor could we select all dispositions from one or two weeks, because that would have contaminated our data with the peculiarities associated with those particular weeks. Consequently, we needed to sample.

We sampled defendants rather than cases. Our interest was in the fate of defendants, and they constituted an unambiguous unit. Indictments and cases are full of definitional ambiguities that vary from city to city. Some defendants are named in multiple indictments whereas others are not; many defendants are washed out of the process before being indicted but after receiving some punishment. Cases may involve a single defendant or many, and tend to be linked together if there are overlapping defendants or indictments. The concept of "defendants" suffers from none of these ambiguities. Using defendants as our unit of analysis permitted us to discern the number of indictments each defendant faced, the number of court cases in which each was involved, and the ultimate fate each faced. In each city we set out to sample approximately 1,500 defendants against whom charges were placed in the first nine months of 1972.

Each city's record-keeping system for criminal courts was unique and reflected the structure of courts and the vagaries of the clerks. None of the three cities — and very few in the entire United States — collected and published reliable summary information about the operation of the criminal courts. In Detroit, official reports gave us the number of defendants flowing through the courts in 1972; such elementary information was unavailable in Baltimore and Chicago. The peculiarities of record-keeping in the three cities forced us to use quite different sampling techniques in each one of them.

Detroit. Detroit provided accurate counts of the number of defendants disposed at any particular stage and of defendants flowing through the entire felony disposition process. Every felony defendant was assigned a case number. A strict random sample of defendants could have been obtained by drawing on the list of case numbers. However, because courtrooms disposed cases quickly, this technique would have precluded our observing actual courtroom proceedings of any of the defendants drawn. Consequently, we relied on an observational sample. In the preliminary hearing courtrooms, we included every defendant who was a party to every other case called on the days we observed the courtroom. At the pretrial conference, we took every defendant whose case was discussed while we were in the office. Finally, our sample included the defendants in every case on the docket of a trial courtroom for each day an observer was present. We allotted our time in proportion to the percentage of cases disposed at any given stage. Our observations took place in the preliminary examination courts, the pretrial conferences, and the trial courts. Within each stage, we spent approximately the same amount of time in each location where that stage took place.

The Detroit sample seems to represent the flow of cases accurately, with one exception. Defendants dismissed at the preliminary exam exited from the process, and we were not able to pick up their cases when we drew our sample of cases from pretrial conferences and trial courtrooms. Consequently, the proportion of defendants in the total sample dismissed at the preliminary exams is too low. When we make generalizations about all felony defendants in Detroit, therefore, we weight the defendants dismissed at the preliminary exam so they will reflect the correct proportion of all defendants.[2]

Chicago. Chicago's record-keeping ranged from nil to minimal. No one counted the number of persons brought to court on felony charges or kept track of what happened to them. We found counts only for those who pleaded guilty to a felony at the preliminary hearing and those who were indicted. Further, the circuit courts had jurisdiction over all of Cook County, and the record-keeping system did not distinguish between those who committed offenses in Chicago and those who committed them in the suburbs.

Consequently, we relied on a variety of sampling methods. In order to sample all defendants brought to court, we stationed ourselves in the five courtrooms that handled preliminary hearings for offenses committed in Chicago. We placed in our sample the defendants we observed there. However, those courts processed cases so quickly and were so chaotic that we found it impossible to take down names and case number for every case that was processed. Rather, we included in our sample every second, third, or fifth defendant, depending on our ability to take down the information and the speed with which events occurred. To compensate for this unevenness, we have weighted this observational sample so that each courtroom is represented by the proportion of defendants it actually handled. Our observations took place within a two-month period; there is some danger that such a brief sampling period introduces some elements of seasonality, and short-run aberrations. As no official statistics exist against which we can compare our results, we do not know whether such biases were introduced. However, our conversations with others who are familiar with those courts gives us confidence that this is a reasonably good sample of defendants for these courtrooms.

Persons whom the grand jury indicted or who pleaded guilty at the preliminary hearing court were listed in the indictment, or information, file. We sampled each of them for the first nine months of 1972 by random selection, throwing out all cases involving suburban incidents. We are confident that this is a random sample in the full technical meaning of that term. That sample provides us with detailed information about defendants who were carried further through the felony disposition process; it is a vast oversample of all felony defendants, because so few of the total reached indictment in Chicago. Consequently, we cannot combine these samples with the preliminary hearing sample.

Finally, we observed each trial courtroom in Chicago for approximately one week during the first three months of 1973. Our sample included each defendant who appeared during our observation in a courtroom where the proceedings involved more than the granting of a continuance. We collected the same file information for these observational cases as for the random sample. In some instances, we combined this observational sample with the random sample; in others we analyzed it separately.

Baltimore. The Baltimore situation was like Chicago's. No listing of felony defendants existed and no official statistics provided a count. However, Baltimore courts handled only Baltimore defendants; suburbanites flowed through a separate court system. Moreover, unlike Chicago, files were kept of defendants who passed through the preliminary hearing courtrooms. We thus had to screen 20,000 district court cases and eliminate those defendants who did not face felony charges; the official files did not make that distinction for us. We were also forced to use a systematic, rather than random, sampling technique. We included every third defendant against whom felony charges were filed between January and June 1972.

That process, however, yielded too few cases. Consequently, we extended our sample to October 1972 and then found that we had more defendants than we had money to code. Thus, we took a random sample of the second subsample, which yielded the correct number but oversampled preliminary hearing dispositions. For the analysis in Chapter 8, we therefore weighted the subsample to produce the correct proportions.

Sampling Summary. Table 7.1 summarizes the samples and the

TABLE 7.1   DEFENDANT SAMPLES
IN THREE CITIES

Sample	Number of Defendants (before weighting)
Baltimore	
File sample	1,127
Observational sample	152
Chicago	
Observational sample from preliminary hearing courtrooms	514
Random sample of Chicago defendants pleading guilty to informations January–September 1972	144
Random sample of Chicago defendants indicted January–September 1972	596
Observational sample of Chicago defendants in trial courtrooms	222
Detroit	
Observational sample of preliminary hearings	357
Observational sample of pretrial hearings	513
Observational sample of trial courtrooms	746

number of defendants in each of them. Despite our intention to draw identical samples in each city, circumstances forced us to use quite different techniques. In each instance we adapted our methods to the situation confronting us. Because the court records were so chaotic, no cleaner alternative was available. We believe these sampling techniques produced collections of defendants that are not systematically biased in any known way. But they are not the kind of random samples that are usually found in opinion surveys.

MEASUREMENT PROBLEMS

Having identified whom we wanted to study, we stationed ourselves in the clerks' offices of the courts in the three cities and examined the court file for each of the 4,371 defendants in our samples. Sometimes, however, the state's attorney's office or the public defender's office had information that we needed, and where possible, we consulted those files as well. Our assistants stayed so long in these offices and vaults that they were almost accepted as full-time employees by the regulars. No restrictions were placed on us in gathering this information or recording it on our forms, except our promise not to identify individual defendants in our publications. However, the files themselves constrained us, because they often contained incomplete or undecipherable information. The data from such files are complex.

Dependent Variables. In our analysis we seek to explain court outcomes for individual defendants. For most of the study, our dependent variables therefore represent dispositions. In every instance, we have concerned ourselves with the *ultimate* outcome for the defendant. If a defendant had one charge dismissed but was convicted on another, we counted it as a conviction. Our indicators of outcome, however, are straightforward. We measured dismissals, acquittals, and convictions. Among the convictions, we distinguished between those obtained through a plea and those obtained at a bench or jury trial. For those who were convicted, we measured the penalty imposed in terms of amount of fines, length of probation, length of suspended sentence, and length of prison sentence. When several prison sentences were imposed at the same time, we took the longest of sentences to be served concurrently or the sum of all sentences to be served consecutively.

Some intermediate outcomes also serve as dependent variables in our analysis. Some defendants who were not convicted nevertheless spent time in jail, had to raise bond money, or had to hire an attorney. Pretrial detention was measured by days elapsed between arrest and release. We measured the cost of bond by the type of bond required (zero for recognizance bonds and a specified amount for monetary bond, the exact amount depending on the bond system in use in each city). The cost of attorneys had to be estimated from the kind of attorney who represented the defendants. It was generally zero for public defender or assigned counsel and several hundred dollars when representation was by a private counsel.

Independent Variables. We want to determine how well we can explain outcomes by factors that other researchers have asserted to be important — such as race and social status of defendant, the kinds of proceedings that occur, the kind of attorney who represents defendants, and so on. In addition, we want to determine whether there is statistical as well as observational support for the organizational perspective that we developed. For those purposes, we needed indicators of independent variables. Some are straightforward, whereas others turned out to be extraordinarily complex.

1. Defendant Characteristics. Police arrest reports provided most of our information about defendants. These reports provide presumably reliable indicators of race, age, and sex. Socioeconomic status is not indicated in a straightforward fashion. Police reports often indicate occupation and employment status, but both are often stated in such ambiguous terms that we could not interpret them without further information that was generally not available. For instance, engineer may mean janitor or a civil engineer; salesman may mean clerking at a dime store or selling computers for IBM. Many housewives have part-time jobs. In addition, the police report and court files provided no information about education or income.

We devised two measures of a defendant's wealth that also may have independent effects on outcomes. First, the type of defense counsel reflects wealth, because defendants with retained attorneys have greater resources than those represented by public defenders or assigned counsel. But as we suggested in Chapters 4, 5, and 6, differences in incentive structures for retained and appointed counsel (including public defenders) may lead to differences in courtroom behavior independent of the defendant's wealth. Second, whether defendants are jailed or released prior to trial also reflects wealth. Bailed defendants generally possess more assets than defendants who linger in jail. But bail status may have a significant effect on case outcomes in its own right. In the absence of less tainted measures of defendant resources, we used these measures, but with caution.

Finally, prior criminal record has often been considered a characteristic with significant implications for a defendant's fate. We were able to find "rap sheets," which listed prior arrests or convictions for many defendants. The amount of information on these rap sheets, however, varied considerably from one defendant to another. After much experimentation and a correlational analysis showing that the simple fact of a prior arrest was highly correlated with the number and seriousness of arrests, we decided simply to use any indication of a prior arrest as our prior record variable. We were then able to reduce drastically the number of defendants with missing information and had a measure that appeared to be as reliable as one based on fuller information.

In the chapters that follow, we will frequently report the contribution of defendant characteristics in tables and diagrams. When we do this, we will be reporting the combined effects of race, age, nature of defense attorney, bail status, and prior criminal record.

2. *Evidence.* Criminal cases are supposed to hinge on the quality of the evidence, but it is difficult to judge evidence without firsthand investigation of each case. That task was clearly impossible for us. Instead, we looked for indicators of evidential quality. The indicators we used are the presence or absence of

physical evidence (such as fingerprints, stolen property, contraband drugs); the presence or absence of eyewitnesses; the recording of a confession; the identification of the defendant by witnesses, through a lineup or through photographs at the police station; and the presence or absence of motions in the file attacking the admissability of evidence or challenging the legality of the arrest. We used these variables as a group in our analyses rather than combining them in any arbitrary way. Intercorrelation between them is low, because some items are important in some kinds of cases whereas others are significant in others. For instance, one frequently finds search and seizure motions in narcotics and weapons cases but almost never in assault cases; lineup or photo identifications abound in assaults but almost never exist for burglary defendants.

Another problem with our evidential measures is that they are based entirely on information in court files. They indicate whether eyewitnesses to the crime existed, but they do not tell us whether those eyewitnesses are credible, or what they saw. Similarly, it was impossible to judge the validity of searches or the relevance of corroborating physical evidence. Consequently, evidence may play a smaller role in our analysis than in the actual case.

3. *Disposition.* We measured disposition in several ways. On the one hand, we were interested in the stage at which dispositions occurred. We concentrated on two stages: preliminary hearing and trial. On the other hand, we also wanted to examine the effect of particular kinds of disposition. We therefore categorized cases according to whether the disposition followed a dismissal, guilty plea, bench trial, or jury trial.

4. *Courtroom.* Every disposition occurs in a courtroom. We could choose between identifying courtrooms by the room number or by the judge who presided. The latter had the disadvantage of creating a new "courtroom" each time a judge transferred in or out, even though the other members of the courtroom workgroup remained the same. Nevertheless, we chose that method, because the files we worked with did not consistently identify courtrooms by room number. Each judge presiding over a stage of the felony disposition process, therefore, is counted as one courtroom. Our analysis, however, focuses on judges handling

large numbers of cases. Because judges were not shifted from one courtroom to another, our method somewhat underestimates the stability of courtroom workgroups; we are also not able to examine statistically what happened when a new judge entered a courtroom workgroup.

5. *Offense.* We could choose between offense originally charged or the offense of which the defendant is eventually cleared or convicted. We chose the former because it is closer to the original incident and less contaminated by the disposition process we were trying to explain.

Many defendants, however, faced multiple charges. We had to choose a method for characterizing those defendants. The combinations and patterns are almost infinite. Again we chose a fairly simple indicator. We ranked the offenses according to seriousness, and characterized the defendant and case according to the most serious charge facing him.[3] Thus, if a defendant was charged with both murder and armed robbery, we characterized him or her as facing a murder charge; if the defendant faced theft and marijuana charges, we counted him or her as a thief rather than a marijuana user. Again, our indicator does some violence to the complexity and richness of the data, but we would have had too few cases with distinct patterns of charges had we preserved the data in its original richness.

All the decisions we made in measuring variables may have affected the statistical analysis that follows. All of them involve compromises, and many of them reduce the data into few categories. However, with each choice we attempted to optimize reliability or validity in the face of what we had learned about the quality of the information that we were extracting from the official files. For instance, given the erratic character of rap sheets, we thought it unwise to construct a finely-tuned measure of prior criminal record, which would produce a large number of missing cases and which would be based on unreliable original files. In many instances we had to simplify complex phenomena in order to preserve a large enough pool of defendants to warrant statistical analysis. To some extent, these decisions may be responsible for our difficulties in accounting for most of the variability in the felony disposition process.

METHODS OF ANALYSIS

As we have already shown, felony dispositions result from a very complex set of social interactions. No single variable or factor can explain them. Consequently, we cannot simply classify dispositions according to race of defendants, their prior record, or their bail status, and expect to demonstrate a strong relationship. These characteristics — together with others — interact in complex ways to produce the final results. Consequently, we need to undertake a multivariate analysis, which will include the simultaneous effects of these variables on dispositions. We will use two statistical techniques for this purpose.

The first is multivariate correlation. It is appropriate when the dependent variable is continuous — for instance, the length of time between arrest and disposition, or the length of a prison sentence. We used a computer program, which permitted us to enter independent, explanatory variables one at a time in a sequence that we controlled.[4] Because the felony disposition process we were trying to explain has a certain order — establishing the charge first, then processing a defendant with particular personal characteristics, considering the weight of evidence, and choosing a disposition mode in a particular courtroom — we entered the variables in that order. However, we also experimented with other sequences and found that the results were not substantially altered.

What does the correlation analysis tell us? First, the multiple correlation coefficient — when squared — indicates how much of the total variance is accounted for by the variables entered into the analysis.[5] If this indicator is .53, 53 percent of the variance is accounted for. Secondly, we can discover how much of this explained variance is accounted for by particular variables. Thus, we can determine whether the original charge or evidence is more important in helping explain what we *can* explain about variations in dispositions.

We cannot, however, estimate the effect on the dependent variable of a change in an independent variable. We cannot do so because most of the independent variables in our analysis are measured as categories rather than as continuous entities. For instance, it makes no sense to say that a little more femaleness would lead to a lower sentence; defendants are either male or female according to our data. In addition, many of our independent variables are sets of "dummy" variables. For instance, the identity of the courtroom is a large set of variables, one for each courtroom, coded 0 for *no* and 1 for *yes*. The whole set together helps explain part of the variance, but the mathematics of the statistical procedure does not permit us to extract regression coefficients for the entire set; it only produces meaningless coefficients for each component of the set.

A second procedure we used is called multiple discriminant function analysis. It is most appropriate when the dependent variable is broken down into categories rather than being a continuous function. We use it when we want to analyze conviction/nonconviction, prison/no-prison, guilty plea/trial, and other dichotomous outcomes. The procedure also contains a standardized computer routine that permits entry of variables in the same fashion as multivariate correlation.[6] However, instead of predicting a continuous set of values, it separates cases into the two categories with the help of the information contained in the independent variables. When the prediction is considerably improved by this additional information, we can conclude that there is a relationship between the independent variables and the phenomena we are trying to explain. The strength of the relationship is measured by a correlation coefficient (canonical correlation squared) that is roughly analogous to the multiple correlation coefficient produced by the first procedure. A second measure for this is *tau*, which indicates how much we will improve our classification of the cases by including the information from the independent variables.[7]

Finally, discriminant function analysis also produces estimates of the power of particular variables. These are measures of the distance which a particular variable moves cases to one category or another. We shall report one such coefficient in our table — *Rao's V* — in terms of the percentage of the total distance that is accounted for by any particular variable. If most of the distance that the whole set of variables moves a case is the result of race, the percentage figure for race will be high; if race does not move the cases very far into a category (for instance, convict) its percentage will be low.

Our use of these procedures is not textbook perfect. Our data cannot meet all the specifications that statisticians demand from perfect data. However, our application is well within the usual bounds of social science usage and we are unaware of better alternatives.

There is one concern, however, that we can assuage. Multivariate analysis would be invalid if the independent variables were not independent of one another. If race and offense, for instance, were closely related so that knowing race one could easily predict the offense, both should not be used in the analysis, because that would only be confusing and would lead to uninterpretable results. We examined a correlation matrix of all our independent variables and found none closely related to another. The problem (technically called multicollinearity) does not exist in our data.

One final difficulty must be surmounted. How do we know whether the coefficients really mean something or are the product of chance combinations in our data? The standard answer lies in probability theory and statistical significance. When samples are random, statistical significance means that the observed relationships could not occur by chance except in one out of a hundred cases (significance at .01 level) or any other chosen level of significance. Our samples, of course, are not usually random. However, if we assumed them to be random, we would calculate statistical significance quite readily. We have done that to provide a rough guide to our analysis. All of the coefficients we report in the following chapters are significant at the .01 level. Even though our samples are not random, statistical significance is the best available rule of thumb to guide our interpretation of the statistical analysis. And in any case, we must be careful not to confuse statistical significance with substantive significance. As we shall indicate in several places, our analyses sometimes produce statistically significant results that are substantively *in*significant because they do not explain enough.

CONCLUSION

The defendants we selected in the three cities constitute — as far as we know — an unbiased sample of felony defendants processed through the criminal courts. By examining case files and observing courtrooms, we were able to collect much information about these defendants and the proceedings they experienced while their cases were being considered. That information allows us to examine two alternative ways of explaining felony dispositions. The first is the traditional one: that defendant characteristics, weight of the evidence, or traits of the process explain the outcomes. The second comes from our organizational perspective: that courtroom workgroups have an indispensable role in structuring the relationship of these other variables and that they exert an independent force in producing dispositions. The statistical tools we use to examine these alternative explanations are multivariate correlation and multiple discriminant function analysis.

We can now turn to our statistical analysis of each stage of the felony disposition process. Instead of following one defendant through the process in each city, we will use approximately 1,500 defendants to guide us through the maze.

NOTES

1. For a fuller discussion of some of these problems, see James Eisenstein and Herbert Jacob, "Measuring Outputs of Urban Criminal Courts," *Social Science Quarterly* 54 (1974): 713–724.

2. Comparison of case characteristics in our sample with comparable information provided in the *Annual Report: The Recorder's Court of the City of Detroit, Michigan, 1972* confirms our sample as accurate. Of the preliminary hearings we observed, 32.5 percent were waived. Statistics for the months of September, October, and November in the *Annual Report* reveal a waiver rate of 33.3 percent. Our dismissal rate at the preliminary exam is within three percentage points of the *Annual Report's* figure. The acquittal rate in jury trials in our sample was 43 percent; in the *Annual Report*, it is 44.5 percent. The proportion of defendants released on personal bond in our sample was 49.4 percent; the *Annual Report* indicates 48.2 percent were released.

3. The ranking of offenses from most serious to least serious in Baltimore and Chicago was:

Baltimore: murder, armed robbery, rape, assault, robbery, heroin dealer, heroin user, burglary-theft, and other.

Chicago: murder, armed robbery, rape, unlawful use of weapons, assault, robbery, heroin dealer, heroin user, unspecified drug dealer, unspecified drug user, burglary, theft, and other.

In Detroit, where multiple charging rarely occurred and where the prosecutors listed the most serious charge first, we used the first charge listed.

4. Norman Nie, C. Hadlai Hull, Jean G. Jenkins, Karen Steinbrenner, and Dale H. Bent, *Statistical Package for the Social Sciences*, 2d ed. (New York: McGraw-Hill, 1975), pp. 320–367.

5. The *variance* is a measure of the dispersion of a phenomenon around its mean.

6. Nie et al., *Statistical Package*, pp. 434–467.

7. For a simple discussion of Goodman and Kruskal's *Tau, see* Hubert M. Blalock, Jr., *Social Statistics* (New York: McGraw-Hill, 1960), pp. 232–234.

Chapter 8

SCREENING IN THE PRELIMINARY HEARING COURTROOMS

Though charged with a felony, many defendants never see the inside of a trial courtroom before their case ends. For them, the preliminary hearing is the final proceeding. For other felony defendants, the decisions made by preliminary hearing workgroups help determine the ultimate outcome in trial courtrooms.

WHAT HAPPENS TO DEFENDANTS

The police made 35,000 felony arrests in Chicago in 1972; the courts convicted 2,500 persons for felonies that year. Such statistics are not extraordinary.[1] They reflect a basic fact of American criminal justice: that courts convict few of the persons the police arrest. Indeed many defendants never reach a trial court.

Table 8.1 summarizes the preliminary outcomes for the defendants in our samples. It is clear that the preliminary hearing courtrooms of the three cities performed quite different functions. Chicago's preliminary hearing courtrooms permitted few

190

TABLE 8.1 OUTCOME OF PROBABLE CAUSE
PROCEEDINGS BY CITY

	Baltimore[a]	Chicago[b]	Detroit[c]
Dismissed	21.0%	63.4%	5.1%
Findings of innocence or no probable cause	4.0	10.8	14.2
Findings of guilt	7.9	4.5	0
Guilty pleas	.3	8.6	0
Sent to grand jury but not indicted	4.0	0	N.A.
Indicted by grand jury or information	62.6	12.7	80.5
	99.8%	100%	99.8%

a. Based on weighted file sample: $N = 1,577$
b. Based on weighted preliminary hearing observation samples: $N = 982$
c. Based on preliminary examination observation sample: $N = 350$

cases to survive to indictment; only 12.7 percent of the defendants we observed were indicted by the grand jury. By contrast the courts took more than three-fifths of the defendants in Baltimore and four-fifths of those in Detroit beyond the preliminary hearing stage.

Guilty pleas, findings of guilt, and acquittals (including findings of no probable cause) were rare. In each city they accounted for only a handful of defendants. Rather it is dismissals that loom large. Chicago preliminary hearing courts may be characterized as dismissal courts; they dismissed as many defendants as Baltimore sent on to the grand jury. Baltimore preliminary hearing courtrooms also dismissed a sizable proportion of defendant's cases. Only in Detroit were dismissals rare in the preliminary stages.

These dispositions, however, reflect only a portion of the total work of these courtrooms. Courtrooms hold several proceedings. They arraign defendants for the violations police or prosecutors originally charge; they set or revise bail; they hear motions; and they decide whether to dismiss charges, accept a guilty plea, try the case summarily, or send it forward to the grand jury or trial court. Many of these decisions were made in substantially different ways in the three cities. Those procedural differences provide a first tentative explanation of the variations in outcomes that we may test.

ARRAIGNMENTS, BAIL, AND MOTIONS

Three proceedings occur in the preliminary hearing courtrooms before disposition (Figure 8.1). Defendants are arraigned; the court determines the conditions under which they may be set free pending a final determination of the charges against them; and defense lawyers may raise legal motions attacking the validity of the proceedings. Each of these proceedings may have some effect on the final outcome.

FIGURE 8.1 Proceedings in Preliminary Hearing Courtrooms.

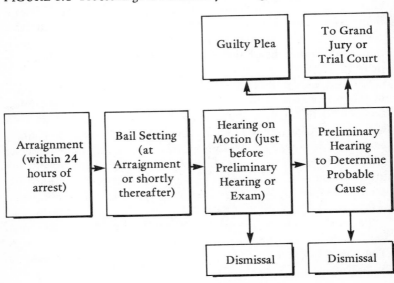

Arraignments. No measurable outcome is associated with arraignments that permits simple correlation between defendant or case characteristics and the manner of arraignment. Arraignments are simple, highly ritualized ceremonies. But the organizational context in which they occur helps explain their significance.

At an arraignment the judge or some other official tells defendants what charges face them. In some courtrooms the judge reads the police charges to the defendant; in others a bailiff pushes the piece of paper into the defendant's hand while the defendant stands before the judge. In a few instances, the courtroom workgroup makes a real effort to help the defendant understand. Mostly, however, the charges are conveyed to the defendant in legal jargon, and no one offers further explanation.

At the same time, the court informs defendants of some of their rights. The judge routinely asks whether they have attorneys; if not, and if they claim indigency, they may be offered attorneys paid by the state. The judge may ask whether they have had a chance to make a telephone call; if not, they may be offered that opportunity immediately after the arraignment.

The arraignment protects defendants because it prevents police from holding prisoners incommunicado. It is also supposed to ensure the provision of legal rights to all defendants at the very beginning of the court process so that they can assert them fully. Those consequences occur in a considerable proportion of the cases. Many defendants undoubtedly come to realize the seriousness of their trouble as the result of the arraignment.

However, the ceremony conveys other meanings as well. It is the first of many occasions at which the defendant must stand in an open courtroom and be identified as a defendant. The courtroom treats him curtly if not roughly. He has to humble himself before the judge; the courtroom workgroup makes it clear that he would also do well to treat all official personnel (clerks, bailiffs, attorneys) with deference. The judge often reminds a bailed defendant that he is only a misstep away from jail; if he is in jail, he is brought to the courtroom under guard. The ceremony demeans; it strips defendants of their self-respect and helps prepare them for entry into the lowest caste of American society, the prison convict's caste. Often not even addressed as "Mr." or "Miss," defendants experience the transition from citizen to subject.[2]

The details of this ceremony varied from city to city. In Detroit, a single judge presided over the arraignments. He would say: "James Dent, you are charged with armed robbery, robbing the Ace Liquor Store yesterday afternoon. How do you plead? Can you afford counsel? Do you have money for an attorney? Have you ever been arrested any place on earth from the time you were born until this moment?" All this took about sixty seconds. If the defendant indicated he was indigent, the judge would command, "Sign the affidavit," while the clerk pushed the paper at him. The affidavit of indigency would be kept in the file for the preliminary hearing, but no attorney was assigned at that moment. Rather, the judge whose turn it was to make the assignments would be notified, and he would appoint a private attorney or the public defender later in the day. The defendant did not see his attorney until a few days later, and sometimes only on the morning of the preliminary examination. Bail was also set at this time as we shall see in the next section. Neither prosecutor nor defense counsel was visible during the arraignment ceremony.

In Chicago, arraignment was brief and uncomplicated by ancillary matters. The judge would look at his file and say, "Donald Charles, you are charged with armed robbery," while the clerk or bailiff shoved a copy of the complaint into the defendant's hands. If the defendant had a defense lawyer, the attorney and prosecutor briefly negotiated about the next hearing date; otherwise, the judge would simply ask the prosecutor when he wished to proceed, taking into account the police officer's schedule. Unrepresented defendants remained unrepresented; public defenders were not appointed until the case was ready for a hearing. That procedure reduced the work load of the public defenders, as they did not need to bother with indigent defendants at intermediate proceedings; it also benefited the prosecution, because the defendant was often held responsible for any delays that occurred (he was not ready since he had no counsel), even though the real reason for the delay was that the prosecution had not assembled its witnesses. Arraignments occurred early in the day in Chicago (so policemen could go home) in terribly overcrowded courtrooms amid general confusion. Each took less than two minutes, just long enough for the defendant to shuffle to the front of the courtroom (or from the lockup), after his name was announced on a loudspeaker, and hear the charges against him.

In Baltimore, arraignment occurred in district courtrooms, but the ordinary courtroom workgroup was absent. A district court commissioner (who was often not an attorney) presided in the presence of a pretrial release officer, who made bail recommendations, and the jail turnkey. The ceremony usually took place at night, a few hours after the arrest. The commissioner read the charges, "gave the defendant his rights," checked to see whether the defendant could hire his own attorney, and set a date for the preliminary hearing. Some commissioners conducted these proceedings quite officiously; others were informal. They convened the group whenever a prisoner was brought in by the police. Because most arraignments occurred intermittently during the night, no public audience witnessed them.[3] They were as brief as those in Chicago and Detroit, rarely taking more than two minutes per defendant.

Arraignments were so standardized that little discretion existed for substantial variations that might favor defendants with particular characteristics. However, arraignments were not empty ceremonies. They protected defendants by forcing police to initiate the judicial process; prisoners could not rot indefinitely in police detention cells. At the same time, however, arraignments served as degradation ceremonies. They helped undermine the self-confidence of defendants and confirmed in a court of law their treatment by the police as criminals. In Chicago and Detroit, arraignments were the first contact between a courtroom workgroup and the defendant, but no opportunity existed for defendants to argue their innocence. In fact, arraigning judges often abruptly silenced those bewildered defendants who tried to ask a question or express their feelings. Finally, although arraigning judges normally exercised little discretion, an interesting exception occurred in Detroit. The presiding judge, who handled most of the arraignments there, often accepted guilty pleas to possession of marijuana charges. Defendants fortunate enough to appear before this judge and smart enough to take his suggestion that they plead guilty received very light sentences — often a $100 fine and a year's probation. Approximately 2.5 percent of all felony defendants fell into this group.[4] Thus, the arraignment performed a minor but highly efficient screening function in Detroit.

Bail. Setting bail is a more significant intermediate proceeding. Bail decisions determine whether defendants return to the street, their neighborhood, their job, and their family within hours of their arrest, or a few days later — or whether they sit in a jail cell until charges against them are dismissed or until they are acquitted or convicted. Many observers of criminal proceedings believe that denial of bail biases later proceedings against defendants; many think that the bail decisions discriminate against the poor and against blacks.[5] When the police arrest a suspect and charge him with a felony, they normally hold him in jail until he is released by the court.[6] A court may release a defendant on recognizance; the defendant is simply required to pledge that he will return to court whenever summoned. In all other cases, release depends on pledging a sum of money determined by the court. Personal bond, used extensively in Detroit, is equivalent to release on recognizance except that the defendant is theoretically liable to pay the face amount of the bond if he does not appear. When the court demands a dollar bail requiring sureties, the defendant must pledge a sum of money by signing over property as security, depositing cash, or buying a bond from a bail bondsman. Whether a defendant can obtain release when a surety bond is set depends on the kind of surety required, the amount, and his ability to pay.

Bail outcomes differed substantially in the three cities, as Table 8.2 shows. About half of all felony defendants remained in jail (at least through the preliminary hearing stage) in Baltimore. In Chicago and Detroit, two-fifths stayed in jail. The cities differed more on how they reached these results. Baltimore made moderate use of recognizance releases but set very high money bail. Recognizance releases were almost unknown in Chicago, but money bail was kept low. Detroit emphasized the use of recognizance release, and when money bail was set, it was fairly low.

Our earlier hypothetical examples of an armed robbery case might make bail proceedings appear to be simple. In fact they

TABLE 8.2 BAIL OUTCOMES AT PRELIMINARY
HEARING COURTROOMS IN THE THREE CITIES

	Baltimore[a]	Chicago[b]	Detroit[c]
Released on recognizance	21.1%	.9%	48.5%
Assessed nominal bail (under $1,000)	6.0%	20.4%	3.1%
Mean bail amount	$7,292	$3,244	$2,812
Released on recognizance or bail at preliminary hearing stage	48%	61.2%	59.8%

a. Based on weighted file sample. N = 1577
b. Based on weighted preliminary hearing observation sample. N = 1015
C. Based on full observational sample. N = 1472

reflected a rather complicated process with many options available to courtroom officials. These options operate under different statutory and organizational constraints in the three cities, reflecting the general variability of bail-setting in the United States.

Bail commissioners or district court judges set bail in the station house district court in Baltimore. The commissioners worked nights, when most arrests were made; they were laymen who often brought police or other law enforcement experience to their job. Bail commissioners were assisted by pretrial release investigators, who obtained personal information about the defendant and made recommendations about whether to release the prisoner on recognizance or whether to recommend a monetary bond. However, the bail commissioner was not bound by the recommendation made by pretrial release; he usually asked his own questions to test the veracity of the defendant. If the bail commissioner ordered release on recognizance, the defendant went free. If he set monetary bond at a level the defendant could afford, the defendant bought a bond from a nearby bail bondsman and again left the station house free. However, if the defendant did not have enough money to buy the required bond, he appeared before the district judge the next morning, when he could ask for a review of the bail; in that case, the defendant often remained in jail until his case was disposed.

The organizational context in which initial decisions were made in Baltimore was very loose. All the personnel except the clerk and policemen rotated out of their district frequently. Nevertheless, the location at which a defendant was processed made a considerable difference to the price of bail and the likelihood of release. In one district, a third of the defendants were released; in another it was two-thirds. The median bail varied from $2,566 to $7,000. These variations were not strongly related to different mixes of criminal charges from one district to another; such differences existed, but they are not consistent with the pattern of bail. Because of the constant shuffling of judges, prosecutors, public defenders, and bail commissioners in the courtrooms where these bail decisions were made, these differences probably reflect the effect of the police in the several districts.[7] Thus, the police not only decided the charges but also had a real effect on whether defendants were released immediately after arrest.

In Chicago, bail was set at the station house, at bond court, or in the preliminary hearing courtroom, depending on the time of the arrest and the type of crime. Bail for property offenses was usually set at the station house. Defendants often did not appear at bond court personally; the judge relied almost entirely on copies of the charge and police record except when he could communicate with the defendant by Picturephone (a gadget that was often broken). Only those persons arrested after bond court closed early in the morning were held over for a bond hearing in a preliminary hearing courtroom. In addition, persons who could not make the bail originally set could ask for a bail hearing in a preliminary hearing courtroom.

Although Illinois law provides for release on personal recognizance (called I Bonds), judges authorized very few of these releases (1 percent in our sample). Rather, they required a monetary bond under another Illinois reform — the 10 percent bail described in Chapter 5. As we said there, instead of buying the bond from a bail bondsman who charged a 10 percent fee, the defendant purchased bail bonds from the court itself for 10 percent of the stated amount; at the end of the proceedings, the court returned 90 percent of the amount paid. Thus a $5,000 bond cost $500 cash, $450 of which the defendant got back at the end of the proceedings.

In Chicago, the amount of bail was closely linked to the seriousness of the charge. Prosecutors and judges in the preliminary hearing courtroom had a table of charges and bail-bond amounts, and they typically made recommendations and decisions based on that table rather than on characteristics of the defendant. Except for indications of prior criminal record, information discovered at the hearing was so unimportant that the hearings themselves were perfunctory events rarely lasting more than two minutes. It was unusual for a defendant or his counsel to win a lower bail because of some information he revealed in court.

In Detroit, a judge of the Recorder's Court set bond at the arraignment immediately after arrest. Under normal circumstances, the amount of bail or the likelihood of release on recognizance depended on the charge and the defendant's police record. Prosecutors were rarely present. Private defense counsel appeared occasionally, believing that such action made a difference. As one attorney put it, "judges do it [reduce bail] more as a favor to the attorney. The judge knows you are trying to make a fee." [8]

Pretrial release thus depended on procedures used in each city and on local norms. In Detroit, the judge granted personal bonds for half the felony defendants; these defendants went free almost immediately. Chicago defendants also were typically released, because they could afford the bonds set; bonds there were not only lower than bonds in Baltimore but cheaper to purchase. Baltimore officials set high bonds that were expensive to purchase. In all three cities, when bonds rather than personal recognizance were required, the offense charged was more important in determining the bail amount than the defendant's race, his police record, the kind of attorney (if any), or the courtroom workgroup that processed his case. [9] Because Baltimore and Chicago police determined (or at least heavily influenced) the particulars of the charge, they had considerable influence over pretrial release. In Detroit, the police had less influence in routine cases.

However, local culture also affected bail. The higher bail required in Baltimore was not the result of more serious offenses committed there. When we examine similar offenses in the three cities, Baltimore usually required the highest bail. For instance, when armed robbery was charged, Baltimore on the average required $23,686 in bail, whereas Chicago asked for $7,719, and Detroit $3,075. When homicide was charged, Baltimore required $7,292 in bail, Chicago $5,000, and Detroit $2,450.[10] Quite apart from formal rules governing bail and the informal procedures for implementing them, Baltimore officials (perhaps more dominated by police than in the other two cities) implemented harsher standards for pretrial release, reflecting the more conservative views held by the city's population and interests active in the criminal justice process. More defendants found it impossible to meet the high bail fees these standards produced.

Bail status sometimes affected case outcome. We did not find the same strong relationships between bail status and final disposition that much previous research led us to expect. But we did find that being in jail sometimes affected whether a case was dismissed early in the proceedings or was carried forward to the grand jury and to trial. For instance, in Chicago we found that for armed robbers and burglars, making bail was more important in determining their fate at the preliminary hearing than the strength of the evidence.[11] However, the effect of bail was quite different for the two offenders. Bailed armed robbers were more likely to have their case dismissed or disposed of at the preliminary hearing than those who were jailed. Burglars released on bail were more likely to be indicted than their jailed counterparts. The difference may lie with the backgrounds of the armed robber and burglar. Although there may be little difference in the professionalism of the jailed and bailed armed robber, it is likely that the bailed burglar was a professional who had the resources to make bail, whereas his amateur counterpart was too poor to raise bond money and thus went to jail until disposition. But the professional burglar faced the more serious charges, which could not be disposed of at the preliminary hearing.[12]

The setting of bail also had important consequences for attorneys. Obtaining a lower bond demonstrated their effectiveness to the client even though the defendant might later be convicted or plead guilty. Bail also demonstrated financial ability, and many judges — especially in Chicago — referred bailed defendants to private attorneys rather than allowing them to be represented by the public defender. In Chicago the bail bond had additional significance. The attorney (with his client's consent) could petition the court to divert the bail refund from the defendant to the attorney; in this way, bail guaranteed a substantial portion of the attorney's fee.

Unlike arraignments, bail proceedings produced quite variable outcomes. They had the powerful immediate consequence of determining whether the defendant returned to the street within hours of his arrest or whether he remained in custody. Custody meant incarceration in overcrowded, outmoded local jails where pretrial defendants suffered the same treatment as convicted prisoners.

Hearing Motions. The decision to send a defendant to trial depends on the state's possession of incriminating evidence. The validity of evidence often is not in question, but when it is, defense counsel may challenge it early in the proceedings. If the judge throws the evidence out as inadmissable, the defendant goes free. Such motions are usually made only when a probable cause hearing is going to be held; if the hearing is waived, motions attacking the evidence are usually saved until the case has been transferred to a trial courtroom. Therefore, it is not surprising that few such motions were made in Baltimore preliminary hearing courtrooms, because preliminary hearings were often not permitted and defendants were moved directly to the next stage of the proceedings. In Detroit, attorneys conducted preliminary examinations in an adversarial manner. Defense attorneys vigorously cross-examined the prosecution's witnesses in many cases. During the preliminary hearing, defense attorneys often moved for dismissal or argued against the prosecution's motion that the defendant be bound over for trial. Defense attorneys sometimes made other motions challenging the prosecution's case (for example, challenging the admissability of evidence or confessions). However, these motions were considered and ruled on in the course of the preliminary examination itself, and did not constitute a separate proceeding.

Motions were handled differently in Chicago. When made, these motions preceded the normal routine followed when examinations were held. However, defense attorneys did not often make such motions. Preliminary hearing proceedings in Chicago were generally less adversarial than in Detroit. The regular preliminary hearing courtrooms were too busy, having to process more than a hundred defendants on many days. Hearings on motions usually took a quarter of an hour; they required some preparation for both defense and prosecution, and called for special attentiveness from the judge. Strong workgroup norms determined when such motions were made. The workgroups considered them unnecessary harrassment and avoided them in all but a very few cases.[13] Only in narcotics courtrooms were motions common. There they were part of the regular plea bargaining in those courts. Physical evidence is 90 percent of an ordinary narcotics case, and the legality of the search that produced the evidence is often in question. In the preliminary negotiations before a case came to preliminary hearing, defense counsel and prosecutor often discussed alternative outcomes, including treatment programs, straight probation, and short time. The quality of the evidence was often a factor in these negotiations. When a tentative bargain had been struck, defense counsel might nevertheless argue his motion on the legality of the search or arrest. If he won, the defendant went free; if he lost, the defendant accepted the prosecutor's bargain and pleaded guilty. Thus, evidentiary motions in fact took the place of trials in many narcotics cases in the Chicago preliminary hearing courtrooms. As in the regular preliminary hearing courtrooms, strong workgroup norms governed the decision about arguing a motion. Disruptive motions were especially unlikely in the narcotics courtrooms, since they had a higher proportion of cases handled by regular defense attorneys than the other courtrooms. Because they specialized in narcotics cases and had a greater commitment to the courtroom workgroup, organizational norms governed them to a high degree.[14]

Motions challenging the validity of the evidence thus directly affected preliminary outcomes in these three cities. When successful, they led immediately to freedom. Several factors determined whether such motions were made. If no preliminary examination took place (either because the defendant waived it or the Baltimore district judge refused to hold it), no motions could be argued. Some charges typically produced motions, particularly when searches produced evidence of a crime (a gun, narcotics, stolen property). Finally, their use depended on the vigor of the defense counsel and the norms of the workgroup conducting the proceeding. Some workgroups tolerated them; others punished those who appeared to invoke such hearings unnecessarily.

The principal preparatory proceedings varied significantly among the three cities. But these variations are not distinctively associated with differences in the outcomes of preliminary proceedings. Detroit, a city with a high proportion of released defendants, sent the highest proportion to trial, which is exactly contrary to what had been expected. Detroit also made the greatest use of pretrial motions. Chicago, with nearly equal pretrial release and more modest utilization of pretrial motions, sent the smallest proportion of defendants to trial. Although the preparatory proceedings are important to the disposition process, they do not distinguish one city's outcomes from another's.

THE EFFECT OF CASE
AND DEFENDANT CHARACTERISTICS
ON PRELIMINARY OUTCOMES

Another tentative explanation of the outcomes may lie in the characteristics of defendants and cases to which courtroom workgroups respond. Those characteristics may be substantially different from one city to another. Our data from case files allow us to examine that hypothesis.

Table 8.3 shows some of the salient characteristics of defendants and the cases they faced. They were not identical in the three cities, but the differences were not large in most instances. Defendants in all three were predominantly black, although the proportion was somewhat lower in Chicago (where the black population is also a somewhat smaller proportion). About a third of all defendants in the three cities were under twenty-one; more than half had a prior record in the two cities where those data were available.

There was more armed robbery in Baltimore; heroin sales charges were exceptionally rare in Detroit. Otherwise, the

TABLE 8.3   CHARACTERISTICS OF DEFENDANTS AND CASES IN BALTIMORE, CHICAGO, AND DETROIT

	Baltimore[a]	Chicago[b]	Detroit[a]
Percentage black	81.5	69.9	82.7
Percentage over 21 years old	66.4	70.2	63.0
Percentage with previous record	58.1	missing	66.0
Offenses			
Murder	3.8	1.7	3.6
Rape	5.1	1.1	1.4
Armed Robbery	16.2	8.5	10.3
Assault	7.3	5.8	7.6
Heroin dealer	11.8	22.0	1.6
Heroin use	2.2	6.7	7.8
Burglary	28.4	8.5	12.5
Theft	n.a.[d]	6.5	4.8
Robbery	10.9	4.1	2.9
Weapons	n.a.[d]	4.0	17.4
Other	14.2	15.0	30.1
Evidence			
Photo identification	8.7	missing	4.6
Lineup identification	1.2	missing	13.0
Eyewitnesses	13.0	10.0	4.7
Confession	9.7	2.8	26.0
Physical Evidence	68.1	78.3	86.0

a. Weighted file sample: $N = 1577$.
b. Weighted preliminary hearing observation sample: $N = 1,015$.
c. Weighted observation sample: $N = 1,640$.
d. Burglary and theft are combined for Baltimore; there is no weapons offense comparable to those in Chicago and Detroit.

charges facing defendants were roughly similar. Evidence appeared to be slightly stronger in Detroit, where police obtained confessions from 26 percent of the defendants as compared to 12 percent in Baltimore and 2.8 percent in Chicago. But differences in evidentiary indicators are not consistent from city to city.

These data indicate that, roughly speaking, defendants in the three cities had similar personal characteristics. Charges lodged against them were similar. The police generated similar kinds of evidence as measured by our indicators. There is nothing in these data to suggest the vast number of dismissals that occurred in Chicago or the high probability of being sent to a trial court in Detroit.

A more rigorous test of the effect of these characteristics is possible by comparing them within each city rather than across the three cities. The question we may ask of these data is: Do these characteristics explain who among all the defendants in any one city is released during these proceedings, and who is sent to a trial court?

For Baltimore and Chicago, we can explain much of the variance in the decision to send a defendant to trial; only in Detroit do our variables almost totally fail us. But defendant and case characteristics explained very little of the decision to send to trial. As Figure 8.2 shows, only the nature of the offense in Chicago played a discernible, even though small, role. The other characteristics of defendant and case had an almost invisible effect. By contrast, the identity of the courtroom was the most important variable in each of the cities. Where defendants were processed was clearly more important than who they were or what they did.

THE EFFECT OF WORKGROUP ORGANIZATION AND CONTEXT

A third explanation of the different outcomes in the three cities rests on the structure and norms of the workgroups operating in the preliminary hearing courtrooms. We have already seen that differences in procedure and differences in defendant or case characteristics did not go far in explaining outcomes. But that

FIGURE 8.2 The Decision by Preliminary Hearing Courtrooms to Send Defendants to Trial[a] Showing the Relative Contribution of Variables to Total Discriminating Power.

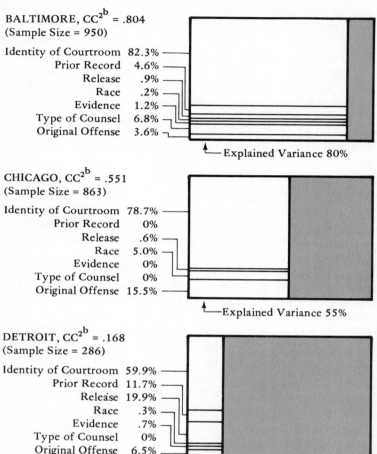

BALTIMORE, CC^2[b] = .804
(Sample Size = 950)

Identity of Courtroom	82.3%
Prior Record	4.6%
Release	.9%
Race	.2%
Evidence	1.2%
Type of Counsel	6.8%
Original Offense	3.6%

Explained Variance 80%

CHICAGO, CC^2[b] = .551
(Sample Size = 863)

Identity of Courtroom	78.7%
Prior Record	0%
Release	.6%
Race	5.0%
Evidence	0%
Type of Counsel	0%
Original Offense	15.5%

Explained Variance 55%

DETROIT, CC^2[b] = .168
(Sample Size = 286)

Identity of Courtroom	59.9%
Prior Record	11.7%
Release	19.9%
Race	.3%
Evidence	.7%
Type of Counsel	0%
Original Offense	6.5%

Explained Variance 17%

[a]Multiple discriminant function analysis was used. This statistical routine discriminates between two categories (here sending defendants to trial rather than disposing of their cases in the preliminary hearing courtrooms) with the aid of a set of independent variables. The amount of the explained variance accounted for by independent variables is estimated by Rao's V. See text for a fuller explanation.

[b]Canonical Correlation Squared.

Samples. Baltimore — weighted file sample; Chicago — weighted preliminary hearing observation sample; Detroit — preliminary examination observation sample.

analysis did suggest that courtroom identity was a major factor among those which could be identified.

We may examine the effect of courtroom organization in two ways. We can describe the structure of courts and the context in which they operated; we can also demonstrate their effect statistically in Chicago, where our data are most appropriate for that kind of analysis.

One effect of courtroom workgroups is that they perceive defendants and cases differently and treat them differently. Table 8.4 shows those differences for four Chicago preliminary hearing courtrooms which heard enough cases to permit this kind of analysis. The different norms of each courtroom emerge in striking fashion. In the north side courtroom, the offense charged was most important; defendant's race was a distant second. However, decisional patterns are not well captured by these variables for that courtroom, both as measured by the correlation coefficient and by the measure of improvement in our predictive ability. In the south side courtroom, offense charged was less important, and race and bail status were much more important; all the variables again explained little of the variance. In one

TABLE 8.4 CHICAGO COURTROOM ANALYSIS OF DECISION TO DISMISS CHARGES[a]

	South-side	North-side	Narcotics No. 1	Narcotics No. 2
Canonical correlation squared	.05	.12	.30	.42
Percentage of explained variance accounted for by:				
Offense	79.0	43.2	18.1	54.6
Race	14.3	25.4	64.5	6.0
Release	0	27.2	3.8	39.3
Evidence	1.3	4.0	13.5	0

a. Multiple discriminant function analysis using weighted preliminary hearing observation sample. Percentage of explained variance accounted for by independent variables is estimated by Rao's V. See page 186 for a fuller explanation.

narcotics courtroom, offense charged had little importance, but the race of the defendant had a large effect: whites were sent to trial more frequently than blacks. In the other narcotics courtroom, race had no significance, but the workgroup reacted to the offense charged and bail status. The only feature common to these four courtrooms was that weight of the evidence as we measured it did not explain much of the variance in the decision to dismiss charges at the preliminary hearing.

We can gain a better insight into the behavior of the Chicago courtroom workgroups and those in the other cities by looking at their structure and examining the full context in which they operate. For that purpose, we must rely on the data we collected while we observed these courtrooms in action.

Chicago Preliminary Hearing Workgroups.* Chaos confronts the casual observer of the Chicago workgroups. Each morning the preliminary hearing courtrooms are packed with people; they buzz with noise and motion that scarcely diminishes when the judge enters and begins proceedings. Clerks call defendants to the bench over a loudspeaker. Those in custody come from the back of the bench and usually meet their family and friends before the judge; those on bail meander from the spectator section with their relatives. Complaining witnesses and police stand a few steps to their left, but a casual observer would think that all the participants form a single cluster. These clusters form, melt away, and reform every two or three minutes as the clerk calls one case after another. Unless a person is standing in their midst (as the court reporter does), he or she cannot hear what is going on. On many days, workgroups in these courtrooms must handle more than a hundred defendants. They work with short coffee breaks from 10 A.M. until 6 or 7 at night on busy days; on days with few defendants, they often finish by 2 o'clock.

The Chicago preliminary hearing courtrooms were highly specialized. One courtroom handled all offenses except narcotics and homicides occurring on the north side of the city; a second handled similar south side offenders. A third courtroom handled all narcotics cases for jailed defendants, but also handled bailed

---

* See pages 106–107 for earlier discussion of these workgroups.

defendants; another handled only bailed narcotics defendants. A fifth courtroom (working only afternoons) processed all homicides. As a consequence, courtrooms 1 and 2 handled a much greater variety of offenses than the narcotics workgroups. A much higher proportion of defendants in courtroom 2 were black than in the other courtrooms, because most of Chicago's black ghettos were located in its area.

As we noted in Chapter 2, another important characteristic of workgroups is their stability. Chicago's preliminary hearing workgroups were more stable than Baltimore's or Detroit's. Unlike judges in Baltimore and Detroit, Chicago's judges were assigned to the preliminary hearing courtrooms for a year or two at a time; no visiting judges worked there, and the regular judges did not rotate through these courtrooms. When a substitute judge was needed, he came from a limited set of alternates, so that even the replacement judges grew familiar with the operations of these courtrooms. A stable set of assistant prosecutors also worked in these courtrooms. Two or three assistants in each courtroom handled the ordinary proceedings. A more senior assistant took responsibility for negotiating pleas for the north side and south side courtrooms, appearing on alternate days in each. A pair of public defenders, who worked in the courtroom for many months, represented indigent clients. In addition, defense attorneys who specialized in preliminary courtroom proceedings represented a discernible number of defendants.[15] As a consequence, preliminary hearing courtrooms were a good deal more stable in Chicago than in Baltimore and Detroit. Judges and attorneys were familiar with one another, and the resulting cohesion allowed them to develop distinctive norms and operating procedures.

Further, the preliminary hearing courtrooms were closely integrated with the trial courts. Although the judges in preliminary hearing courtrooms worked in the municipal division rather than the criminal division of the Cook County Circuit Court, the same presiding judge supervised both. As we noted earlier, the preliminary hearing courtrooms occupied the same building as the trial courtrooms, enabling the personnel to develop at least some awareness of the effect of their actions on the later processing of cases. Preliminary hearing workgroups were keenly aware of the need to prune cases so that trial courts would not be overwhelmed. Chicago prosecutors in 1972 had little opportunity to influence the charging process. Except in one experimental district, policemen brought whatever charges they thought appropriate, without consulting a prosecutor. Hence, the first opportunity to weed out cases occurred at the preliminary hearing. Every preliminary hearing courtroom recognized this weeding out as a major task. The 63 percent dismissal rate of these courtrooms reflects their effectiveness.

Chicago preliminary hearing courtrooms dismissed more of the minor charges than the major ones, with the exception of rape (see Figure 8.3). No murder or narcotics dealer charges

FIGURE 8.3 Dismissals in Chicago Preliminary Hearing Courtrooms: By Original Charge as Compared to Chicago Mean.

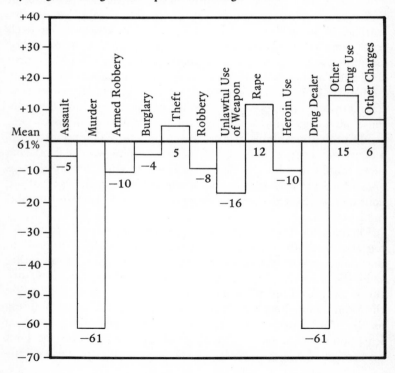

were dismissed in our sample, and distinctly fewer armed rob-bery and unlawful use of weapons charges were dismissed than the average for these courtrooms. On the other hand, the pre-liminary hearing courtrooms dismissed more theft, narcotics user, and minor felony charges. However, the *average* dismissal rate for these courtrooms was 63 percent. Thus, although these workgroups dismissed fewer alleged armed robbers than was usual in these courtrooms, more than half the persons accused of armed robbery left the courtroom with their charges dis-missed; 56 percent of those charged with assault and 73 percent of those accused of rape went free.

Because the workgroups dealt with a specialized set of cases, they developed distinctive dismissal patterns. Dismissals were rare in homicide court. Once the police had made an arrest in a murder case, they usually gave the courtroom enough evidence to send the case to the grand jury. In addition, homicide cases were taken seriously, and the work load of the homicide court-room was much lighter than that of the other courtrooms; conse-quently, the participants developed their cases in a much more formal, adversarial manner than did the other courtrooms. Homi-cide cases also had a greater visibility than most others, and their dismissal at this early stage could well provoke hostile reactions from the courtroom's external environment. The low homicide dismissal rate did not (as we shall see later) auger a high con-viction rate; rather, the preliminary hearing workgroup shunted these cases forward, both because of their strength and because of their delicacy.

The narcotics courtrooms dismissed most of their cases by a legalism called SOL (Stricken Off with Leave to reinstate). That practice reflects the nature of the crimes with which they dealt. In most narcotics cases, policemen were the formal complainants, and dismissal usually indicated failure by the police to prose-cute. By contrast, the north and south side courtrooms, which handled all other offenses, relied on a different legalism — DWP (Dismissed for Want of Prosecution) — for most of their dismis-sals. DWPs were entered when citizen complainants failed to appear, or when they stepped forward and indicated their re-fusal to take the matter further. DWPs accounted for all the rape dismissals and many armed robbery and theft dismissals.

The courtroom workgroup threw some of these cases out because the defendant either compensated or reconciled with the complaining witness. Court records do not reflect this phenomenon, but we witnessed such dismissals daily during our observations. Especially in theft cases, once the complaining witness had his property back or had been paid for it, he lost interest in pursuing the case; without the complainant's testimony, the prosecutor had to drop the case.

Thus charge, victim interest, and the courtroom to which a case was sent had the most influence on the courtroom workgroup's decision to dismiss a case. When cases appeared strong to the prosecution, or when complainants (whether civilian or police) pursued them with vigor, the preliminary hearing workgroup usually sent them to the grand jury or took a guilty plea. Other cases lingered and were eventually dismissed. Thus, curiously enough, dismissed cases stayed longer on the docket than cases sent to the grand jury. Cases disposed of by a preliminary hearing took three and a half months, on the average; cases that were dropped because the civilian complaining witness lost interest took four months; cases dropped because of police disinterest stayed on the docket almost five months, on the average. The screening process in Chicago consequently was largely passive. Rather than eliminate cases that were unworthy of further attention, Chicago preliminary hearing courtroom workgroups focused their efforts on those which warranted prosecution and let the rest sink into oblivion.

Although there were many dismissals, almost 9 percent of all defendants pleaded guilty in the preliminary hearing courtroom, mostly to an information filed after probable cause had been determined. Specialization also marked these guilty pleas. All these guilty pleas represented the interaction between defense attorneys, one prosecutor who specialized in plea bargaining for the north and south side courts or the courtroom prosecutors for the narcotics courts, plus (to a limited degree) the judges. Preliminary hearing judges did not regularly participate in the plea bargaining, because of their work load. However, they kept an eye on the negotiations and signaled to the participants what they were likely to accept or reject. The judges' variable cooperation with plea bargaining led to almost three times as many such pleas in the north side court as in the south side one, and twice as many in one narcotics court than in the other. Guilty pleas at this stage were almost entirely on the offense originally charged.

No one kind of offender was singled out for this treatment, as shown by the comparison between the distribution of offenses brought to the preliminary hearing courtrooms and the offenses to which defendants pleaded guilty (Table 8.5). Only armed robbery, burglary, and robbery were decidedly overrepresented among the guilty pleas, and in each case the guilty pleas did not represent a substantial portion of defendants charged with one of these crimes.

A probationary or short prison term apparently was the incentive for pleading guilty. Although our evidence does not sub-

TABLE 8.5   DISTRIBUTION OF OFFENSES: CHICAGO

	All Defendants Coming to Preliminary Hearing Courtroom[a]	Defendants Pleading Guilty to Information[b]
Assault	5.8	8.3
Murder	1.7	1.4
Armed Robbery	8.5	19.4
Burglary	8.5	17.4
Theft	6.5	2.8
Robbery	4.1	10.4
UUW (weapons)	4.0	3.5
Rape	1.1	.7
Heroin use	6.7	9.7
Heroin dealing	1.2	4.9
Other drug use	12.1	.7
Other drug dealing	—	4.9
Other	37.4	15.3
	97.6%	99.4%

a. Weighted observation sample: $N = 1,015$
b. Random file sample of informations: $N = 143$

stantiate it, the participants strongly believed that pleading at this stage would produce a better deal than pleading later or being sentenced after a trial. Prosecutors continually repeated to defense attorneys and defendants their determination to exact a higher price at a later stage. Their persuasion resulted in low-visibility, low-risk guilty pleas in the preliminary hearing courtrooms. But it did not produce numerous guilty pleas. Defendants who had probable cause determined against them and faced grand jury indictment did not often have enough incentives for pleading guilty as a matter of course. Although most eventually pleaded guilty, they usually preferred to wait until their case reached the trial court.

Chicago preliminary hearing workgroups attained the widely shared goal of disposing of cases by dismissals, rather than by guilty pleas or findings of probable cause. They operated very defensively. They dismissed cases through default, waiting for complainants or policemen to signal that a case was important enough to pursue with vigor. Only cases pursued with some vigor through a probable cause proceeding became targets for plea negotiations, and negotiations succeeded in only a few of these cases. But the workgroups were sensitive to the needs of the trial courts for a severe pruning of cases that entered the disposition process. Consequently, the passive screening resulted in the dismissal of three-fifths of all defendants brought in by the police. Finally, the stability and specialization of each of the preliminary hearing courtroom workgroups resulted in quite distinctive patterns of disposition. Some workgroups paid much closer attention to defendant characteristics than others; some processed a greater variety of charges and used charge as an important cue.

Baltimore Preliminary Hearing Workgroups.[*] In Baltimore, the organizational structure of preliminary hearing courtroom workgroups was entirely different. Police brought charges to one of the district courts scattered throughout the city. These courts held trials for misdemeanors and some felonies as well as preliminary hearings for felonies, but they could not hear jury trials. If they did not dispose of felonies, they sent them to the grand jury, and if the case survived grand jury screening, it went to

---

[*] See pages 72–75 for our earlier description of these workgroups.

the criminal division, a court with nine sections located near downtown Baltimore.

As we indicated in Chapter 4, the judges of the district court were organizationally separate from those of the criminal division. They served for a different term, were supervised by their own administrative judge, and stood lower in the judicial hierarchy than criminal bench judges. They had a heavy work load and worked in generally shabby surroundings.

Moreover, the district court workgroups had only a transient existence. The judges generally sat in a particular courtroom for only a month at a time; they then rotated to one of the other districts. Assistant prosecutors and public defenders stayed in the district courts only briefly; as soon as they could, they transferred to one of the other divisions of their office. Private attorneys also did not like to practice in the district courts, because their location was inconvenient for most of them; unless all their clients came from one neighborhood, attorneys had to chase from one section of the city to another when handling district court cases. Consequently, district court workgroups rarely had a chance to develop norms that might sustain complex collective actions. Instead, these workgroups sent most of their felony cases to the grand jury.

Baltimore's preliminary hearing workgroups rendered very different decisions than Chicago's. As Table 8.1 indicated, two-thirds of the defendants had their cases sent to the grand jury. It was the simplest, most certain, and least costly action for the district courtroom workgroups. Moreover, they accomplished this action without holding a preliminary examination. As noted in Chapter 4, a defendant in Maryland had no right to insist on a preliminary exam as he did in Michigan and Illinois. Holding it was up to the discretion of the judge, and most district court judges found preliminary hearings a waste of time. Rather, they used three simple criteria for deciding whether to dispose a case in their courtroom or send it to the trial courts: the kind of defense counsel, the defendant's prior record, and the seriousness of the charges (whether they involved murder, heroin dealing, armed robbery, or something else). The effect of these three characteristics together with some others is shown in Table 8.6; that analysis excludes the courtroom itself.

TABLE 8.6   THE DECISION TO SEND CHARGES
TO TRIAL COURT: BALTIMORE[a]

Canonical correlation squared	.423
Percentage of explained variance accounted for by:	
Type of counsel	56.7
Prior record	29.6
Murder, armed robbery, Heroin dealing charges	9.6
Evidence	2.7
Pretrial release	1.0
Defendant's race	0

a. Multiple discriminant function analysis using weighted file sample. Percentage of explained variance accounted for by independent variables is estimated by Rao's V. See page 186 for a fuller explanation.

Type of counsel had the greatest effect. Public defenders took only 28 percent of their clients to trial courts, whereas assigned counsel took 99 percent, and private counsel took 70 percent; thus type of counsel accounts for 57 percent of the variance in Table 8.6. The effect of the type of counsel demonstrates the significance of the slight degree of permanence among public defenders in these highly unstable courtroom workgroups. Specific combinations of judge, assistant prosecutor, and public defender worked together long enough to begin to develop mutual dependence and familiarity. Public defenders were apparently able to take advantage of this leverage and of their knowledge of district court proceedings to secure an early disposition for their clients. They may also have used these dispositions to break the monotony of handling misdemeanors. Retained attorneys took their cases to the criminal division, where it was more convenient for them but where their clients often fared worse.

District court workgroups also responded to prior criminal record. They sent defendants with a prior criminal record to trial court more often than those with no record. Finally, the kind of offense was significant; murder, armed robbery, and heroin dealing charges usually were sent to the trial courts, whereas all others were disposed of with some regularity in the preliminary hearing courtrooms. Notice that pretrial release, the evidence, and the defendant's race by themselves had little or no relationship to whether a defendant was sent to trial court or not.

Hence, the workgroups screened a few defendants with less serious charges or with no prior criminal record; among such defendants, whites were somewhat more often screened out than blacks. But the sieve remained gross. No member of the district courtroom workgroup had an interest in pruning cases. It would have been in the interest of the state's attorneys office for the district court to prune cases more effectively. They did not do so, in part because prosecutors assigned to district courts were inexperienced, worked for a separate division in the state's attorney's office that had little organizational interest in the work load of trial prosecutors, and anxiously awaited promotion to a higher-paying position in the trial division.

Even reducing charges to misdemeanors did not always lead to screening the case out. Experienced defense counsel would sometimes seek such a reduction and then request a jury trial. That request again brought the case to the criminal division, where subsequent bargaining could further reduce the charge and the sentence. Further, the district courts had the reputation of being conviction-minded and heavy sentencers. Thus, there was little inducement for the defense to agree to keep the case in the district, unless the charges were dismissed. Finally, private counsel often had not yet been paid when a case came before the district court; they had every incentive to delay disposition by not resisting transfer to the grand jury. It was much more productive for most private counsel to have a case transferred to the criminal division or sent to the grand jury, where it could be handled together with the other criminal matters on the attorney's calendar.

The grand jury also screened few cases out of the disposition process; it indicted 94 percent of the defendants referred to it. It might have served as a more sensitive screen if the state's attorney had wished to use it in this fashion; all cases presented to the grand jury were reviewed by a team of assistant prosecutors. Although we have no direct evidence, we think so few cases were screened because having the grand jury refuse indictments would expose the ineptness of the police or state's attorney's office. It would not take long for the Baltimore press to become aware of a large number of "no true bills" (rejected indictments) in part because nonprofessionals — the grand jurors themselves — would have to concur in such an action. It was much safer for weak cases to be dismissed at a later stage, before a trial judge. There, only members of the courtroom team need to be involved; the activity would be scattered over nine courtrooms rather than concentrated within one jury room. And it would be sanctioned by a judge, whereas grand jury actions operated independently. Another reason for low dismissal rates at the grand jury was that the two assistants in the grand jury section lacked adequate information about the cases. An internal memo of the state's attorney's office put it bluntly:

Since, with the small exception of rape cases, witnesses are not usually interviewed prior to going before the grand jury, the members of our Division are completely dependent upon the offense reports. . . . It is not possible to know that an offense report is not accurate until the witnesses are spoken with . . . Even reading offense reports prior to going before the grand jury will not indicate either a weak case or where problems may exist, and that these problems only come to the fore in the subsequent preparation of the case for trial . . . Receiving incomplete offense reports a day or two prior to going before the grand jury is a problem that has still not been solved.

Generally, prosecutors working with the grand jury did not look at cases until the morning they were to be presented. They then saw the original police report and spoke to the policemen who were directly involved; only rarely did they speak to the principal civilian witnesses. Furthermore, the two assistants working with the grand jury processed several dozen cases each day and could pay little attention to any one. Consequently, it was much simpler to let the grand jury indict than to attempt to distinguish between cases that should be dismissed and those that should go to trial.

The Baltimore organizational structure thus produced results almost the opposite of those in Chicago. The preliminary hearing workgroups did not usually prune cases, because it was not in the interest of any member of the workgroup to do so. The judges had no stake in the work of the criminal division; the prosecutors were too inexperienced; private counsel wanted the convenience of a central court and the delay that led to their receiving their fee. The workgroups, moreover, were too transient to develop strong norms of their own. The simplest action in these circumstances was to send cases to the grand jury. Only public defenders obtained dispositions for most of their clients in the district courts. The grand jury also did not screen cases, because prosecutors had inadequate information and because they feared unfavorable publicity should the grand jury reject large numbers of charges. Consequently, in Baltimore, most original charges went to the trial courts.

Detroit Preliminary Examination Workgroups. * Detroit courtroom workgroups at the preliminary hearing stage worked in quite a different context. Before felony charges could be filed in court, the police had to obtain the approval of the warrant section of the prosecutor's office. The warrant section's six attorneys scrutinized the police's arrests. They refused to prosecute some potential felony cases at all. Others were knocked down to misdemeanor charges. When prosecutors lodged formal charges, they usually chose the specific charge carefully to fit the facts. Thus, only cases that the prosecutor felt were sufficiently important and serious and had strong enough evidence survived this early screening. Only those cases produced an arrest warrant and a formal charge that was sent to court for a preliminary examination. The Detroit prosecutor's office was so confident that its decisions at the warrant stage would survive judicial scrutiny, that the forms detailing the charges at the warrant stage were backed with carbon and simultaneously produced the informations that formally charged the defendant with a felony after the preliminary examination. It was rare for charges to be altered because of a preliminary examination, and as our data indicate, charges were infrequently thrown out.

The case load of the warrant section was high. The best evidence we found indicates that it processed approximately fifty-three requests for a felony warrant each working day.[16] The criteria prosecutors used to decide whether to press misdemeanor or

---

* See pages 134–136 for our earlier discussion of preliminary hearing workgroups.

felony charges or to drop the matter entirely included both the legal distinctions — which determine whether sufficient evidence exists to win a conviction — and pragmatic criteria, such as the insistence of a complaining witness, the commitment of police, and the most desirable outcome from the point of view of the victim and the society. The latter consideration sometimes led to surprising results. For instance, an offender who appeared to be dangerous and was already out on bail for another felony might be charged with a misdemeanor, because a misdemeanor conviction could be obtained that same day or within the week, and the offender could be immediately incarcerated. The felony disposition process was perceived as more problematic and less likely to result in quick incarceration. On the other hand, when an incident involved a family fight, the prosecutor in the warrant office might convince the victim to drop charges or to accept a misdemeanor complaint, because a felony disposition would be too devastating to the ongoing relationship between victim and defendant. In addition, the prosecutors knew that in many such instances the complaining witness would lose interest in pursuing the matter, and it would have to be dropped later on.

The members of the warrant office knew that they handled complaints differently. One described himself as sympathetic to the police and concerned with relationships between his office, police, and complaining witnesses. A colleague was described as much more rigorously committed to formal legal standards. These variations in outlook made it likely that the prosecutor's discretion would not be uniformly applied by the warrant office. The screen that was applied varied in its mesh.

Approximately 20 percent of all complaints brought to the warrant office were denied outright, and an additional 36 percent were filed as misdemeanors. Half of the misdemeanors might have been felonies, had the discretion of the prosecutors been exercised differently. Thus about 35 percent of all potential felony cases brought to the warrant section led to no felony prosecution and never came to preliminary hearing courtrooms. Unlike cases in Chicago and Baltimore, cases coming to the courtrooms in Detroit had already been screened by the prosecutor's office. Thus, Detroit preliminary hearing workgroups both felt less pressure and had fewer occasions to prune weak cases. Much of the explanation for Detroit's lower screening rate at the preliminary exam lies in this fact.

The structure of preliminary hearing courtroom workgroups, presented in Chapter 6, also differed from the other cities in important respects. Their distinctive features included the presence of temporary visiting judges with no organizational ties or long-range commitment to Recorder's Court, the presence of considerable uncertainty introduced by the visiting judges, the participation of regular defense attorneys, who were familiar to clerks and career prosecutors, and the mix of career prosecutors and novices.

As we would expect from this situation, the preliminary examination in Detroit was a rather formal proceeding, and it occurred frequently. Only one-third of all defendants waived it. The decision to hold or waive it was the defense counsel's. Private attorneys were slightly more likely to hold exams than the defenders.[17] For private counsel, the preliminary exam provided an early opportunity to show their clients how hard they were working for them. In addition, about one-quarter of the defendants had their charges dismissed after a preliminary exam, and that success rate encouraged the majority to hold the exam, especially if they thought the prosecutor's case vulnerable because of evidentiary problems or because of unimpressive witnesses. If the complaining witness was not in court, the defense might ask for an exam in the hope that the case would be dismissed for want of prosecution. But even when the case appeared fairly strong, some counsel liked to hold exams to pin down the state's witnesses. If the witnesses gave different testimony several months later at trial, the defense could use the preliminary exam transcript to impeach their truthfulness.

Whether a defendant held or waived his preliminary exam also appeared to be related to the adversariness of his attorney. Although the substance of the cases held and waived did not seem to differ systematically with respect to seriousness of charges, weight of evidence, or characteristics of defendant, a substantially higher proportion of those who held exams subsequently insisted on a trial, as Table 8.7 shows. Conversely, those defendants who waived exams frequently pleaded guilty when their case went to the trial courtroom.[18] The adversarial pose

TABLE 8.7 TRIAL COURT DISPOSITION MODE
IN DETROIT BY PRELIMINARY EXAMINATIONS[a]

| Preliminary Exam | Trial Court Disposition Mode | | Total |
	Went to Trial	Guilty Plea	
Held (N = 113)	25%	75%	100%
Waived (N = 79)	7%	93%	100%

x^2 = 10.6, significant at .001 level.

a. Preliminary examination observation sample used.

which those defendants and attorneys struck in the preliminary exams apparently carried over to the trial courtroom as well.

When the examination was held, it was a clear adversarial proceeding. The prosecutor had to mount a sufficient case to show probable cause. He was likely to call the complainant (if there was one) and the arresting officer to the witness stand. They were subjected to a routine direct examination and cross-examination, which were followed by a brief summary and argument on legal points. The median time of the examinations we witnessed was fifteen minutes. Most preliminary examinations resulted in a finding of probable cause, not only because most cases were fairly strong but also because in questionable cases the safest decision for the visiting judges was to find probable cause. If they were wrong, a trial court could later dismiss or reduce the charges. Moreover, the visiting judges often were unfamiliar with the routine violence in the city and applied somewhat different standards to the seriousness of crimes and to police behavior (particularly lying by the police, a practice about which many defense attorneys complained). Many of the defense attorneys we interviewed indicated that they thought visiting judges were more likely to find probable cause than were indigenous judges. Our data are inadequate to test these perceptions fully. Almost all the preliminary examinations we observed were handled by visiting judges; the one regular judge who appeared often in our sample dismissed a third of the cases; the visiting judges in our sample who handled twenty or more preliminary examinations dismissed 5 percent fewer (not a statistically significant difference). However, since visiting judges heard most of the cases, they apparently set the norm for these proceedings.

The predispositions of the career assistant prosecutors assigned permanently to preliminary exams also discouraged screening at this stage. Unlike their counterparts in Chicago, they felt no inclination or obligation to dispose of cases. They knew that a colleague had already approved the charges in the warrant office. They subscribed strongly to the office view described earlier — that many defendants deserved to go to jail. Their anticrime, antidefendant viewpoint encouraged them to seek a finding of probable cause in all but the weakest cases.

Conclusion.　The structure of the preliminary hearing courtroom workgroups and the context in which they worked in these three cities clearly affected their methods and outputs. Stable workgroups in Chicago developed informal methods for screening cases. They held few formal preliminary examinations. But because of their links with the trial courts, they felt obliged to prune cases severely. In Baltimore, unstable workgroups, less well integrated with the trial courts, responded to similar pressures by sending most defendants forward to the grand jury, from which the prosecutor sent them to the trial courts. Those options were also promoted by the fact that Baltimore courts were not obliged to provide preliminary examinations to all defendants who wanted them. Unstable workgroups in Detroit operated in a very different context. The prosecutor had already screened cases before they reached the courtroom. Defendants had the right to ask for preliminary examinations, but defense attorneys had mixed feelings about exams. Assigned counsel received fifty dollars whether they held or waived the exam. The uncertainties introduced by the visiting judges could best be avoided by waiving the exams. Adversarial attorneys, however, preferred to hold exams in most cases, even in the face of financial incentives to waive them. The general atmosphere of adversariness produced by such attorneys forced all attorneys to hold exams frequently. However, preliminary exams did not account for most felony defendants screened at the early stages in Detroit. The prosecutor's warrant section performed this function. We estimate that about 44 percent of potential felony defendants arrested by the police did not get to the trial stage, either because of warrant screening or dismissal at the preliminary hearing.

SUMMARY

Our data provide some striking but clear answers to the questions we posed at the beginning of this chapter. The most probable disposition for defendants in some cities is not conviction but dismissal. Defendants return to the streets because the courtroom workgroups dismiss charges against them. Neither race, nor charge, nor evidence, nor bail status alone determines which defendants go free. Rather, differently structured workgroups responding to their own incentives apply unique standards. In Chicago, the policeman and the victim had the most influence in determining who goes free. In Baltimore, defendants represented by the public defenders, who stayed as long as anyone in the unstable workgroups there, more often received a disposition in the preliminary hearing courtroom. Prior record and seriousness of the charges also had some effect. But over 60 percent of the defendants were held over for trial simply because of the structure of the Baltimore courtroom workgroups. In Detroit, the prosecutor screened out cases in which the victim was likely to fade away after a short time, or which the prosecutor himself deemed insufficiently important. That screening occurred before cases entered court; thereafter, few were screened out except by formal proceedings in which for some reason the evidence proved insufficient to sustain further proceedings.

Consequently, courtroom workgroup structure and context play crucial roles in determining the character of these early proceedings. They also have an important effect on later proceedings, because all the cases sent forward by the preliminary hearing courtrooms become the input of the trial courtrooms.

NOTES

1. In 1965, the President's Crime Commission estimated that, of the 467,000 adults apprehended for serious crimes in that year, only 30,000 were convicted. President's Commission on Law Enforcement and Admin-

istration of Justice; *The Challenge of Crime in a Free Society* (Washington: Government Printing Office, 1967), pp. 262–263. See also Isaac D. Balbus, *The Dialectics of Legal Repression* (New York: Russell Sage Foundation, 1973), pp. 73, 145, 212.

2. Herbert Garfinkel, "Conditions of Successful Degradation Ceremonies," *American Journal of Sociology* 61 (1956): 420–424; Maureen Mileski, "Courtroom Encounters," *Law and Society Review* 5 (1971): 530.

3. The occasional daytime arraignments were squeezed in between other proceedings. They happened so quickly and inconspicuously that inattentive observers would not even know they occurred.

4. This estimate is based on an analysis of arraignments for a week in the fall of 1972. The 1972 *Annual Report* of recorder's court indicates that 11,547 defendants in 1972 were given personal bond or a surety bond, or were remanded, although 11,838 defendants were arraigned. The missing 291 defendants, 2.4 percent of the total, probably were defendants allowed to plead guilty at arraignment.

5. See for instance, Charles Ares, Ann Rankin, and Herbert Sturz, "The Manhattan Bail Project," *New York University Law Review* 38 (1963): 68–70; "A Study of the Administration of Bail in New York City," *University of Pennsylvania Law Review* 102 (1954): 1035–1038; plaintiff's brief, *Roballo et al.* v. *The Judges and Justices of the New York City Criminal Court* (U.S. District Court, Southern District of New York), 74 CIV 2113 MEL, pp. 46–58.

6. The chief exception is that sometimes defendants are allowed to post bail at the station house if they can come up with the bail amount indicated. Bail is determined by a schedule based on the nature of the charges.

7. The mix of charges did not vary significantly from district to district and cannot explain the differences discussed here.

8. Personal interview.

9. A multivariate correlation analysis on bail amount produced R^2s ranging from .16 in Baltimore to .32 in Detroit. The low R^2s suggest that much of the variation in bail amount was random — that is, not associated with characteristics we measured — although those characteristics are the ones usually thought to be most closely related to the bail decision. The amount of explained variance accounted for by offense was 86 percent in Baltimore, 89 percent in Chicago, and 68 percent in Detroit. No other variable accounted for more than 10 percent of the variance, except in Detroit, where courtroom workgroups accounted for 20 percent.

10. The lower bail for murder than for armed robbery reflects the fact that in most murders no bail is set. When it is, strong extenuating circumstances exist, and the offense is viewed as "not so serious."

11. But neither variable in the context of others was determinative. See footnote 9.

12. Compare the portraits of robbers given by John E. Conklin, *Robbery and the Criminal Justice System* (Philadelphia: J. P. Lippincott, 1972), pp. 59–78 and of burglars given by Harry A. Scarr, et al., *Patterns of Burglary*, 2d ed. (U.S. Department of Justice, Law Enforcement Assistance Administration, June 1973), pp. 63–102.

13. A further complication in Chicago resulted from an Illinois Supreme Court ruling during the course of our research that a motion could only be made once during the course of a criminal proceeding. If successful at the preliminary hearing stage, it could not be reasserted at the trial stage. Hence, attorneys increasingly saved their motions for later proceedings, unless they felt certain that they could win release of their client through a motion in the preliminary hearing courtroom.

14. We are indebted to Janet Gilboy for these observations of narcotics preliminary hearing courtrooms in Chicago.

15. Janet A. Gilboy, "Perspectives and Practices of Defense Lawyers in Criminal Cases," unpublished Ph.D. dissertation, Northwestern University, June 1976.

16. This estimate is based on actual warrants issued in November 1972 (See *Annual Report of the Recorder's Court of the City of Detroit, Michigan, 1972*, p. 15) and our estimate that 39 percent of the warrant requests are denied.

17. The relationship between holding or waiving the preliminary exam and type of counsel was as follows for the defendants on whom we have these data:

	Type of Counsel		
	Public Defense	Assigned Counsel	Private
Held	59.2%	70%	69.9%
Waived	40.8	30	30.1
	100.0%	100%	100.0%
	N = 49	N = 170	N = 123

18. This finding supports the belief reported to us by defense counsel that if one were planning to plead guilty, one did not ask for a preliminary hearing.

Chapter 9

THE DECISION TO CONVICT

The scene is Room 702 in the Criminal Courts Building at Twenty-sixth and California on Chicago's southwest side. It is 2 o'clock in the afternoon. The courtroom workgroup began the day at 10 o'clock in the morning. After three cases were continued to another date, defense counsel, state's attorney, and judge retreated to the judge's chamber for a conference. They emerged when a private defense attorney appeared just before lunch to continue another case. The judge is now taking his place on the bench; the state's attorney and defense counsel stand before him, and a defendant comes from the counsel's table to join his attorney.

> THE COURT: Is the state ready to proceed?
> STATE'S ATTY.: The state is ready, your honor.
> THE COURT: Is the defendant ready to proceed?
> DEFENSE ATTY.: Yes, your honor. At this time the defendant wishes to withdraw his plea of not guilty, and enter a plea of guilty.

THE COURT: Is this a negotiated plea?

STATE'S ATTY.: Yes, your honor.

THE COURT: Mr. Donald Charles, the court cannot accept your plea of guilty to the charge of armed robbery as set forth in the complaint, without first informing you, and determining that you understand the consequences of your plea.

THE COURT: What is your name?

DEFENDANT: Donald Charles.

THE COURT: Is that your birth name, your proper name?

DEFENDANT: Yes, it is.

THE COURT: How old are you?

DEFENDANT: Twenty-three.

THE COURT: Mr. Charles, are you represented by a lawyer?

DEFENDANT: Yes, your honor.

THE COURT: Have you talked to your lawyer about your case?

DEFENDANT: Yes, your honor.

THE COURT: Mr. Charles, you are charged in indictment number 72-1880. It alleges that on or about September 10, 1972, at and within said county, Donald Charles committed the offense of armed robbery in that you intentionally, knowingly, took property from Robert Smith, by force, while armed with a dangerous weapon in violation of a state statute. Do you understand that?

DEFENDANT: Yes, your honor.

THE COURT: Now, your lawyer has advised me that you wish to withdraw your plea of not guilty and enter a plea of guilty. Is that your wish?

DEFENDANT: Yes.

THE COURT: Do you understand that you are entitled to be tried by a jury of twelve men and women who would determine your guilt or innocence, and by entering your plea of guilty you give up that right? Do you understand that?

DEFENDANT: Yes.

THE COURT: I have asked your attorney to have you sign a jury waiver in open court. Let the record show that a jury waiver has been signed by the defendant, Donald Charles. The jury waiver will be attached to and made a part of the record.

Mr. Charles, you understand that in addition to a jury

trial, which you have waived, you are entitled to have the judge determine your guilt or innocence? Do you understand that?

DEFENDANT: Yes.

THE COURT: And you also wish to give up that right, is that correct?

DEFENDANT: Yes.

THE COURT: I must also inform you that you have the right to have the state attempt to prove this case as required by law, a right to offer evidence on your own behalf, and a right to cross-examine the state's witnesses. Do you understand that?

DEFENDANT: Yes, sir.

THE COURT: Furthermore, that by your plea of guilty you give up your right not to testify and your right not to incriminate yourself. Do you understand that?

DEFENDANT: Yes, your honor.

THE COURT: I must further inform you that on your plea of guilty to this charge of armed robbery, I could fine you $10,000 or more or imprison you in a penal institution for an indefinite period, but not less than four years; or I could do both — that is, I could fine you and sentence you to a penal institution. Do you understand that?

DEFENDANT: Yes, your honor.

THE COURT: Now, Mr. Charles, we — that is, your attorney, the state's attorney, and myself — have had a pretrial conference out of your presence and off the record. Do you understand that?

DEFENDANT: Yes, your honor.

THE COURT: And I take it that this conference was with your consent?

DEFENDANT: Yes.

THE COURT: Do you understand that you are not bound by that conference?

DEFENDANT: Yes.

THE COURT: What is your recommendation Mr. State's Attorney?

STATE'S ATTY.: We recommend that the defendant be incarcerated for a period of six to ten years.

THE COURT: And what is your recommendation, Mr. Stohl [defense attorney]?

DEFENSE ATTY.: Your honor, we recommend the defendant be placed on probation.

THE COURT: Now, Mr. Charles, I have indicated in the conference with your attorney and the state's attorney that I would dispose of this matter by sentencing you to a term of four to six years in the state penitentiary. Do you still wish to pursue your plea of guilty?

DEFENDANT: Yes, your honor.

THE COURT: Mr. Charles, do you understand that you have the right to plead not guilty and you have the right to persist in that plea?

DEFENDANT: Yes.

THE COURT: Has anyone threatened you, to get you to say you are guilty?

DEFENDANT: No.

THE COURT: Mr. Charles, has anyone forced you, to get you to say you are guilty?

DEFENDANT: No, your honor.

THE COURT: Has anyone promised to reward you, to get you to say you are guilty?

DEFENDANT: No, your honor.

THE COURT: Are you making this plea voluntarily, as a result of your own decision, after discussing the matter with your attorney?

DEFENDANT: Yes, your honor.

THE COURT: Now, Mr. Charles, what is your plea to the offense of armed robbery?

DEFENDANT: Guilty, your honor.

THE COURT: All right. Enter a plea of guilty to the complaint. Is the state prepared to proceed in the stipulation?

STATE'S ATTY.: Yes, your honor.

[*State's attorney recites into the record the facts in the case.*]

THE COURT: Mr. Charles, do you still wish to plead guilty?

DEFENDANT: Yes, your honor.

THE COURT: On the plea of guilty there is a finding of guilty, and there is a judgment on the finding of guilty.

Courtroom workgroups repeat such scenes thousands of times each day throughout the United States. The details vary, but the ritual is essentially the same. The guilty plea ceremony may take anywhere from two to twenty minutes. It occurs far more frequently than jury or judge trials.

Because trial workgroups must make final dispositions, they operate under quite different conditions than the preliminary hearing workgroups. Their input is different, the options available to them differ, and the frequency with which they specialize differs. Trial courtroom workgroups process defendants sent them by the preliminary hearing courtrooms via the grand jury or, as in Detroit, by an information issued by the prosecutor; they also process a few cases coming directly from the grand jury.[1] Usually, defendants already have been given bail hearings and have been categorized as eligible or ineligible for a public defender. Often they have appeared several times before the preliminary hearing courtroom; by the time they reach the trial courts, they wear the stamp of criminal defendants.

Survival through the prior processing — even when the screening is not very stringent — marks these defendants' cases as serious. Evidence against them sufficed to overcome the potential challenge of the preliminary hearing and (where applicable) the grand jury's scrutiny. Prosecutors or judges deemed the matter serious enough to send it forward. In all likelihood, complaining witnesses persisted. Almost everyone perceives trial defendants as being in serious trouble.

Trial courtrooms cannot simply send defendants forward as the preliminary hearing courtrooms did. They must decide on a final disposition — one that is final except for possible reversal on appeal. But the trial workgroups nevertheless have several options. They may dismiss, acquit, or convict defendants. Dismissals may occur on a variety of grounds. Evidence may turn out to be insufficient because of a challenge to the legality of its seizure, because witnesses fail to appear, or because the witnesses no longer remember the details of the incident clearly enough. At other times, workgroups dismiss cases because of procedural irregularities, such as violation of a time limit or the prosecution's failure to provide required information to the defense. When defendants are not dismissed, however, they must be acquitted or convicted. Convictions may come through guilty pleas in ceremonies like the one we have described, or they may occur through a trial. Some are bench trials, held before a judge alone; he hears the evidence and decides guilt or innocence. Others — the decided minority — are jury trials, in which the jury decides guilt or innocence while the judge presides and decides matters of law.

Finally, trial courtrooms differ from preliminary hearing courtrooms in the degree to which they specialize in particular kinds of cases or sorts of tasks. Trial courtrooms mostly are *less* specialized. They hear all kinds of felony cases and may use any of the dispositions generally available. But exceptions exist; in some jurisdictions, particular courtrooms specialize in hearing motions, dismissing cases or receiving guilty pleas; in others, certain offenders are channeled to particular courtrooms.

DIFFERENCES IN DISPOSITIONS

Courtroom workgroups in the three cities produced remarkably similar dispositions, although the methods they used to reach their dispositions differed substantially. As Table 9.1 shows, the trial courtroom workgroups convicted approximately the same proportion of defendants in each of the three cities.[2] However, the similar numbers conceal substantial differences. One must remember that Baltimore trial courts processed largely unscreened cases sent them by the district courts and the grand jury. By contrast, 40 percent of felony arrests had been screened out by Detroit courts, and 85 percent had been pruned by the Chicago preliminary hearing courtrooms. Consequently, Baltimore convicted a higher proportion of felony arrests than either of the other cities.[3] But in the trial courtroom itself, the conviction rate for the three cities was essentially similar.

The trial courtroom workgroups arrived at these results in quite different manners. Detroit workgroups operated faster than workgroups in the other two cities. They completed their processing in less than two months for half their cases. By contrast, Baltimore workgroups took almost six months for the median

TABLE 9.1 TRIAL COURTROOM DISPOSITIONS
FOR FELONY DEFENDANTS

	Baltimore[a]	Chicago[b]	Detroit[c]
Defendants sent to trial, which court convicted	68.0% (N = 549)	75.5% (N = 519)	72.2% (N = 1,202)
Median number of days between grand jury indictment or information and trial courtroom disposition	178 (N = 459)	151.5 (N = 626)	56 (N = 1,114)
Median number of days between arrest and trial courtroom disposition	226 (N = 451)	267.5 (N = 604)	71.2 (N = 1,114)
Disposition methods			
guilty pleas	34.7%	61.7%	63.9%
bench trials	33.9%	19.9%	6.8%
jury trials	9.4%	6.7%	7.3%
dismissals	22.0%	11.7%	22.0%
	100.0% (N = 549)	100.0% (N = 519)	100.0% (N = 1,208)

a. Unweighted file sample.

b. Indictment sample used except for estimates of disposition time which is based on combination of indictment and information samples.

c. Trial court sample.

case, and Chicago courtroom workgroups required almost five months. Notice that these are median figures; many cases in each of the cities took much longer to process. Indeed, when one adds the time that preliminary hearing courtrooms required, the differences between the cities become larger, and Chicago becomes the slowest city.

Finally, Table 9.1 shows differences between the three cities in disposition method. Again, the differences are substantial. Chicago and Detroit relied primarily on guilty pleas, whereas Baltimore processed more cases through trial than through pleas.

Both Baltimore and Chicago courtroom workgroups used bench trials more frequently than did Detroit. Workgroups in all three cities shunned jury trials; even in Baltimore, jury trials accounted for fewer than 10 percent of all trial courtroom dispositions. Finally, the use of dismissals is remarkably similar in the three cities. We expected a higher dismissal rate in Baltimore, because of the failure of Baltimore district courtrooms to winnow cases. But Baltimore trial courtrooms did not apply a more severe screen either. Only Chicago trial courtroom workgroups used dismissals somewhat sparingly, but they did so after the severe culling that occurred at earlier stages.

These data make it clear that the principal activity of trial courtroom workgroups is to convict. Very few defendants win acquittals. If they leave the trial courtroom free, they are more likely to be the beneficiaries of dismissals than of acquittals. Yet, because one-quarter to one-third of all felony defendants at the trial level avoid conviction, we must ask how the courtrooms distinguish between the guilty and innocent or between the guilty and the unconvictable. In addition, because the length of time that charges hang over a defendant's head may be a significant sanction by itself, we need to ask why workgroups dispose some cases quickly while others linger for months and months.

CASE AND DEFENDANT
CHARACTERISTICS AS EXPLANATIONS
OF DISPOSITION TIME,
DISPOSITION MODE, AND CONVICTION

Our data permit us to test some of the hypotheses that have been offered to explain the time, technique, and outcome of dispositions. Several of the explanations introduced in Chapter 1 are especially amenable to testing. One concerns the characteristics of defendants. Some observers of criminal dispositions have alleged that the more affluent defendant who is out on bail induces his attorney to procrastinate so that evidence will grow weaker as the memory of witnesses dims. Moreover, such defendants presumably ask for bench or jury trials more frequently, because their attorneys can be paid adequately and because they are not part of the courthouse negotiation cabal. By contrast, poorer defendants — especially those in jail — want quick dispositions, because they want to get out of jail — either to go free or to go to the penitentiary (where conditions are often better than in the local jail) — and because they can at least begin serving their time. Because of the desire of jailed defendants for quick dispositions, because public defenders cannot risk trials and courthouse regulars cannot afford them, poorer defendants are said to plead guilty more frequently. They are supposed to be the chief consumers of so-called bargain justice.[4]

Traditional legal factors offer another possible explanation of outcomes. In this view, defendants' fates depend on the nature of the evidence against them. If the evidence establishes guilt beyond a reasonable doubt, the defendant will be convicted. As the evidence weakens, the likelihood of conviction decreases. If the strength of evidence controlled whether convictions were obtained, it also would be associated with disposition mode. Very weak cases would be dismissed; questionable cases would go to trial; strong cases would usually be disposed by a guilty plea.

A third explanation combines elements of the first two. While every offense must be proved "beyond a reasonable doubt," the statutory provisions of the criminal code require varying kinds of evidence that make some crimes easier to prove than others. This variation may affect how quickly cases are processed and the kind of evidence needed to produce convictions. Since the penalties associated with various offenses differ markedly, the calculations surrounding the choice of disposition mode can also change as the nature of the charge changes. Differences in the characteristics of defendants who commit various crimes might also produce differences in outcomes to the extent that these characteristics themselves are relevant.

A fourth factor's effect on case outcomes can be tested with our data — the identity of the courtroom workgroup. Although we used the judge's name to define this variable, we are not measuring the effect of the judge alone. Because judges do not move from courtroom to courtroom, the judge's name was a convenient way to identify the courtroom workgroup and to test the

FIGURE 9.1 Regression on Number of Days from Arrest to Disposition by Selected Characteristics Showing the Relative Contribution of Variables to Total Explained Variance.

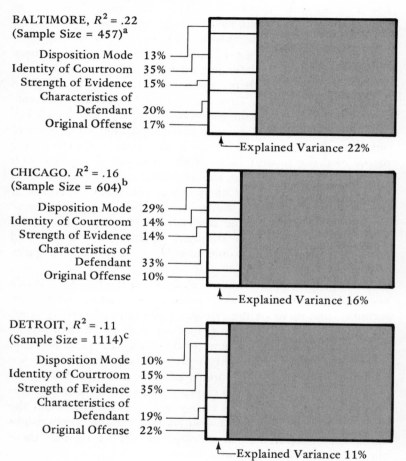

BALTIMORE, $R^2 = .22$
(Sample Size = 457)[a]

Disposition Mode	13%
Identity of Courtroom	35%
Strength of Evidence	15%
Characteristics of Defendant	20%
Original Offense	17%

Explained Variance 22%

CHICAGO. $R^2 = .16$
(Sample Size = 604)[b]

Disposition Mode	29%
Identity of Courtroom	14%
Strength of Evidence	14%
Characteristics of Defendant	33%
Original Offense	10%

Explained Variance 16%

DETROIT, $R^2 = .11$
(Sample Size = 1114)[c]

Disposition Mode	10%
Identity of Courtroom	15%
Strength of Evidence	35%
Characteristics of Defendant	19%
Original Offense	22%

Explained Variance 11%

[a]File–sample defendants disposed at trial court level.

[b]Indictment and trial court observation sample.

[c]Trial court observation sample.

importance of differences between workgroups in shaping dispositions.

Disposition Time. Most of the variance in disposition time occurs between rather than within cities. Consequently, there is less left to explain in analyzing each city separately as we do in Figure 9.1, and we are able to account for only a small portion of the remaining variance: 22 percent in Baltimore, but only 11 percent in Detroit.

Each of the variables we used accounts for some of the variance in the three cities; none dominates. In Baltimore, the identity of the courtroom is the most important variable; the weakness of sponsoring organizations permits considerable variation in the operation of individual courtroom workgroups. In Chicago, defendant characteristics are the most important variable; bail status (an indicator of relative wealth) worked as hypothesized — those on bail waited longest for their dispositions. In Detroit, strength of the evidence was the most influential variable, because, in cases with weak evidence, defense counsel refused the proferred plea and insisted on a separate hearing on their evidentiary motions. If they lost the motion, their client could still plead guilty or ask for another date for a trial. By contrast, in cases with strong evidence, many defendants took the plea offered at the pretrial hearing and entered their plea that same afternoon.

Although the Chicago data provide weak support for the hypothesis that defendant characteristics are an important determinant of the speed of dispositions, the data from other cities do not. And even the Chicago evidence provides only weak support, because defendant characteristics account for only a third of the 16 percent of the variation that we can account for. These data make it clear that none of the variables in Figure 9.1 — alone or in combination — account for differences in disposition time.

Disposition Mode. Table 9.2 displays the same kind of analysis for the decision to plead guilty rather than choose a trial of some sort. Again our analysis explains only a small portion of the variance — ranging from 9.2 percent in Detroit to 18.5 percent in Chicago (as indicated by the canonical correlation

TABLE 9.2 THE RELATIONSHIP BETWEEN
THE DECISION TO PLEAD GUILTY
AND SELECTED CASE CHARACTERISTICS[a]

	Baltimore	Chicago	Detroit
Canonical correlation squared	.148	.185	.092
Improvement in ability to predict (Tau)	30%	43%	40%
Relative contribution of discriminating variables:			
Original offense charged	28%	50%	20%
Characteristics of defendant	8%	9%	11%
Strength of evidence	40%	15%	47%
Identity of courtroom	24%	26%	22%
	100%	100%	100%
	(N = 299)	(N = 462)	(N = 724)

a. Multiple discriminant function analysis with variables forced in order of
presentation above. Defendants whose cases were dismissed were excluded from
the analysis, and remaining defendants were classified as "pleaded guilty" or
"did not plead guilty." Relative contribution of discriminatory variables is measured by Rao's V: see page 186.

squared.) In the portion of the variation that we can explain,
defendant characteristics play a uniformly small role. In two
cities, strength of the evidence is the principal explanatory variable; in the third (Chicago) the original offense charged accounts
for half of what we can explain.

Many observers of criminal courts allege that courts use
guilty pleas resulting from plea bargains because of their heavy
case load.[5] Our data do not support that contention. Baltimore
courtrooms — which disposed only one-third of their cases by
guilty pleas — had 671 defendants per courtroom on the average
in 1972. Chicago courtrooms — which used guilty pleas twice as
often — had 307 defendants per courtroom. Detroit, with the

same guilty plea rate as Chicago, had the heaviest courtroom work load: 735 defendants per courtroom.[6] These data indicate that there is no clear relationship between courtroom work load and use of guilty pleas.[7]

We may also examine the choice made between bench and jury trials when defendants refused to plead guilty. The differences among the three cities in the use of the two modes of disposition are again substantial. In Baltimore, only one-fifth of all defendants not pleading guilty or dismissed opted for a jury trial; in Chicago, it was one-fourth. But in Detroit, more than half such defendants asked for a jury trial.

Figure 9.2 shows our statistical analysis of that choice in each of the three cities. The characteristics of defendants once more play a minor role. But the analysis reveals quite different patterns for the three cities. In Baltimore, most of the decision hangs on the original offense charged; some offenses were tried much more frequently before a judge, whereas others went more often before a jury. The weight of the evidence and the identity of the courtroom made up most of the rest of the explanation. Altogether, these variables accounted for 31 percent of the variance and permitted a 54 percent improvement in our ability to predict correctly which kind of trial would be chosen. In Chicago, the analysis hinges entirely on the nature of the offenses, but it accounts for only 5 percent of the variance and permits only a 27 percent improvement in our ability to predict. In Detroit, most of the explanatory power lies in the identity of the courtroom; the rest is divided between the offense charged and the defendants' characteristics. The weight of the evidence plays no role. The analysis accounts for almost half the variance and permits a 56 percent improvement in prediction.

Conviction. Although workgroups in the three cities convicted about the same proportion of defendants sent to trial courts, the cases sent up by preliminary hearing courtrooms differed markedly. In Baltimore, little prior screening had taken place, so some really weak cases remained for the trial workgroups to dispose of. In Chicago and Detroit, prior screening had eliminated most questionable cases; the defendants who remained were perceived by the trial workgroups to be serious threats to

FIGURE 9.2 The Relation Between the Decision to Choose a Bench Trial Over a Jury Trial and Selected Characteristics[a] Showing the Relative Contribution of Variables to Total Discriminating Power.

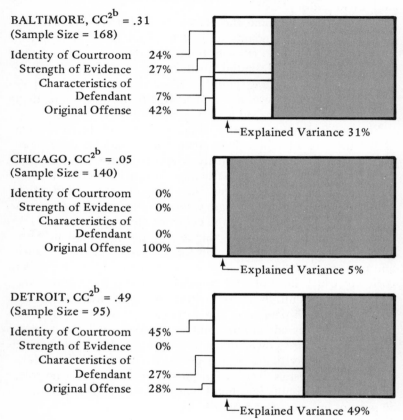

BALTIMORE, CC^{2b} = .31
(Sample Size = 168)

Identity of Courtroom	24%
Strength of Evidence	27%
Characteristics of Defendant	7%
Original Offense	42%

Explained Variance 31%

CHICAGO, CC^{2b} = .05
(Sample Size = 140)

Identity of Courtroom	0%
Strength of Evidence	0%
Characteristics of Defendant	0%
Original Offense	100%

Explained Variance 5%

DETROIT, CC^{2b} = .49
(Sample Size = 95)

Identity of Courtroom	45%
Strength of Evidence	0%
Characteristics of Defendant	27%
Original Offense	28%

Explained Variance 49%

[a]Multiple discriminant function analysis with variables forced in reverse order of presentation above. Defendants whose cases were dismissed or who plead guilty were excluded from the analysis. The samples used were: Baltimore, weighted file sample; Chicago, random indictment plus observational trial courtroom sample; Detroit, observational sample. Relative contribution of variables to total discriminating power is measured by Rao's V. Improvement in ability to predict was 54 percent in Baltimore, 27 percent in Chicago, and 56 percent in Detroit.

[b]Canonical Correlation Squared.

public order and welfare. Consequently, it is not surprising that different variables explain the decision to convict in the three cities.

As Figure 9.3 indicates, defendant characteristics explain much of the explainable variance for the decision to convict in Baltimore, but not in the other two cities. Defendant characteristics account for 55 percent of our ability to discriminate between conviction and acquittal in Baltimore, but about 10 percent in the other cities. In Baltimore, almost all of the discriminatory power of defendant characteristics is due to the effect of bail status; those who are released are more likely to win acquittal than those in jail. This was not true in the other cities. Moreover, neither in Baltimore nor in the other cities did other defendant characteristics have a significant effect on acquittal or conviction. Prior criminal record had its effect, if at all, in the preliminary hearing courtrooms. The many allegations of racism, and the inadequacy of public defenders, would lead one to expect that blacks and clients of public defenders are convicted more often than whites or clients of retained attorneys. Our multivariate analysis, which holds the effects of other variables constant, suggests that this was not the case. Nor were workgroups systematically biased against defendants according to their age. Other factors were more important for the defendants who got as far as the trial courts.

In Chicago, original offense discriminated most clearly between convictions and acquittals. Certain charges almost automatically led to acquittal; others led to conviction. That variable alone accounted for two-thirds of the discriminatory power of all the variables. On the other hand, in Detroit, the identity of the courtroom and the strength of the evidence played large roles. This difference reflects considerable variation in conviction rates from one courtroom to another; it also reflects the importance of strong evidence in some cases and not in others in Detroit.

Summary. If one knows something about a defendant's characteristics, the evidence, the charge, and the identity of the courtroom that processed his case, how well can one predict case outcomes? In other words, how well does this information,

FIGURE 9.3 The Relation Between the Decision to Convict or Acquit and Selected Characteristics[a] Showing the Relative Contribution of Variables to Total Discriminating Power.

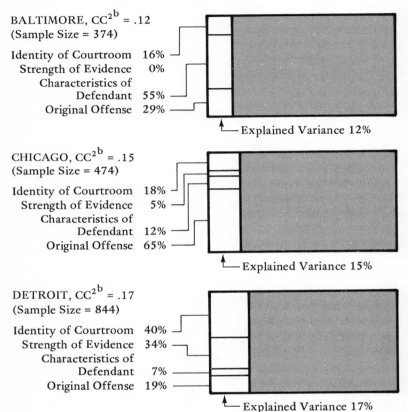

BALTIMORE, CC^{2b} = .12
(Sample Size = 374)

Identity of Courtroom	16%
Strength of Evidence	0%
Characteristics of Defendant	55%
Original Offense	29%

Explained Variance 12%

CHICAGO, CC^{2b} = .15
(Sample Size = 474)

Identity of Courtroom	18%
Strength of Evidence	5%
Characteristics of Defendant	12%
Original Offense	65%

Explained Variance 15%

DETROIT, CC^{2b} = .17
(Sample Size = 844)

Identity of Courtroom	40%
Strength of Evidence	34%
Characteristics of Defendant	7%
Original Offense	19%

Explained Variance 17%

[a]Multiple discriminant function analysis with variables forced in reverse order of presentation above. Only defendants who were convicted or acquitted were included. The samples used were: Baltimore, weighted file sample; Chicago, random indictment sample plus observational trial courtroom sample; Detroit, observational sample. Improvement in our ability to predict (Tau) was 32 percent for Baltimore, 42 percent for Chicago, and 43 percent for Detroit.

[b]Canonical Correlation Squared.

which forms the basis of many traditional explanations of case outcome, actually help in understanding what happens to defendants?

The analysis just described is multifaceted. We discussed the effect of four sets of variables for three outcomes (disposition mode, disposition time, and ultimate outcome) in three cities. Within the rich array of data produced, several general trends emerge.

By far the most significant finding is that using all of these data in combination, we are unable to make very good predictions. We do best in predicting whether defendants in Detroit who neither pleaded guilty nor had the charges dismissed would be tried by a jury or by a judge (49 percent of the variance is explained). But few defendants fell into this category. In most instances, we could account for only 10 to 20 percent of the variance in outcomes. Thus, defendant characteristics, evidence, the original charges, and the identity of the workgroup are related to outcomes, but not very strongly.[8] Contrary to popular rhetoric and some research, a defendant's race, age, bail status, wealth (as measured by the kind of attorney he has), and prior criminal record did not determine outcomes. Likewise, the identity of the workgroup, the strength of the evidence, and the nature of the original charge provide only limited — though real — help in understanding outcomes.

Another conclusion about these variables (keeping in mind their limited overall ability to explain outcomes) is that all had some effect on some outcomes under certain circumstances. For instance, characteristics of defendants in Chicago were best able to explain how long it took for a case to be disposed. Bailed defendants' cases took longer there. The nature of the charges lodged affected whether defendants in Baltimore and Chicago opted for a bench or jury trial, and whether Chicago defendants were convicted or not. The strength of the evidence affected whether Detroit defendants chose a jury trial or bench trial, and whether they and their Baltimore counterparts pleaded guilty or not. Knowing the courtroom that disposed a case helped explain whether Detroit defendants were convicted and how long Baltimore defendants' cases lingered.

The most general characteristic of the felony dispositions these relationships reveal is the intricacy of the process. Variables interact in many different ways. No simple or single explanation is possible.

The felony disposition process is intricate in part because defendants' traits, case characteristics, and legal provisions affect case outcomes in the context of interactions in courtroom workgroups. Thus, a defendant's characteristics do not directly shape outcomes. Those characteristics are perceived by workgroup members; they shape outcomes only as they affect participants' behavior. Because these variables are mediated through workgroups, it is essential to review their structure in each of the three cities along with the contexts in which they operated.

WORKGROUPS AND PLEA BARGAINING

The structure of workgroups had a direct effect on the incidence and character of plea bargaining.[9] Negotiations are by necessity a group activity. As we have already noted, the composition of bargaining groups varied markedly from city to city. The characteristics of courtroom workgroups and the context in which they operated can help us understand the variations in plea bargaining that existed in these three cities.

Workgroup Familiarity. As we suggested earlier, workgroup familiarity is a key variable in the structure of courtroom organizations. When members know each other well, they can take into account each other's idiosyncracies, norms, and habits. They can understand the pressures imposed by the sponsoring organizations of other participants. They can reduce uncertainty by negotiating with each other, because they know whom they can trust and with whom they must deal at arm's length. They can exchange favors or accommodations, because they know they will be dealing with each other for a long time. However, these behaviors cannot occur when workgroups are composed of strangers.

Wide differences existed in the stability of trial courtroom workgroups in the three cities. Two measures of these differences are shown in Table 9.3. The first applies to defense counsel. In Baltimore and Detroit, defense attorneys rotated from courtroom to courtroom. But in Chicago, the attorney with the most clients in each courtroom represented an average of 30 percent of defendants, between four and five times the figure for Baltimore and Detroit. The second measure reflects prosecutorial assignment policies. Baltimore prosecutors were less likely to stay in one courtroom, whereas in Chicago and Detroit a single assistant prosecutor usually handled about half of the defendants.

These figures confirm what we would expect from the descriptions in chapters 4 through 6. The Baltimore practice of reassigning cases to an "open courtroom" if the scheduled courtroom was busy, led to the formation of workgroups composed of unfamiliar participants. In addition, instead of a single public defender for each courtroom, numerous attorneys paid by the public defender operated in each. Some of these attorneys were

TABLE 9.3   MEASURES OF COURTROOM
WORKGROUP STABILITY IN BALTIMORE,
CHICAGO, AND DETROIT TRIAL COURTS

	Baltimore	Chicago	Detroit
Mean percentage of defendants in each courtroom represented by defense attorney who handled the *most* defendants	8	30	6.4
Mean percentage of defendants in each courtroom prosecuted by assistant state's attorney who handled the most defendants	22	48	45

full-time public defenders, whereas others were private lawyers assigned to a particular indigent's case. Defense lawyers also had limited opportunities to cluster cases in favorite courtrooms, because the Baltimore courts used a central case assignment procedure. Finally, the state's attorney's office assigned assistants to trial teams. Though nominally assigned to a courtroom, trial team members followed their cases all over the courthouse after the frequent breakdown of their courtroom's docket.

By contrast, Chicago public defenders remained in their assigned courtrooms along with two or three assistant state's attorneys. Retained defense attorneys were often able to cluster their cases. In Detroit, prosecutors worked in a single courtroom, whereas defense attorneys went to whatever courtroom came up in the blind draw.

Judges also had shorter tenure in the Baltimore courtrooms than in the other cities. In Baltimore, judges rotated through the criminal bench every year. The chief judge in Chicago assigned jurists to the criminal division for an indefinite tenure, which usually lasted more than two years. Detroit judges were elected to Recorder's Court for six-year terms, and many judges won reelection; hence they became almost permanent fixtures in their courtrooms.

Table 9.4 summarizes the structural differences that determine courtroom familiarity. But we need to consider other factors as well. As we asserted in Chapter 2, intermittent interaction over several years produces the same level of familiarity and reduces uncertainty as much as more intense interaction over a shorter period. The lower turnover among both judges and prosecutors in Detroit than in Chicago and Baltimore increased familiarity among workgroup members. In addition, we observed that the more defense attorneys specialize in criminal cases, the more likely they are to acquire a working knowledge of the personal characteristics of prosecutors and judges. In Baltimore, our evidence showed that defense work was concentrated among a slightly smaller set of defense attorneys than in the other two cities.[10] Finally, the extent to which defense attorneys share information about prosecutors and judges also affects how long it takes participants to learn about one another. Both the physical

TABLE 9.4   SUMMARY OF FACTORS
AFFECTING COURTROOM WORKGROUP STABILITY
IN BALTIMORE, CHICAGO, AND DETROIT

	Turnover of Assistant State's Attorneys	*Tenure of Judges on Criminal Court*	*Method of Assigning Defendants and Defense Counsel and Courtrooms*
Baltimore	highest	1-year rotation	Last-minute reassignment to "open" courtroom if scheduled court is filled; public defender (and assistant state's attorney) follow defendant.
Chicago	moderate	indefinite, usually 2 to 3 years	Chief judge assigns defendants to courtrooms; retained counsel able to "cluster" cases in certain courtrooms; public defender remains in one courtroom and represents indigents assigned to it.
Detroit	lowest	6-year term; frequent reelection	Strict random draw; difficult to transfer case from "blind draw" judge; defense counsel (including assigned counsel and public defender) follow defendant.

layout of the courthouse and local tradition facilitated informa-
tion-sharing much more in Detroit than in Baltimore or Chicago.

   In sum, Baltimore workgroups were much less stable than
those in the other two cities. Defense attorneys were less likely
to be familiar with the judges sitting on the Criminal Division of
the Supreme Bench in general and the prosecutor and judge in

any particular case. The annual circulation of judges in and out of the criminal court and the rapid turnover among assistant state's attorneys reduced the likelihood of familiarity.

Another characteristic of courtroom workgroups introduced in Chapter 2 is the dependence of one workgroup member on another. The higher the proportion of dispositions accounted for by the same set of participants, the more interdependent they become. Even defense attorneys who practiced almost exclusively in Detroit Recorders' Court appeared only sporadically in any one courtroom and were responsible for a small fraction of a courtroom's cases. Mutual dependence and reciprocal influence were consequently much lower in Detroit than in Chicago. In Chicago, both public defenders and retained regulars appeared consistently before the same judge, worked with the same prosecutors, and accounted for more of the case load. On the other hand, there was greater mutual dependence in Detroit than in Baltimore, especially since assistant prosecutors in Detroit mostly remained in one courtroom.

These differences in workgroup familiarity and mutual dependence, we believe, were closely associated with the frequency of plea bargaining. Guilty pleas are almost always the product of negotiations. The prosecution and defense must communicate with one another in an atmosphere minimizing uncertainty in order to conduct negotiations. There must be little uncertainty about the expected behavior and intentions of the other side and about the likely outcome in terms of sentence. Furthermore, each party's incentives must impel him to prefer a bargained plea to the alternative dispositions, even if the conditions for negotiations are met.

Baltimore workgroups lacked both the preconditions and the incentives for bargaining. Courtroom workgroups there were the least stable. In a high proportion of cases, the principal members of the courtroom organization were unfamiliar with each other's behavior and intentions. Procedures for assigning cases compounded the uncertainty. It was often impossible to tailor bargains to the preferences of the judge, because no one knew who the judge would be. Even when the identity of the judge was known, his or her response to a bargain was less predictable than where courtroom organizations were more stable. Furthermore, the courthouse's physical layout and case assignment procedures did not provide prosecution and defense with convenient opportunities to negotiate before the day of disposition. They did not encounter each other regularly as in Chicago, and were not able to rely on a formalized bargaining session as in Detroit. Thus, both prosecution and defense in Baltimore had to prepare for trial, since they could not safely rely on obtaining a satisfactory plea bargain. Having invested time and effort into preparing for trial, neither side was able to reap the savings provided by pleas that their counterparts in Chicago and Detroit could. This further reduced the incentives to plea bargaining.

By contrast, the stability of courtroom workgroups in Chicago facilitated negotiations and hence guilty pleas. The same prosecutors and public defenders (and often private counsel) worked with a single judge for months at a time. Cases almost never migrated from one courtroom to another. They were docketed in the courtroom and given a trial date several months away. During the interim, prosecutors and defense counsel had frequent opportunities to talk about the case and negotiate informally. On days the case was formally docketed, each side knew what would be happening; at a mutually agreeable time, they requested a conference with the judge if a guilty plea was possible. That conference formally committed the judge to a precise sentence bargain. Under these circumstances, uncertainty about the outcome could almost be eliminated. Neither side needed to prepare for a trial until negotiations had failed. Both sides often knew whether a trial date would result in a guilty plea or a trial. These circumstances optimized the conditions for plea negotiations.

Detroit produced a high guilty plea rate under different conditions. Plea bargaining occurred outside the courtroom in the pretrial conference for every case. The three assistant prosecutors there negotiated with defense counsel. They knew which judge the case had been assigned to; they usually knew each other. They constituted a stable out-of-court workgroup, which promoted plea negotiations.

About half of the pleas entered in Detroit can be attributed directly to the pretrial conference.[11] But many defendants adopted the strategy pursued by our hypothetical defendant, and initially refused the plea offered at the pretrial conference. Although courtroom workgroups were not as stable as in Chicago, external forces (described in Chapter 6) often produced a common interest in disposing cases. The pleas offered at the pretrial conference served as a starting point for negotiations conducted within the courtroom between defense and prosecution. Often, the initial plea offered was finally accepted, but more lenient pleas sometimes emerged.

The same structural characteristics also help explain the high preference for bench trials in Baltimore and Chicago and the favoring of jury trials in Detroit. In Baltimore, bench trials became a functional equivalent to the guilty plea; they were sometimes called a slow plea. Prosecutors and defense counsel presented their evidence to the judge hastily; the formal trial was interspersed with off-the-record remarks which presaged the outcome. Such slow pleas helped reduce uncertainty in the same way negotiations did in Chicago and Detroit, though to a lesser degree. They excluded unpredictable jurors; they permitted participants to proceed with considerable informality and with minimal preparation. Informal exchanges between counsel and with the judge softened the formal adversarial process. All participants, but especially the judge, had far more control over the proceedings and outcomes than in a jury trial. The high conviction rate in bench trials gave assistant prosecutors reasonable assurance that the process would produce a conviction. Defense attorneys felt bench trials provided better opportunities to minimize the sentences of guilty defendants. Finally, the size of the docket gave Baltimore workgroups an additional incentive to prefer bench trials. Sixty-eight percent of all indicted defendants remained for disposition after guilty pleas and dismissals. It would have been difficult to handle the work load if they had had to conduct jury trials for most of these remaining defendants. Jury trials required more preparation; they took at least one full day instead of the hour to two of the normal bench trial. Thus, to produce the dispositions expected of prosecutors and judges and the income required by defense counsel, the workgroups chose bench trials for 80 percent of the cases going to trial.

Chicago courtroom workgroups preferred bench trials for some of the same reasons. The workload incentive did not exist since most defendants pleaded guilty. Only 26 percent of Chicago's trial level defendants remained after guilty pleas and dismissals. But because of the highly stable workgroups, Chicago bench trials considerably reduced uncertainty, even when the defendant insisted on a trial. All the participants knew each other; only witnesses introduced uncertainty. Many judges conducted bench trials with considerable flexibility. If not all witnesses were present on one day, the judge adjourned the trial until another day. Some judges talked about the trial in chambers with defense counsel and prosecutors; others in chambers participated in these discussions about ongoing cases. Judges also interrupted bench trials to hear motions or take guilty pleas in other cases. All this activity permitted counsel to learn how things were going during the trial and to steer it to an acceptable outcome in many instances. Although bench trials could be very formal, ritualistic proceedings, they often assumed the characteristics of a slow plea.

Conditions were quite different for Detroit workgroups. The two-stage plea bargaining process plus dismissals left only 14 percent of trial defendants for disposition, a small enough proportion to remove most of the docket pressures that predisposed Baltimore workgroups to favor bench trials. Detroit's workgroups also exhibited less familiarity and cohesion than Chicago's, weakening the gain in uncertainty reduction that bench trials offered. By contrast, positive incentives to ask for a jury trial existed. Many judges strongly believed in a defendant's right to a jury trial and did not seek to discourage them either overtly or covertly. A larger portion of the Detroit defense bar (both private and the defenders) expressed a strong commitment to adversarial dispositions. When their clients did not plead guilty, they felt inclined to go "all the way." Finally, the widespread perception that juries, which included many black members, viewed black defendants favorably encouraged jury trials. The result was that half of the defendants who remained after guilty pleas and dismissals received a jury trial.

Summary. Both choices, guilty plea over trial and bench trial over a jury trial, appear to be closely related to two organizational characteristics of courtroom workgroups in the three cities:

the familiarity among them and the incentives motivating their behavior. Familiarity produced pleas, because with familiarity negotiations reduced uncertainty. Production and financial incentives as well as uncertainty reduction promoted bench trials in Baltimore. When trial courtroom workgroup members were less familiar, and when incentives for bench trials were missing, jury trials became more prevalent — as in Detroit.

WORKGROUPS AND THE DECISION TO CONVICT

Workgroup characteristics also help explain the differing significance of defendant characteristics, original charge, and evidentiary strength in the three cities. The organizational context gives meaning to the complex relationships described earlier.

As Figure 9.3 revealed, in Baltimore defendant characteristics contributed most to our ability to discriminate between convicted and nonconvicted defendants. The entire effect came from one variable: whether the defendant was out on bail or in jail at the trial date. Jailed defendants received convictions more often. They pleaded guilty more than bailed defendants, and they were convicted more often when they went to a bench trial. In the other two cities, bail status had virtually no effect on outcomes.[12]

The interaction of workgroup characteristics and general features of Baltimore's felony disposition process produced this bias.[13] First, more defendants were "eligible" for differential treatment, because Baltimore freed fewer of its defendants. Long delays in disposing cases intensified the pressures on these persons to escape conditions in the Baltimore City Jail by pleading guilty. Second, judges enjoyed wide lattitude in their courtrooms. They were not constrained by a strong sponsoring organization. Unstable workgroups and members' lack of familiarity with one another gave judges more influence over outcomes than they had in more cohesive workgroups in the other cities. Third, these judges generally held conservative views toward crime and criminals. Differences in outcomes between courtrooms, as evidenced by the modest contribution of the "identity of courtroom" variable, were not great, lending support to the proposition that Baltimore workgroups responded in similar ways. Finally, their decisions reflected the bias toward jailed defendants and the characteristics associated with their jail status. Dismissals, which depend at least in part on judges' preferences, were granted to more than twice the proportion of bailed than jailed defendants (29.8 percent versus 12.8 percent). Decisions in bench trials, made without the intrusion of a jury, freed 29 percent of bailed defendants but only 14 percent of jailed defendants.

In Chicago, original offense accounted for most of the ability to discriminate between convicted and unconvicted defendants. Defendants charged with heroin delivery or theft were far more likely to be convicted than those charged with murder, assault, or rape.[14] Knowing which courtroom organization disposed a case contributed only 18 percent of the power to discriminate. As in Baltimore, courtroom organizations did not differ much in their propensity to convict, despite their relative autonomy from sponsoring organization control, which created the potential for distinctive patterns. As in Baltimore, judges displayed similar attitudes, which helped create uniformity of conviction rates. It was much more helpful to know what the defendant was initially charged with than which courtroom workgroup handled his case if we wanted to predict whether he was convicted or not. For the most part, Chicago's courtroom organizations handled like offenses similarly.

However, when we look at each courtroom separately, strength of evidence becomes distinctly more important than in the city-wide analysis; it increases from 6 percent of the predictive power to an *average* of 31 percent. This finding suggests that Chicago courtroom workgroups developed different responses to evidential strength. Some workgroups weighed it much more heavily than others. Such variation was possible in Chicago because the workgroups enjoyed considerable autonomy and developed enough stability to nurture distinct norms.

In Detroit, the importance of evidence strength was consistent with the adversarial tendencies of defense attorneys there. As we noted earlier, they were likely to insist on a preliminary hearing, and these hearings were usually quite formal and relatively long. The attorneys who insisted on preliminary exams also usually asked for trials when evidentiary strength became conspicuously important. At trial, they often made motions attacking the prosecution's evidence.

The importance of courtroom identity in Detroit reflects other characteristics of the workgroups. Detroit judges shared decision-making less than judges in Chicago and somewhat more than those in Baltimore. Courtroom workgroups were weaker in relation to sponsoring organizations, but Detroit judges represented a wider social and political spectrum than Baltimore or Chicago judges. They were sharply divided in their attitudes toward defendants and the proper balance between the protection of society on the one hand and the rights of defendants on the other. These divisions were reflected in wide variations in the conviction rate from one courtroom to another in Detroit, much wider than in the other two cities.

Moreover, Detroit courtrooms responded to different offenses in unique ways. When we analyzed all the courtrooms together as in Figure 9.3, offense charged had little discriminatory power, suggesting that either it was unimportant or that wide differences from courtroom to courtroom canceled each other out. Analyzing each courtroom in Detroit separately makes it clear that they canceled each other out. Instead of contributing 32 percent of the discriminating power (as in the citywide analysis with identity of courtroom eliminated as an explanatory variable) offense contributed an *average* of 44 percent to the ability to predict conviction or acquittal. We attribute this difference in the handling of offenses to judges rather than to other members of the courtroom workgroup, because of the dominant position of Detroit judges in the courtrooms as described on pages 137–139.

Our data support the centrality of courtroom organizations in still another way. When we performed the same multivariate analysis as in Figure 9.2 for each courtroom separately in the three cities, our ability to predict conviction or acquittal increased markedly. Those results are shown in Figure 9.4. Moreover, as our focus on courtroom workgroups predicts, the relationship between the variables we measured changes from one courtroom to another. In some, the original offense charged was most important; in others some aspect of defendants' characteristics was significant; in still others, the weight of the evidence enjoyed primacy. This analysis shows the least improvement for Detroit, because identity of the courtroom was the most important variable predicting conviction in Detroit; hence, when we control for it by analyzing each courtroom separately, our ability

FIGURE 9.4 Comparison of Discriminant Function Analyses for Entire City and for Individual Courtrooms in Each City.

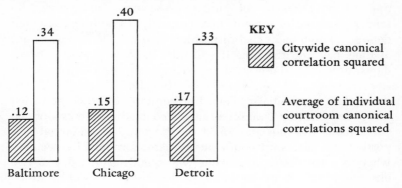

KEY

▨ Citywide canonical correlation squared

☐ Average of individual courtroom canonical correlations squared

to predict does not increase substantially. Individual courtroom organizations in Baltimore and Chicago are more distinctive, but for different reasons. In Chicago, distinctiveness resulted from differences in the mix of cases heard, the types of defendants encountered,[15] and the cohesiveness that emerged from the interaction of stable organization members. In Baltimore, courtrooms were distinctive because they were less stable and less constrained by the sponsoring organizations which sent them their principal personnel. As a group, they did not show marked differences in their responses to the various charges or to the attributes associated with bail status. But the specific mix of variables that affected conviction did show individual variation, just as the kind of disposition defendants chose varied by courtroom identity.

WORKGROUPS AND DISPOSITION TIME

As we noted earlier, enormous differences existed in the length of time a defendant stood in jeopardy of a conviction in the three cities. What took seven and a half and nine months in Baltimore and Chicago took a little over two months in Detroit for the median defendant. These differences are important, because all participants in the felony disposition process are sensitive to the length of time it takes to dispose cases. Pressures from the task environments of judges, prosecutors, and public defenders account for some of this sensitivity. In addition, retained defense counsel know that disposition time will affect the amount of their pay and the time it will take them to get it.[16] Defendants, especially those awaiting trial in jail, are often eager to resolve their case, if only to obtain a transfer to the better facilities a state penitentiary offers. Furthermore, the time at which things happen in a case often affects conflicting interests of the participants and thus may affect the outcome. A substantial proportion of a trial courtroom's energies are consumed by deciding when to make decisions. Anyone who spends even a day or two observing trial courtrooms in any of the three cities will be struck by the number of postponements. Although we did not specifically try to measure this phenomenon, we have fragmentary data that convey the prevalence of postponements. Our research assistants randomly assigned to Detroit trial courtrooms observed 788 defendant's cases called. Of these, 132 (16.8 percent) merely had their case adjourned, and another 76 (9.6 percent) appeared only to have a trial date set. Over one-third of Detroit defendants had one or more postponements indicated on their court files, and this certainly underestimated the actual number. In Baltimore, 23.8 percent of our defendants had a postponement indicated, and in Chicago the proportion was much higher.

However, the common administrative difficulties surrounding the scheduling of cases do not account for delay. Significant differences existed among the three cities. An analysis of variance on the mean number of days from arrest to courtroom disposition for thirty-four courtrooms in the three cities confirms the magnitude of intercity differences. They are significant at the .001 level, and the ratio of explained variance (between city variation) to total variance in mean length of case is .81.[17]

These differences are consistent with the organizational context in which the courtroom workgroups operated in the three cities. A combination of factors facilitated rapid disposition in Detroit. They included provisions for prosecutorial screening of cases before issuing formal arrest warrants, a well-staffed and fairly experienced warrant screening section, a moderately effective preliminary hearing process with a mandated maximum of twelve days between arrest and the hearing, the pretrial bargaining conference, which facilitated obtaining pleas in a timely manner, and adequate judicial manpower provided by the state supreme court's "crash program" to reduce case backlog. Widespread concern with the condition of the docket and the size of the jail population encouraged most participants to use these mechanisms effectively. Finally, many defendants' attorneys were appointed, and consequently found it advantageous to speed disposition.

In Baltimore, the length of dispositions reflected the time required for cases to pass through the three separate steps in the disposition process. District court proceedings took at least two weeks and sometimes longer. Bringing charges through the grand jury required a month or more. After grand jury indictment, prosecutors and defense counsel were allowed a minimum of six weeks to prepare for trial. Often, attorneys won more time. Neither the judges' sponsoring organization nor the state's attorney's office had enough power to produce quicker action.

The snail's pace of felony cases in Chicago is ironic, because Illinois had a statutory rule that *required* final disposition of charges or the beginning of the trial within 120 days after arrest for jailed defendants and within 160 days for released defendants. In reality, even preliminary hearing proceedings often were not completed in that time span. Rather, those rules encouraged courtroom members to use the prescribed limits in their negotiations. Part of the "get-along, go-along" norm of many of the courtroom workgroups required defense counsel's acquiescence to delays that broke the "term;" in exchange, jailed defendants sometimes won their release. The state's attorney's office regarded losing a case because of the term's expiration as a sign of gross negligence on the part of the courtroom assistant; the assistant could be dismissed because of it. All members of the workgroup (except an occasionally recalcitrant defense attorney) worked to avoid such dispositions. We witnessed one case in which a trial began at 5 o'clock on the afternoon of the 119th day with testimony from a court reporter in order to avoid dismissal of the charges. Consequently, the principal effect of the term rule was to promote the release of some defendants who would otherwise have remained in jail pending final disposition of their charges. It clearly did not lead to speedy dispositions.

CONCLUSION

Trial courtrooms convicted approximately the same proportion of the defendants in each of the three cities. Did the differences in procedures and organization then have any effect? As our analysis shows, the answer is both yes and no. Baltimore trial courtroom workgroups managed their case load with a low guilty plea rate and convicted almost the same proportion of their defendants as in Chicago and Detroit. But different characteristics of the case were important in Baltimore. Baltimore was the only one of the three cities in which defendants who sat in jail before trial were penalized with a higher proportion of convictions. In each of the other cities, different combinations of characteristics accounted for the decision to convict, for the choice between guilty plea and trial, and for the choice of a bench trial or jury trial. This produced an extraordinarily complex decision process that cannot be neatly summarized in a single statistical equation.

Further, there were distinct differences in the length of time for felony disposition in each city. Detroit, with its management-oriented judges and prosecutor, organized the process so that half the cases were disposed in just over two months. In Baltimore it took three times as long; and in Chicago almost four times as long, with half the cases remaining undisposed after nine months had passed since the arrest. Such delays cannot be attributed to case load; both cities had lighter case loads than Detroit. Rather, they reflected the lack of external controls on the courtroom organizations and the structure of those organizations. Much of the delay was the result of courtroom members protecting each other's interests so that dispositions were not pushed if retained counsel had not been paid or if the prosecutor was unprepared.

As with preliminary hearing outcomes, differences between the three cities — and within them as well — reflected variations in the organizational structure of the courtroom workgroups. Where workgroup members were familiar with one another and the workgroups were stable (as in Chicago and Detroit), plea negotiations occurred frequently; where they were not (as in Baltimore), fewer guilty pleas appeared. But Baltimore workgroups could and did reduce uncertainty with bench trials. Detroit trial workgroups had a higher proportion of adversarial defense attorneys who made a greater use of jury trials in those few cases which were not pleaded. Another evidence of courtroom workgroups' significance was the variable effect of defendant characteristics, the strength of the evidence, and the nature of the offense on the decision to convict or acquit. Finally, the time it took to dispose cases reflected the environment in which the workgroups operated and the bargaining counters available to them.

NOTES

1. In a few instances, the grand jury votes indictments before an arrest is made; such defendants go directly to the trial courtroom.

2. The differences are not statistically significant for the sample sizes involved.

3. Of every hundred felony defendants arrested and passed on for further processing by the police, the actual number convicted of any crime at any stage was fifty-one in Baltimore, forty-three in Detroit, and twenty-three in Chicago.

4. Cf. Stuart S. Nagel, "The Tipped Scales of American Justice," in Abraham S. Blumberg (ed.), *The Scales of Justice* (Chicago: Transaction Books, 1970), pp. 31–49; and Dallin Oaks and Warren Zehman, "Lawyers for the Poor," in ibid., pp. 91–104.

5. See for example *The President's Commission on Law Enforcement and Administration of Justice, Task Force Report: The Courts* (Washington, D.C.: Government Printing Office, 1967), pp. 4, 10; and assumptions underlying recommendations to abolish plea bargaining in *National Advisory Commission on Criminal Justice Standards and Goals: Courts* (Washington, 1973), pp. 46–49.

6. The number of defendants per courtroom is based on the number reported in 1972 official reports. For Baltimore, see *Report of the States Attorney's Operations in the Criminal Court of Baltimore, 1972,* mimeographed, p. 1; for Chicago see *1972 Annual Report of Circuit Court of Cook County,* mimeographed; for Detroit see *Annual Report of Recorder's Court,* 1972, p. 11.

7. The same results are reported for Connecticut jurisdiction, both in the past and at present by Milton Heumann, "A Note on Plea Bargaining and

Case Pressure," *Law & Society Review* 9 (1975): 518–524; and by Malcolm Feeley, "The Effects of Heavy Caseloads," paper presented to the 1975 Annual Meeting of the American Political Science Association at San Francisco, Calif., September 5, 1975.

8. The modest association between our independent variables and case outcome deserves some comment. Without question an unknown but substantial amount of error is present in our analysis. We believe error introduced in the process of recording the data, keypunching, and creation of analysis variables is largely random. We are not so sure error attributable to incomplete or inaccurate information found in prosecutor and court records is random, however. Another problem is that we were simply unable to capture good information on key variables. This is especially true of evidence strength. Our measures, based on available information in prosecutor and court records, are extremely crude. We may know whether there were eyewitnesses to the offense, but we do not know how credible they are or how much they actually saw. Similarly, it is impossible to judge the validity of searches or the relevance of corroborating physical evidence. Some cases' outcomes are determined by factors entirely extraneous to those measured by our independent variables. For instance, dismissal may result from the defendant's conviction on another case or the refusal of a witness to testify. Such reasons are not consistently reported in court or prosecutor records. The strength of the relationships measured may also be depressed by combining in our analysis outcomes from the various courtroom organizations within each city. We will return to this point shortly. Finally, some independent variables that affect outcomes have already exerted their influence by the time cases reach trial court. Cases in which the evidence is especially weak are often eliminated at the preliminary exam. In Baltimore, we found that district court judges used the defendant's record as one of the two criteria for deciding whether to dispose a case or pass it on to the grand jury. It is not surprising to find prior record has little bearing on trial courtroom dispositions. Those cases in which prior record is most likely to shape the outcome have already been taken out of the system.

9. Our emphasis on workgroup structure as an explanation of plea bargaining is in some respects like Blumberg's emphasis on the social context of plea negotiations; see Abraham Blumberg, *Criminal Justice* (Chicago: Quadrangle, 1967). Our emphasis, however, differs substantially from most previous discussions of plea bargaining, which typically focus on an individual participant (such as judge or prosecutor) or unspecified elements of the workgroup structure. Cf. Albert Alschuler, "The Prosecutor's Role in Plea Bargaining," *University of Chicago Law Review* 36 (1968): 50–112; David W. Neubauer, *Criminal Justice in Middle America* (Morristown, N.J.: General Learning Press, 1974); and Donald J. Newman, *Conviction: The Determination of Guilt or Innocence Without Trial* (Boston: Little, Brown, 1966).

10. Although our disposition sample in Baltimore was smaller than in the other two cities, 31 percent of defendants were represented by an

attorney who also represented more than ten other defendants in the sample; in Chicago the proportion was 26 percent and in Detroit 23 percent.

11. This figure was obtained by analyzing *when* guilty pleas were entered. Any plea accepted within a week of the pretrial conference was assumed to result directly from the conference itself. In fact, most of these pleas were entered on the day of pretrial. The 50 percent figure corresponds closely with the estimate given to us by one of the two judges who had (prior to September 1972) handled all pretrials.

12. The relationship between bail status and case outcome in Baltimore is summarized in the following tables:

	Jail	Bail		Jail	Bail
Not convicted	20.3%	41.3%	Jury trial	12.2%	5.6%
Convicted	79.7%	58.7%	Bench trial	32.7%	35.1%
	100%	100%	Guilty plea	42.3%	29.4%
			Dismissed	12.8%	29.8%
				100%	99.9%
	$N = 207$	$N = 259$		$N = 196$	$N = 248$

In Chicago the equivalent tables are:

	Jail	Bail		Jail	Bail
Not convicted	22.2%	27.5%	Jury trial	8.7%	6.6%
Convicted	77.8%	72.5%	Bench trial	15.7%	19.7%
	100%	100%	Guilty plea	62.4%	55.3%
			Dismissed	13.2%	18.4%
				100%	100%
	$N = 301$	$N = 317$		$N = 287$	$N = 304$

The equivalent tables for Detroit are:

	Jail	Bail		Jail	Bail
Not convicted	21.7%	29.3%	Jury trial	11.1%	5.9%
Convicted	78.3%	70.7%	Bench trial	7.9%	6.8%
	100%	100%	Guilty plea	65.6%	63.8%
			Dismissed	15.4%	23.4%
				100%	99.9%
	$N = 253$	$N = 774$		$N = 253$	$N = 774$

13. However, the general literature on bail led us to expect Baltimore's results in all the cities. See especially Ann Rankin, "Effects of Pretrial Detention," *New York University Law Review* 39 (1964): 641–655; Charles

Ares, Ann Rankin, and Herbert Sturz, "The Manhattan Bail Project: An Interim Report on the Use of Pre-trial Parole," *New York University Law Review* 38 (1963): 67–92, and the "Plaintiffs' Memorandum on the Merits" in the New York Legal Aid Society's suit challenging the constitutionality of the bail system in *Johnny Roballo, et. al.* v *The Judges and Justices of the New York City Criminal Court, et. al.* For a summary of other studies which relate bail status to outcome, see Daniel Freed and Patricia Wald, *Bail in the United States: 1964*, Report to the National Conference on Bail and Criminal Justice (Washington, D.C.: 1964), pp. 46–47.

14. The percentages convicted for these offenses are: heroin delivery, 92%; theft, 86%; murder, 48%; assault, 60%; and rape, 51%.

15. When individual courtrooms are compared according to the proportion of cases heard which fall into each offense category, the range and standard deviation for Chicago and Baltimore courtrooms are considerably greater than those of Detroit.

Percentage:	Baltimore			Chicago			Detroit		
	mean	S.D.	range	mean	S.D.	range	mean	S.D.	range
Assault charge	7.5	5.6	20	8.6	7.4	22	7.5	2.5	8
Armed robbery	24.8	9.1	32	21.3	12.5	33	12.6	5.6	22
Burglary-theft	19.8	5.1	32	16.7	9.7	32	25.5	6.0	17
Murder	5.9	3.3	10	13.2	8.2	29	3.9	2.4	9

Chicago also shows more variation on case characteristics between courtrooms, including the proportion of defendants released, the number with no prior record, and the nature of defense counsel. Clearly the mix of cases found in Chicago varies more from courtroom to courtroom than in either Baltimore or Detroit.

16. For a fascinating study of defense counsel, see Albert W. Alschuler, "The Defense Attorney's Role in Plea Bargaining," *Yale Law Journal* 84 (1975): 1181–1206. See also Abraham Blumberg's classic article, "The Practice of Law as a Confidence Game," *Law and Society Review* 1 (1967): 15–39.

17. This measure is known as *eta squared* and reflects the amount of variance in the number of days from arrest to disposition in the thirty-four courtrooms that is accounted for by differences in the three cities.

Chapter 10 | SENTENCES AND OTHER SANCTIONS

Criminal courts do more than decide which defendants to convict and which to release.[1] They also mete out a range of punishments. In the name of the state, courts may deprive offenders of their liberty and property. But the task environments in which courtroom workgroups operate and the organizational characteristics of the workgroups themselves severely constrain their authority to invoke sanctions.

CONSTRAINTS AND SOURCES OF FREEDOM IN THE SANCTIONING DECISION

The task environment of courtroom workgroups conditions their use of authority to punish. Two elements of the task environment are particularly important: the legislature as the source and definer of sanctioning authority, and public opinion as the context in which workgroup members develop expectations about punishment.

Legislatures pass laws that both authorize and limit sanctions. Imprisonment, supervision, and fines are the normal punishments authorized by American law. In 1972 the death penalty was not available in Illinois, Maryland, or Michigan.

Imprisonment is the most visible sanction. Criminal statutes generally indicate the length of time that an offender may be incarcerated if he is convicted of particular offenses. Typically, criminal codes associate particular sentences with particular crimes, but usually the law does not specify the exact length of incarceration. Instead, legislatures provide a range from which judges may choose. In some states, courts may impose both a minimum and maximum sentence; in others they may set only the maximum. In either case, the number of years a court metes out to a convict is limited by the statutes. The court also determines where the convict is to be sent. Sentences of less than a year usually mean the local jail; longer sentences generally send the prisoner to the state penitentiary. If an offender is convicted of several crimes, he may receive a sentence for each of them. Statutes generally permit courts to impose these additional sentences concurrently or consecutively. Concurrent sentences are all served at one time; in the case of consecutive sentences, after one sentence is completed, the convict must begin serving the next.

Statutes also permit courts to sentence convicted defendants to supervision in place of or in addition to imprisonment. Supervision takes several forms. The court may suspend the sentence for a certain period of time. If the offender gets into trouble again, the suspension is lifted and the sentence executed; if he stays out of trouble, the sentence is without effect. Greater supervision occurs when the convict is placed on probation. He generally must adhere to rules established by the probation department and must report to a probation officer periodically. Violation of the rules or failure to report may be grounds for lifting probation and imposing a prison sentence on the offender. A new arrest for another crime may also lead to revocation of probation.

Fines are usually imposed for minor offenses, but they are often available for serious offenses as well. They may be imposed in conjunction with prison terms or by themselves. The criminal code specifies the minimum or maximum amount of a fine for each crime, leaving the court free to impose the exact amounts.

The criminal codes thus provide three dimensions of punishment: prison sentences ranging from a day to life; supervision ranging from a day to many years in length and from no prohibitions to intense regulation and close supervision; and fines ranging from zero to several thousand dollars. Each sanction has a lower and upper limit; these limits vary according to the offense a person is convicted of. The legislature thus gives courtrooms considerable discretion in sentencing convicted defendants, but the law also imposes bounds that may not be exceeded.[2] No matter how heinous the circumstances, if the maximum penalty for a crime is five years, the court may not impose a sentence of ten years. In practice, however, the bounds are quite generous and do not impose severe limitations on courtrooms.

A second effect of the task environment emanates from public opinion about the purposes of sanctions and the norms that have developed concerning their use. Ambivalent expectations and understandings of the general public indirectly help to shape sentencing behavior.

Some people believe that sanctions are imposed for the purpose of rehabilitation. Rehabilitation means resocialization; the offender should learn to accept the social norms of the general public and adhere to them. Those who believe in the rehabilitative function of sanctions find it important to consider the offender's social background, his or her moral character, and the chance that he or she might reform. Such information will also guide them in choosing the kind of facility to which they send the convict (if there is a choice). Their expectation is that when the offender has been rehabilitated, he or she will be released and begin a productive and law-abiding life.

A contrary understanding is that sanctions should punish, in order to deter the offender from committing another crime or to deter others who hear about the punishment from committing a crime. Persons with this understanding place more emphasis on information about the offense than about the offender. The severity of the sanction (and perhaps its certainty) should serve the deterrent function. The length of incarceration should depend on what is needed to deter rather than the prisoner's readiness to lead a law-abiding life.

Still another view of sanctions is that they should prevent the occurrence of crimes by disabling the offender for a period of time. Imprisonment removes offenders from the streets; while they are in prison, they cannot commit new crimes on the general public. Temporary removal of some criminals is, therefore, thought to be the goal of the sentencing process.

Finally, some people believe that sanctions should function as retribution or as a socialized form of private revenge. In this view, criminals should be punished because they are bad and have injured innocent victims. The courts substitute authorized punishment for private vengeance.

None of these views has won a clear mandate in legislation or public opinion, although for many years the rehabilitative view was the dominant one. Some court personnel base their actions on one of these perspectives; many are guided by a pragmatic although inconsistent combination of several. In addition, many courtroom participants are guided by a feeling that sentences ought to be the same for equally heinous crimes or equally dangerous offenders. However, there is no simple way to operationalize the seriousness of the offense or the danger of the offender. Consequently, courtroom personnel are pulled in inconsistent directions by what they understand sanctions ought to do and by their commitment to equal treatment for all those who appear before them.

An additional element of discretion results from the fact that information about the effects of sentences is fragmented and inconsistent. Few of the people who work in the courtrooms follow the scholarly research on the consequences of imprisonment. Like the general public, court personnel are exposed to accounts in the popular press and on television. In addition, they see some defendants repeatedly over a number of years, even though those defendants have been sent to prison for rather long periods of time. They rarely encounter a rehabilitated ex-criminal, because such people do not come to court.

If judges, prosecutors, defense counsel, and probation officers did read the scholarly literature, they would not be much enlightened. Our present understanding of the consequences of a variety of prison programs is that they are equally ineffective.[3] Because people placed under supervision have very different backgrounds and have committed very different crimes than those sent to prison, comparisons between supervision and incarceration are usually invalid. Consequently, the court personnel involved in the sentencing decision have no reliable factual basis for preferring one sentence over another. That may limit rational decision-making, but it is a generous source of freedom for the decision-maker not concerned with the final outcome of the sentencing decision.

The organizational structure of the courtroom workgroup guarantees that those who contribute to the sentencing decision have little concern for the ultimate fate of defendants except in a few highly publicized cases. Neither the judge nor anyone else in the courtroom is held accountable for what happens to a convict after he enters a prison. Prisons rarely inform courtroom personnel when a prisoner is released, and unless he commits another crime in the same jurisdiction, no one in the original courtroom will know that he has become a recidivist. Only when convicts are released on supervision immediately after trial may the judge or other courtroom personnel be held accountable by the press if the offender commits another crime. On the other hand, there is no mechanism for publicizing successful supervision sentences and rewarding those who imposed them. Finally, most courtrooms and sponsoring organizations do not keep score of the sentences that are meted out. Neither judges nor assistant prosecutors are evaluated and promoted (or punished) for the sentences to which they contribute. However, defendants may informally evaluate defense attorneys by the success they reputedly have in avoiding severe sentences for their clients. Occasionally, unsuccessful defense counsel are also known by this trait; for instance, we ran across one attorney derisively called Statesville Charlie because so many of his clients were sent to the state penitentiary.

The organizational structure of the courtroom establishes other, severe constraints on the sentencing decision. Contrary to the protestations of many prosecutors and judges, sentences are collective decisions in which all participants have some influence. Defense counsel may have considerable influence over the sentencing decision.[4] Prosecutors normally have an even greater influence. Consequently the judge sometimes formally shares his decision-making powers with these persons and almost always finds his decision-making discretion constrained by their prior actions.

To a considerable degree, these constraints flow from the collective decision-making process leading to a guilty plea. In some jurisdictions, such as Chicago, the plea hinges on an agreement to a sentence. Most pleas are "on the nose" — to the offense originally charged. During plea negotiations the prosecutor and defense counsel agree on a sentence. Chicago judges normally participated in the bargaining and pledged a specific sentence contingent on the plea. In that situation, the judge was one of three participants in the bargaining session. He had more or less influence depending on his personality, but he rarely dictated the decision. In other cities (Baltimore and Detroit are among them), the plea bargain more often involved a reduction in the offense or the selection of a lesser offense among all those charged against the defendant. Conviction on a lesser offense normally constrained the judge to impose a less severe sentence; it almost always meant a lower maximum. In addition, plea bargains in Baltimore sometimes involved a pledge by the prosecutor to recommend a particular sentence. Past experience with the judge hearing the case gave the prosecutor and defense counsel a good idea of what sentence to expect in such circumstances.

Prosecutors and defense counsel also have considerable control over the information on which the judge may base his sentence. Especially when there has been no trial, the information they convey to him in chambers before sentencing or in formal proceedings (arguing aggravation or mitigation) may be the only knowledge he has of the case when he passes on the sentence. This is particularly true where, as in Chicago, defense counsel avoid presentence reports by waiving that "right," thus making the judge even more dependent on the attorneys than he would be otherwise. In Detroit, preliminary hearings are sometimes waived to keep gory details about a crime off the record and thus improve the defendant's chances for a light sentence.

Thus, the sentencing decision is a shared decision, announced from the bench but arrived at collectively. Although statutes generate some constraints, and public expectations produce an area of discretion, the organizational context in which the decision-makers operate set the real limits on the sentencing decision.

THE USES OF SANCTIONS

Our concern for defendants should not blind us to the possibility that sanctions may also be used by courtroom workgroups to facilitate maintaining their work routines. There is ample evidence that such is the case.

Sentences are sometimes used symbolically, to reward prosecutors and defense counsel. Observing those participants at sentencing proceedings, this use becomes apparent through their response to the sentence that is given. When a defendant receives a particularly light sentence, courtroom participants chalk it up as a victory for the defense counsel, a reward from the judge. That reward is likely to be useful when the attorney recruits additional clients. Unusually heavy sentences serve a slightly different function for prosecutors. They feel that their efforts have been rewarded, that they are appreciated by the judge. But the length of the sentence rarely plays a major role in the prosecutor's chances for promotion or his evaluation by supervisors. It simply provides symbolic satisfaction; especially long sentences are likely to be the subject of conversation for days thereafter.

An even more important use of sentences leads to the impression in many courtrooms that guilty pleas are rewarded by lighter sentences whereas an insistence on trial, especially a jury trial, results in a heavier sentence. This belief appears to be almost universally fostered in trial courtrooms, although in some instances it is stated less brazenly than in others. Many judges who talked to us in Baltimore, Chicago, and Detroit justified the differential in terms of the penance displayed by defendants who plead guilty; the judges insisted that such an attitude was the first step toward rehabilitation and should be rewarded. In addition, some judges indicated that a defendant who insisted on a trial and then appeared to perjure himself by insisting on his innocence in testimony should receive additional punishment for the perjury (although he was not tried or convicted of that offense). A few judges were forthright in indicating that they wanted to promote guilty pleas by offering lighter sentences; if there were no premium for guilty pleas, they feared that more defendants would insist on a jury trial with its attendant expense and consumption of court time.

At first sight, the data seem to support the belief that defendants convicted after a trial receive harsher sentences (Table 10.1). Mean sentences are longer for jury trials than for bench trials or guilty pleas. That finding supports the courthouse (as well as predominant social science) lore, although the difference between bench trial and guilty plea sentences is slight. However, when we take a closer look and consider not only the type of disposition but also the offense on which a person is convicted, his personal characteristics, the strength of the case against him, and the identity of the courtroom workgroup that sentenced him, the effect of dispositional mode is insignificant in accounting for the variance in sentence length. It accounts for as little as 3 percent, and at the most 7 percent, of the variance that can be accounted for by all these factors.*

That result should not surprise us, because guilty pleas are not a random sample of all cases. Rather there are distinct cir-

TABLE 10.1 MEAN LENGTH OF PRISON SENTENCE (IN YEARS) BY DISPOSITION TYPE IN THREE CITIES

	Baltimore		Chicago		Detroit	
Jury Trial	9.7	$(N = 43)^a$	13.8	$(N = 37)$	4.6	$(N = 35)$
Bench Trial	4.9	$(N = 299)$	2.9	$(N = 75)$	2.2	$(N = 24)$
Guilty Plea	4.8	$(N = 193)$	2.5	$(N = 361)$	2.1	$(N = 306)$

a. Numbers in parentheses indicate N on which mean is based. Analysis is based on all defendants who were convicted. In Baltimore we used the weighted file sample; in Chicago, the indictment sample; in Detroit, the observational sample.

* For a fuller discussion, see page 282 and Figure 10.2.

cumstances, as indicated in the previous chapter, which tend to select cases for guilty pleas or trial. More serious offenses more often went to trial; "dead-bang" cases were more likely to be pleaded. Moreover, characteristics of judges also affected the choice between guilty plea and trial. Judges known to prefer severe sentences were more likely to have trials, because defendants have little to lose if they insist on a trial. Light sentencers were likely to have more guilty pleas.

However, what is important is the impression that is left with court officials and defendants alike: that they give a premium for guilty pleas and impose the risk of a heavier sentence if defendants insist on a trial and are convicted. Court participants saw that impression as instrumental in promoting a steady flow of guilty pleas. Many of them believed that a contrary perception might substantially reduce the number of guilty pleas. Although empirically false, this impression was nurtured by the occasional heavy sentence after a jury trial or an exceptionally light sentence after a guilty plea.

Sanctions have another important function. Courts impose unauthorized punishment on the vast number of unconvicted defendants by requiring bail, by the need to hire an attorney, and by the threat of prison which hangs over those arrested. These sanctions are often imposed in conformance with the belief that even if defendants are not convictable (because of technical flaws in the cases against them), they are factually guilty and ought to receive some punishment. For example, a policeman who illegally stops and searches a "suspicious"-looking vehicle with "suspicious" occupants and finds illegal weapons concealed under the front seat may press charges even though a conviction is improbable. The defendants are guilty of possession of the weapons in a factual sense, but unless the officer is willing and able to lie convincingly (or the defense attorney convinces the accused to cop a plea), a conviction is unlikely. However, the officer and prosecutor who handle the case are aware that the very fact of prosecution results in some punishment. We suspect that other courtroom personnel also recognize these facts and condone or perhaps even encourage the punishment of the unconvicted to make certain that most persons arrested by the police receive some punishment. Such defendants are seen as being a little guilty, and receive punishment short of conviction or a prison sentence.

The punishment suffered by defendants jailed prior to their release is obvious, but even those who won pretrial release and were not convicted suffered punishment. Not only was the arrest a blot on their record that may follow them for years, but defendants were sanctioned more immediately and directly. We cannot easily measure the psychic costs or the damage to social relationships, but we can indirectly measure other dimensions of their punishment: the amount of time their case lingered in court, the amount of money they had to post for bail, the proportion who waited in jail while their case was being processed, and for two cities, the length of time unconvicted defendants were imprisoned before being bailed or having their charges dismissed. Table 10.2 presents these data. It indicates that in

TABLE 10.2 SANCTIONS IMPOSED
ON UNCONVICTED DEFENDANTS

	Baltimore[a]	Chicago[b]	Detroit[c]
Percentage not released on bail	38.1	19.2	33.8
Percentage of those released on bail who spent a week or more in jail	48.2	22.9	n.a.
Percentage with bond set at $5,000 or more	31.6	19.4	25.1
Median number of days from arrest to disposition	42.0	102.0	65.5
Estimated number of unconvicted defendants in 1972 or 1973	2,100	21,100	7,700

a. Based on weighted file sample. Total number of unconvicted defendants for 1973 obtained from internal report of the state's attorney's office.

b. Based on weighted preliminary hearing sample.

c. Based on Detroit sample adjusted to reflect proportion of dismissals at preliminary examination.

these three cities, between one-fifth and two-fifths of those not convicted never made bail; that a fifth to almost a half of those making bail spent at least one week in jail while attempting to raise their bail, and that the proceedings that had been initiated against them lasted on the average between one and a half and three and a half months. We are, of course, speaking of proportions and averages; some defendants escaped with lower costs, whereas others suffered considerably more.

We do not have direct data on attorneys' fees or bondsmen's fees paid by unconvicted defendants, but most of those who post bond or hire their own attorney undoubtedly find the costs difficult to bear. Retained counsel often charge a minimum of several hundred dollars.[5] Our data also reveal a costly choice for a number of unconvicted Baltimore defendants. There, over 30 percent of those not convicted were asked to post bail of $5,000 or more. They then had a choice of raising at least $500 for the bondsman's fee or sitting in the Baltimore City Jail. In Chicago considerably fewer facer a $5,000 or higher bond. Costs in Chicago were further reduced because defendants posted 10 percent of the face value of the bond with the court and received a rebate of 90 percent of this fee when their case was closed. In Baltimore and Detroit, defendants typically purchased bail from bondsmen who charged 10 percent of the required amount and kept it all. Ironically, what Chicago defendants saved in bail fees they often paid in attorneys' fees, since many of them agreed to assign their bail refund to their attorney as part of his compensation. Consequently, unconvicted defendants in the three cities who did not suffer pretrial detention often bore the considerable financial burden of posting bail, paying an attorney, or both.

Defendants who are not convicted but punished constitute a sizable group. In Chicago, where the courts coped with their work load principally by dismissing cases, released felony defendants numbered 21,000 by our estimate in 1972. At the other extreme, the smaller city of Baltimore with its lower screening rate had only approximately 2,100 released defendants one year later. Detroit had an estimated 7,700 released defendants in 1972. Standardizing these figures by the 1970 population, Chicago had the highest proportion of unconvicted defendants, 6.24 per thousand. Detroit's rate was 5.09 per thousand, whereas Baltimore's was 2.32 per thousand.

The law does not authorize punishment of unconvicted defendants, and the practice runs counter to the mores of the Anglo-American legal tradition. It occurs under the guises of requiring bail bonds to ensure the appearance of defendants, the necessity for legal representation in court, and the administrative convenience of keeping police records. None of these practices are designed as sanctions, although many people know that they have that effect. Little sympathy for the unconvicted but punished defendant existed in the courtroom workgroups we observed, because of the widespread belief that all defendants brought to court were guilty of something. Most courtroom regulars believed that the unconvicted were lucky to escape with such mild punishment; they grumbled about the technicalities and other circumstances that led to the release of these defendants. By imposing sanctions on the released, courtroom workgroups expressed their evaluation of these defendants' moral character.

THE DISTRIBUTION OF SANCTIONS TO CONVICTED DEFENDANTS

Workgroups reserved the most severe sentences for convicted defendants. However, as we already have seen, sentences were not limited to incarceration. Indeed, prison sentences were not always the most common sanction. In Detroit, most convicted defendants did *not* receive a prison sentence, but rather were fined or placed under supervision. In both Baltimore and Chicago, prison sentences were more common, but only three-fifths of the convicted defendants were sent to prison. No city routinely sent convicted defendants to prison.

Courtroom workgroups rarely imposed fines on felony defendants. Fines accounted for less than 5 percent of the sanctions in any of the three cities. There is nothing in the literature to indicate that they are widely used anywhere in the United States for felony convictions.

The data in Table 10.3 reveal another important difference. Baltimore relied heavily on suspended sentences, whereas Chicago and Detroit almost exclusively used probation for convicted defendants not sent to prison. Probation generally involved much closer supervision than suspended sentences, although a formal hearing is usually required to revoke it; a hearing may not be necessary to revoke a suspended sentence. In both cases, no new

TABLE 10.3   SENTENCES IMPOSED
ON CONVICTED DEFENDANTS

	Baltimore[a]	Chicago[b]	Detroit[c]	
Percentage of convicted defendants sentenced to prison	63.1	60[d]	34.8	
Percentage of convicted defendants not sentenced to prison	36.9	40	65.2	
Percentage of those not sentenced to prison given:			Felony Division[e]	Misdemeanor Division[f]
fine/restitution	3.9	1.5	2.6	39.2
suspended sentence	83.2	—	5.4	34.2
probation	12.9	98.5	92.0	26.5

a. Based on weighted file sample.

b. Based on weighted indictment and information samples and weighted preliminary hearing samples.

c. Based on observational sample and estimate of potential felony defendants prosecuted, convicted, and sentenced in misdemeanor division.

d. Includes an estimate of the proportion sentenced to prison after conviction in the preliminary hearing courtrooms. No such estimate was made for Table 3 of Jacob and Eisenstein, "Sentences and Other Sanctions in the Criminal Courts of Baltimore, Chicago, and Detroit," (*Political Science Quarterly* 90 [1975] : 624), which reports only the percentage of *trial* court–convicted defendants sent to prison.

e. Based on entire observational sample.

f. Calculated from Annual Report of the Recorder's Court of the City of Detroit, Michigan, 1972, statistics on the misdemeanor division.

crime needs to be proved; one only needs proof that the conditions of the release have been violated. As there are many more conditions associated with probation, it is much easier to go astray and be sent to prison despite the originally favorable sanctioning outcome. We do not have data about probation revocations in the three cities, although they occupy a prominent place on each city's court dockets every week. Nor should one conclusively declare probation to be more onerous than suspended sentences. Many probation departments are so overworked and understaffed that the supervision they impose is little more than an empty gesture.

Explaining which defendants obtain supervision and which are sent to prison is much more complex than one might guess. None of the cities had precise guidelines that could be followed by courtroom workgroups. Rather, the outcome depended on the course of the bargaining if there was any, on the apparent seriousness of the crime, and on the perceived degeneracy of the defendant. As Figure 10.1 shows, only 19 percent of the variance can be accounted for in Chicago, whereas 43 percent and 37 percent are accounted for in Detroit and Baltimore respectively; however, we can improve our predictive ability by about half the maximum possible. Figure 10.1 represents an analysis of all the "obvious" factors that might be thought to be significant in deciding whether to send a convict to prison or release him under supervision.

Although the proportion of convicted defendants sent to prison varies greatly among the three cities, the basis for making that decision appears nearly the same in the statistical analysis shown in Figure 10.1. Two of the six variables — original charge and identity of the courtroom — explain much of the variance in each of the three cities. In addition, defendant characteristics are important in Baltimore and Detroit, but not in Chicago. In Detroit most of the explanatory power of that variable comes from our bail indicator, reflecting a propensity in Detroit to give probation to convicted defendants who had won pretrial release and to send the rest to prison. Figure 10.1 also presents strong evidence that courtroom workgroups did not systematically discriminate against defendants who were convicted at a jury or bench trial as compared to those who pleaded guilty; disposition mode explains

FIGURE 10.1 The Relation Between the Decision to Sentence
Convicted Defendants to Prison and Selected Characteristics[a]

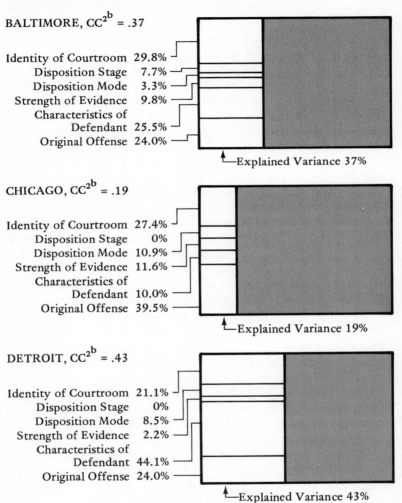

BALTIMORE, CC^{2}[b] = .37

Identity of Courtroom 29.8%
Disposition Stage 7.7%
Disposition Mode 3.3%
Strength of Evidence 9.8%
Characteristics of
Defendant 25.5%
Original Offense 24.0%

Explained Variance 37%

CHICAGO, CC^{2}[b] = .19

Identity of Courtroom 27.4%
Disposition Stage 0%
Disposition Mode 10.9%
Strength of Evidence 11.6%
Characteristics of
Defendant 10.0%
Original Offense 39.5%

Explained Variance 19%

DETROIT, CC^{2}[b] = .43

Identity of Courtroom 21.1%
Disposition Stage 0%
Disposition Mode 8.5%
Strength of Evidence 2.2%
Characteristics of
Defendant 44.1%
Original Offense 24.0%

Explained Variance 43%

[a]Multiple discriminant function analysis with variables forced in reverse order of
presentation above. Weighted file sample used in Baltimore; random indictment
sample plus observational trial courtroom sample used in Chicago; and observational sample used in Detroit. Improvement in predictive ability (Tau) was 57
percent in Baltimore, 45 percent in Chicago, and 63 percent in Detroit.

[b]Canonical Correlation Squared.

little of the variance for the decision to send convicted defendants to prison.

One important element that is not reflected in Figure 10.1 is the point of the queue at which a sentence is meted out. A defendant is not sentenced in a temporal vacuum. Courtroom workgroups produce sentences on a day or during a week in which other sentences are meted out. An armed robber sentenced after several murderers may do better than if his turn comes up after a series of concealed weapons offenders. We do not have systematic evidence about this queuing effect, but noticed it when we observed courtrooms. Further, sentences may become harsher when the press talks about a crime wave or after a particularly heinous crime; at other times — such as during the Christmas season — sentences are usually more lenient.

Our analysis accounts for much of the variance; our failure to account for more reflects the autonomous character of each courtroom organization. Felony sentences are not the product of a single organization, the criminal court. Rather they are the product of the many courtroom organizations. Each has somewhat different goals and operational norms. This within-city variation reduces our ability to explain the decision in the city as a whole, since characteristics that are more significant in one courtroom are less so in others.

The proportion of convicted defendants sent to prison varied widely from courtroom to courtroom in Baltimore and Detroit.[6] The significance of individual courtrooms becomes evident when we replicate the analysis in Figure 10.1 for each courtroom separately, something we can do for Baltimore and Detroit.[7] The analysis yields an average canonical correlation squared of .88 in Baltimore and .69 in Detroit, signifying that we can explain almost all of the variance in Baltimore courtrooms and more than two-thirds in Detroit with the same variables as in Figure 10.1 (excluding, of course, identity of the courtroom). These statistical analyses show that the Baltimore and Detroit courtrooms each had their own norms for making the choice between prison or no prison. In four of the Baltimore courtrooms, the decision hinged mostly on the weight of the evidence; but in two it depended mostly on the defendant's characteristics, and in one it hinged largely on whether the defendant pleaded guilty or took a bench or jury trial. In Detroit there were even greater differences from one courtroom to another, reflecting the diversity of the backgrounds and attitudes of the judges as described in Chapter 6. Three based the prison decision mostly on the original offense charged; three relied on whether the defendant pleaded guilty or took a trial. Two based the decision largely on the weight of the evidence against the defendant; one on the defendant's characteristics; and one courtroom weighted all the factors about evenly. In addition, we can account for less of the variance in Detroit, indicating that other, perhaps random, factors were also significant. These findings reinforce the importance of the individual courtroom workgroups; in both cities they displayed considerable individuality in the prison decision, as they did in many of the other decisions we have examined.

For defendants sent to prison, the key decision related to the length of their sentence. However, we should realize that the sentence pronounced in court is almost never the actual amount of time a convict expects to serve in American prisons. Regardless of whether the sentence is couched in terms of a minimum or maximum number of years, most prisoners win release earlier. They become eligible for parole after a portion of their sentence has been served; they may generally earn a reduction of their sentence by good behavior. As prisons are largely warehousing operations, the size of the "inventory" also helps to determine length of sentence. When the prisons are full, someone must be released for each new convict admitted. A sentence of fifty years is usually no longer than one of twenty-five years; even those given life sentences are generally eligible for parole after ten or fifteen years. However, the length of the sentence pronounced in the courtroom roughly establishes when a prisoner may expect to be freed on parole (assuming good behavior). In Chicago, for instance, a sentence of three years means eligibility for parole in two and three-quarter years. Everyone in the courtroom knows the "real" meaning of sentences; during plea negotiations in Chicago, the real meaning of the sentence is continually referred to in the effort to obtain the defendant's agreement.

Tables 10.4 and 10.5 show the distribution of sentences by offense originally charged for the three cities. Both the mean and the median are presented, because the distribution of the

TABLE 10.4 TRIAL COURT SENTENCES: MEDIAN AND MEAN MONTHS

Offense Originally Charged	Baltimore[a]			Chicago[b]			Detroit[a]		
	Mean	(N)	Median	Mean	(N)	Median	Mean	(N)	Median
Murder	155.8	(22)	102	129.0	(20)	96.0	95.3	(23)	69.6
Armed Robbery	105.1	(121)	84	57.4	(98)	48.6	46.1	(73)	35.3
Assault	77.6	(25)	81	25.0	(25)	15.3	23.6	(22)	14.1
Heroin Dealer	79.7	(52)	50	32.1	(17)	28.0	11.4	(8)	8.4
Heroin User	33.1	(12)	26	25.5	(4)	27.0	6.4	(17)	5.4
Burglary–Theft	52.6	(70)	46.5	16.1	(57)	16.0	15.6	(83)	12.1
Rape	83.7	(11)	48	56.0	(15)	52.5	91.2	(5)	46.5
Robbery	74.8	(41)	63.4	27.5	(26)	19.0	33.9	(10)	31.0
Weapons				21.1	(20)	17.1	9.3	(26)	7.5
Other	30.3	(25)	25.5	19.3	(24)	16.9	16.7	(94)	11.8

Note: Life sentences excluded from calculations.

a. Based on weighted file sample.

b. Based on indictment sample.

c. Based on entire sample.

TABLE 10.5 TRIAL COURT SENTENCES ADJUSTED
FOR PAROLE ELIGIBILITY: MEAN AND MEDIAN MONTHS

Offense Originally Charged	Baltimore[a]			Chicago[b]			Detroit[c]		
	Mean	(N)	Median	Mean	(N)	Median	Mean	(N)	Median
Murder	116.9	(22)	76.5	90.3	(20)	78.0	58.9	(23)	48.2
Armed Robbery	78.9	(121)	63.0	46.5	(98)	44.4	31.5	(73)	25.9
Assault	58.2	(25)	60.8	21.6	(25)	14.0	16.9	(22)	10.6
Heroin Dealer	59.7	(52)	38.0	29.4	(17)	25.7	8.4	(8)	6.3
Heroin User	26.1	(12)	21.5	23.2	(4)	24.5	4.9	(17)	4.1
Burglary–Theft	39.4	(70)	38.9	14.6	(57)	14.5	11.6	(83)	9.1
Rape	62.8	(11)	44.3	49.1	(15)	48.1	50.3	(5)	32.8
Robbery	56.5	(41)	47.8	25.1	(26)	17.0	24.3	(10)	22.9
Weapons				19.0	(20)	15.6	6.9	(26)	5.6
Other	22.7	(25)	19.1	17.5	(24)	15.5	12.3	(94)	8.8

Note: Life sentences excluded from calculations.

a. Based on weighted file sample.

b. Based on indictment sample.

c. Based on entire sample.

sentences is severely affected by a few long sentences. The data show considerable but not perfect agreement from city to city in ranking the offenses according to length of sentence. In all of the cities, murder, armed robbery, and rape was severely punished when a prison sentence was imposed; heroin use and property theft drew fairly light sentences in each city. Regardless of whether we look at the sentences as pronounced or as modified by probable parole eligibility, Baltimore imposed the most severe sentence, whereas Detroit defendants received the shortest prison terms.

Explaining the variation in sentence length by the nature of the offense charged, characteristics of the defendant, the strength of the evidence, the dispositional mode, the dispositional stage, and the identity of the courtroom produces more consistently satisfactory results than our earlier analysis of the decision to send a convict to prison. More than half the variance is accounted for by those variables. In each of the three cities, the original offense charged accounts for more of the variance than any other set of variables.

Figure 10.2 is most remarkable for what it does *not* show. The identity of the courtroom is not a significant explanatory variable except in Baltimore, where individual judges operated under the least constraint, either from the rest of the courtroom workgroup or from plea bargaining. Disposition mode — the manner in which a defendant was convicted — makes little difference when the other characteristics of his case are taken into account. Apparently, in these three cities, defendants convicted by a bench or jury trial were not given longer prison sentences than those who pleaded guilty. Nor did defendants receive a lighter prison sentence if they were convicted at the preliminary hearing stage rather than in a trial courtroom. The strength of the evidence also plays only a small role in explaining the length of the sentence in these three cities.

In addition, most personal characteristics of defendants were unimportant in determining sentence length. In all three cities, the defendant's race and prior criminal record had little effect.[8] Sentencing in these three cities was apparently both colorblind and free of class bias. Only in Baltimore did the kind of attorney significantly affect the length of the sentence, and only in Detroit

FIGURE 10.2 The Relation of Length of Sentence to Selected Characteristics[a]

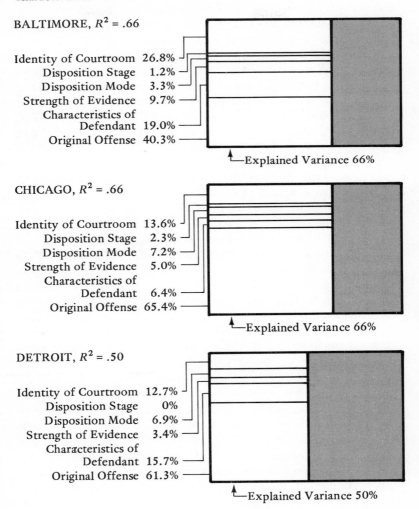

BALTIMORE, $R^2 = .66$

Identity of Courtroom	26.8%
Disposition Stage	1.2%
Disposition Mode	3.3%
Strength of Evidence	9.7%
Characteristics of Defendant	19.0%
Original Offense	40.3%

Explained Variance 66%

CHICAGO, $R^2 = .66$

Identity of Courtroom	13.6%
Disposition Stage	2.3%
Disposition Mode	7.2%
Strength of Evidence	5.0%
Characteristics of Defendant	6.4%
Original Offense	65.4%

Explained Variance 66%

DETROIT, $R^2 = .50$

Identity of Courtroom	12.7%
Disposition Stage	0%
Disposition Mode	6.9%
Strength of Evidence	3.4%
Characteristics of Defendant	15.7%
Original Offense	61.3%

Explained Variance 50%

[a]Stepwise multiple regression was used, forcing variables in reverse order of presentation above. The Baltimore analysis was based on a file sample of defendants sent to prison ($N = 191$); the Chicago analysis was based on weighted indictment and informational samples of defendants sent to prison ($N = 173$); in Detroit we used the entire sample of defendants sent to prison ($N = 256$). Life sentences were excluded. Sentence length (in months) was transformed by taking the natural logarithm.

did pretrial release make a small but discernible difference. The principal determinant of sentence length was the offense *originally* charged, even though in some cases the defendant was convicted of a lesser offense. The original characterization of the crime by police or prosecutors continued to have a decisive effect at the very last stage of the felony disposition process. When convicted, defendants were punished for the crimes they originally were thought to have committed. Patterns of punishment, however, are more complex than displayed by Figure 10.2. The total effect of race, bail, and type of attorney depends on their effect on earlier portions of the process.

We found race to have little effect on any portion of the felony disposition process that we studied. It is, of course, true that police arrest more blacks than would be expected by their proportion of the population. That may be the result of racial prejudice, but it may also simply reflect the greater propensity of blacks to commit the kinds of offenses for which police frequently make arrests. Our data do not permit a test of these alternative explanations. All we can say is that once defendants have been arrested, courtroom workgroups were colorblind in processing the cases against them.

Bail and pretrial release had a regular but unsystematic effect on final outcomes. In Baltimore, jailed defendants were somewhat more likely to be convicted, but once convicted, jail status did not have a strong effect on the likelihood of their imprisonment or the length of the sentence they might receive. In Chicago, pretrial release had little effect on any stage of the process. In Detroit, jailed defendants were not convicted more than those released. But when convicted, jailed defendants were more likely to be sent to prison, although the length of their prison sentence was not strongly related to their pretrial release status.

Bail status both indicates defendant wealth and has independent effects. The poorer a defendant is, the less likely he is to win pretrial release. But in addition, pretrial incarceration pressures defendants to plead guilty. It severs their social ties, which makes them higher probation risks; and coming to court from jail confirms the suspicions of the courtroom workgroup that they are dealing with a dangerous person. Given the potential power of these effects, we were surprised to find that bail had such an inconsistent effect in our analysis. We conclude that bail status did not determine ultimate punishment but that it did sometimes contribute to its definition.

Our other indicator of wealth — type of defense attorney — also had a complex effect. In terms of length of prison sentence, public defenders did better for their clients than other attorneys. Public defenders' clients generally received shorter sentences than defendants represented by private or assigned counsel. However, the conviction rate for public defenders was slightly higher than for other counsel. In terms of ultimate punishment, therefore, the effect of public defenders is ambiguous. Our evidence certainly does not support the charge that public defenders neglect their clients or that they sell their clients short. In fact, private attorneys in Baltimore appeared to penalize their clients substantially by taking more of their cases to trial courts, where their clients received more prison sentences than they might have in the district courts.

Thus, much of the sentencing disparity that other studies emphasize was apparently absent from these three cities. These findings also conflict with beliefs of courtroom participants. That inconsistency is, however, easily explained. Courtroom participants see only the cases that occur in their own courtroom and hear about the exceptional ones that occur in other courtrooms and enter the courthouse gossip mill. In telling us about sentencing decisions, participants dwelt on particular characteristics that were associated with the case — such as a long prior record, a high bail, or (much less frequently) the race of the defendant. Thus, the folklore of the courthouse developed from limited experience and exceptional cases; in none of the three cities did anyone collect and distribute a statistical report that might develop the broader perspective displayed in Figure 10.2.

We should emphasize that all of the variables commonly thought to be significant in affecting the length of the sentence account only for one-half to two-thirds of the variance. The effects of the queuing, measurement error, and random or unidentified factors account for the rest.

Our findings conclusively demonstrate the manner in which individual judges are constrained in their sentencing decisions. Those constraints also became evident from our observations of the courtrooms. Plea negotiations clearly limit the ability of the judge himself to affect the sentence arbitrarily. The courtroom workgroups, through their ongoing interactions among major participants, develop norms and expectations about sentences that constrain all the participants in any individual case. No defendant is sentenced out of context; the sentence he receives becomes part of the courtroom's norm. Workgroup members continuously compared defendants and cases with others that had been processed in that courtroom. Thus, the social organization in which courtroom participants operated limited the scope for arbitrary action as much as the law itself.

CONCLUSION

Sentences and other sanctions that defendants receive are the product of complex interactions within the courtroom workgroup as constrained by their task environments. Sentences were not arbitrarily handed down by the judge. They were not the singular product of backroom negotiations. Rather, they flowed from continuous interactions among courtroom personnel. Laws also set bounds to what sentences can be meted out, and prior agreements — especially in Detroit — affected what the judge and other courtroom personnel could impose.

Some room was undoubtedly left for judges' personal values, but not much.[9] Baltimore judges had perhaps the most room for discretion, because of the weakness of the courtroom workgroups and of the sponsoring organizations operating there. However, Detroit judges brought with them the greatest range of personal values; courtroom workgroups and the strength of sponsoring organizations inhibited them from displaying their personal values more.

Personal traits of defendants and characteristics of the felony disposition process were not consistently important. Defendant characteristics proved most significant for the decision to imprison in Detroit; it had little effect on length of sentence. Disposition mode had little effect on either decision.

Only the original charge and the identity of the city had much effect on the length of the sentence, and as with all the other major decisions we have examined, courtroom workgroups played a prominent role within cities. They generally overshadowed single actors such as the judge, prosecutor, or defense attorney.

NOTES

1. Some of the materials in this chapter were presented earlier in Herbert Jacob and James Eisenstein, "Sentences and Other Sanctions in the Criminal Courts of Baltimore, Chicago, and Detroit," *Political Science Quarterly* 90 (1975): 617–626.

2. In Michigan, it was the Supreme Court which prescribed that minimum sentences could not exceed two-thirds of the maximum.

3. Cf. Robert Martinson, "What Works — Questions and Answers About Prison Reform," *The Public Interest* (Spring 1974): 22–54; Gordon Tullock, "Does Punishment Deter Crime," Ibid., (Summer 1974): 101–111. Tullock is more sanguine about the deterrent effect of punishment than Frank Zimring and Gordon Hawkins, *Deterrence* (Chicago: University of Chicago Press, 1973).

4. The opposite view is taken by Ronald L. Goldfarb and Linda R. Singer, *After Conviction* (New York: Simon and Schuster, 1973), pp. 153 ff.

5. In Detroit, the average fee paid to appointed counsel was $181.94 according to the court's annual report for 1972, p. 13. Retained attorneys can hardly afford to charge much less, and probably charge substantially more. See the much higher estimates in Albert W. Alschuler, "The Defense Attorney's Role in Plea Bargaining," *Yale Law Journal* 84 (May 1975): 1183–1184.

6. The range was from 52 to 83 percent in Baltimore, and from 24 to 52 percent in Detroit.

7. We cannot do it for Chicago, because there are so few no-prison sentences that we do not have enough cases for a courtroom-by-courtroom analysis.

8. This finding is consistent with John Hagan, "Extra Legal Attributes and Criminal Sentencing: An Assessment of a Sociological Viewpoint," *Law and Society Review* 8 (1974): 557–583, who reanalyzes most prior studies. See also James L. Gibson, "Racial Discrimination in Criminal Courts: Some Theoretical and Methodological Considerations," mimeographed, n.d.

9. This conclusion like many of our findings conflicts with John Hogarth, *Sentencing as a Human Process* (Toronto: University of Toronto Press, 1971). The differences may be the result of quite different methodologies and locales. We do not have the attitudinal data Hogarth employed; on the other hand, we have more extensive observational and file data.

Chapter 11 | THE POLITICS OF CRIMINAL JUSTICE

Felony disposition as we have described it is essentially a political process. It explicitly redistributes such highly valued possessions as liberty, reputation, and property. Our data describe what happened to almost 4,500 men and women forcibly taken into custody and subjected to the possibility of extended incarceration. The intrusion of government into the affairs of these people is dramatically played out daily in the courtrooms, lockups, and hallways we frequented. As we revealed in the preceding chapter, even those not convicted are affected by their involvement in the process and often profoundly so. Government's application of officially sanctioned force is nowhere illustrated so vividly and frequently as in the felony disposition process.

Until recently political scientists shunned studying trial courts.[1] In part, this neglect stemmed from a tradition in which only the Supreme Court, among the many components of the legal process, seemed an appropriate object for study. It also resulted from a belief that partisan politics, the electoral process, and policymaking in general did not affect trial courts' operations.

Our analysis suggests that these perceptions are wrong. Local political structures and practices shape courtroom workgroups and especially sponsoring organizations in several ways. The dominant characteristics of the felony disposition process in the three cities reflect fundamental differences in political structures and traditions.[2]

The redistribution of liberty, property, and reputation effected by the criminal courts does not fall evenly across the population. In these three cities, as in most large American cities, defendants in the criminal courts were mostly black, poor, young and male. That tells us much about American politics. The behaviors most severely punished by governmental power are those in which persons on the fringes of American society most readily engage. Black and poor young males have the greatest economic incentive to engage in property crimes, because they are often frozen out of the lawful labor market. Moreover, crimes of violence most readily erupt among the poor, where crowded living conditions and poor health exacerbate the tensions produced by poverty, relative deprivation, and real or imagined discrimination. It is an inescapable fact of American life that crime as defined by law and by police practices occurs mostly among the young poor and that blacks comprise a disproportionate share of the urban poor. Crimes (especially white-collar crimes) committed by other segments of the population attract less public attention, less scrutiny from the police, and less vigorous prosecution.

The felony disposition process mirrors the distribution of political power in American society in another way. Although most defendants in urban felony courts are black and lower- or working-class, most of the people processing their cases are white and middle-class. It is tempting to assume that if most judges, prosecutors, defense attorneys, and other personnel were black, outputs would change significantly. We do not believe this would happen. The black community fears crimes just as the white community does. Having blacks staff the courtrooms would not close the status and class gap between defendants and court officials. But it might reduce the anger and suspicion that many defendants feel about the process.

To a greater extent than many like to admit, political power

290 STAGES OF THE FELONY DISPOSITION PROCESS

and economic rewards are unevenly distributed among different elements of the American population. Although those who commit crime do so to some unknown extent in response to individual personality pathologies, they are also responding to social conditions which the exercise of political power reinforces. The felony disposition process plays an essential role in this drama.

OUTCOMES FOR DEFENDANTS:
AN OVERVIEW

The decisions of felony courts affect defendants profoundly. In the preceding three chapters we dissected the felony disposition process in order to show the contributions of different courtroom workgroups to the ultimate outcome. How one views the final outcome depends on where one stands.

Politicians, police, prosecutors, court officials, and the media typically report on what happens to defendants from the perspective of the trial court. Table 11.1 summarizes outcomes for defendants who survived the preliminary hearing stage and appeared in a trial courtroom. The proportion of defendants convicted in the trial courts of the three cities scarcely varies. More substantial differences emerge from other measures, however. Chicago appears to be the harshest city, sentencing almost all convicted trial-level defendants to prison; by contrast, Detroit sent only about one-third to prison. The data on sentence length reported in Chapter 10 support the finding that Detroit sentenced its defendants less severely, but Baltimore gave longer prison terms than Chicago. Different techniques produced these results in the three cities. Baltimore courtroom workgroups accepted guilty pleas in only one-third of their cases, disposing an equal number by bench trials. Chicago and Detroit both relied on guilty pleas in over 60 percent of trial-level defendants' cases. For the remaining cases, however, Chicago primarily used bench trials, and Detroit, dismissals. Finally, the time consumed between arrest and disposition in the trial courts varied between seven and a half and nine months for the median defendant in Baltimore and Chicago. Detroit cases took little more than two months.

Quite different outcome patterns emerge when we take pre-

TABLE 11.1   CASE OUTCOMES FOR DEFENDANTS
WHO REACHED TRIAL COURT

	Baltimore	Chicago	Detroit
Percentage of trial defendants who were convicted[a]	68.0	75.5	72.2
Percentage of defendants convicted who were sentenced to prison[b]	63.1	87.6	34.8
Method of disposition at trial[c]			
guilty plea	34.7	61.7	63.9
bench trial	33.9	19.9	6.8
jury trial	9.4	6.7	7.3
dismissed	22.0	11.7	22.0
Median number of days from arrest to final disposition for trial-defendants[c]	226	267.5	71.2

a. See Table 9.1.

b. The figures for Baltimore and Detroit, taken from Table 10.3, slightly overstate the proportion of trial-level defendants sentenced to prison, since they include a few defendants convicted at the preliminary exam and sentenced to jail. Unlike the figure reported in Table 10.3 for Chicago, the figure reported here applied only to defendants indicted and subsequently convicted at the trial court level.

c. See Table 9.1.

liminary hearing results into account, as we do in Table 11.2. We find that Detroit convicted more than half of its felony defendants; Baltimore convicted substantially less than half; and Chicago convicted only a quarter. However, the range of convicted defendants sent to prison did not vary greatly. The reason for these differences — when we take preliminary hearing results into account — is shown in the last line of Table 11.2. Chicago had a low overall conviction rate because its preliminary hearing workgroups screened out most cases, as we showed in Chapter 8.

TABLE 11.2 CASE OUTCOMES FOR ALL FELONY
DEFENDANTS REGARDLESS OF STAGE AT WHICH
THE CASE WAS DISPOSED

	Baltimore	Chicago	Detroit
Percentage of defendants convicted	43.7	25.6	57.5[a]
Percentage of defendants sentenced to jail or prison	27.6	15.0	20.0[a]
Percentage of defendants screened before reaching the trial stage	37.4	87.3	56.0

a. The figures for Detroit were calculated by estimating the number of defendants screened by the prosecutor's warrant section either by outright refusal to prosecute or authorization of misdemeanor charges when a felony was possible. Conservative estimates were used. If anything, the conviction rate is lower than 57.5%. The proportion imprisoned includes an estimate of potential felony defendants charged in misdemeanor court, convicted, and given a jail sentence.

Only 12.7 percent of all defendants were sent forward to trial; preliminary hearing workgroups convicted a few and took some guilty pleas; the rest were dismissed. Baltimore preliminary hearing workgroups convicted more and dismissed fewer. Finally, in Detroit most defendants went to a trial court if they got as far as the preliminary exam, but substantial screening occurred before that stage through the work of the prosecutor's warrant office.

Different proportions of convicted defendants were sent to prison from preliminary hearing courtrooms and trial courtrooms. In Chicago, for instance, only two-fifths of those convicted in the preliminary hearing courtrooms received prison sentences, whereas seven-eighths of those convicted in the trial courtroom went to prison. When we combine conviction rates with imprisonment rates, we obtain an overall rate of 15 percent. Thus, in terms of the proportion of all felony defendants sent to prison, Baltimore was harshest and Chicago was the most lenient. These contrasts are highlighted by Figure 11.1.

FIGURE 11.1 Comparison of Trial Court Dispositions with Disposition of All Felony Defendants.

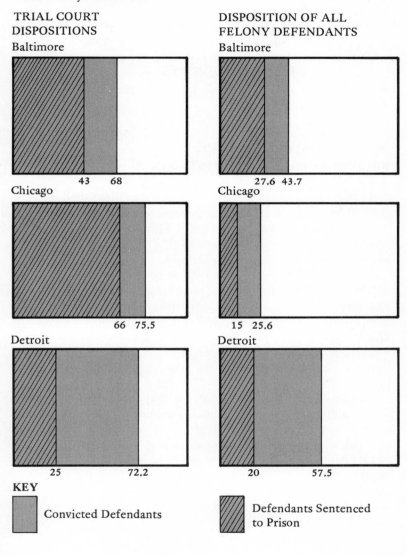

TRIAL COURT
DISPOSITIONS

Baltimore

43   68

Chicago

66   75.5

Detroit

25   72.2

DISPOSITION OF ALL
FELONY DEFENDANTS

Baltimore

27.6 43.7

Chicago

15   25.6

Detroit

20   57.5

KEY

Convicted Defendants

Defendants Sentenced
to Prison

The length of time courtrooms consumed in disposing cases also varied substantially from one city to another as we have shown. Detroit was the swiftest, disposing half its preliminary examinations 9 days after an arrest; by contrast Baltimore took 40 days and Chicago 109 for the median case. Trial courtrooms in Detroit were also the most speedy of the three, whereas Chicago's lagged. Thus although Chicago eventually convicted the fewest defendants, it held defendants in jeopardy for the longest time.

TOWARD UNDERSTANDING
FELONY DISPOSITION PROCESSES

How can we account for the outcomes just described in each city? Why do such striking differences emerge when we compare outcomes between cities? We believe that our focus on courtroom workgroups and sponsoring organizations provides many of the answers to these questions.

Outcomes of the felony disposition process are not the result of singular efforts by judges, prosecutors, or defense counsel. Outcomes result from interactions among these courtroom members and others. They not only interact with one another but also become dependent on one another. They work in a context established by the police, legislatures, appellate courts, correction agencies, the media, and the general political process of the city.

The interdependence of major participants is closely related to the notion of process. The tasks performed by courtroom workgroups require the participation of all members. The policies and behavior of the judges' organization, prosecutor's office, the public defender's office, and the private bar inevitably affect one another. It is important to note, however, that the degree of interdependence and its precise form vary from jurisdiction to jurisdiction, over time in each jurisdiction, and even from courtroom to courtroom.

The interdependence among judges, prosecutors, defense attorneys, defendants, clerks, bailiffs, the police, witnesses, victims, and the press produces intricate patterns of interaction. But this interdependence is only one of several important sources of complexity. The sequence of steps and procedures used to process individual cases is complicated in itself. Workgroups can choose among several disposition techniques at each stage of the process. Furthermore, decisions made at one stage affect subsequent stages. Considerable variation in the characteristics of individual cases also contributes to complexity. Cases differ according to the personal characteristics of the defendant (age, sex, race, prior record, wealth), the status of the defense attorney, the strength of the evidence (including the quality of witnesses and the complaining witness' personal status and credibility), whether the defendant is in jail or on bail, and workgroup members' personal characteristics (legal skills, values, and motivation).

The complexity generated by the simultaneous interaction of all of these variables helps to account for another characteristic of felony disposition processes — its uncertainty. This complexity overwhelms those who try to predict outcomes precisely. Cases differ in uncertainty and participants vary in their tolerance of it. The nature of uncertainties affects the methods workgroups use to handle a case. Furthermore, institutional arrangements and procedures shape both the amount of uncertainty and time at which it is resolved. Members of stable workgroups who are familiar with each other have less doubt about each other's behavior and intentions, and thus can cooperate in disposing cases without resorting to adversarial techniques. Procedures for sending cases to courtrooms and assigning both prosecutors and defense attorneys to defendants determine when uncertainty about the courtroom workgroups' composition will be eliminated.

The task of understanding felony disposition is further complicated by the fact that the process changes continually. In Detroit, the court shifted from a central docket case assignment system to a strict random draw just before we started our observations. This change virtually eliminated opportunities for judge-shopping and ended the practice of taking most guilty pleas to just two of the judges. At about the same time, the prosecutor's office was forced to shift from a trial team form of organization to a zone assignment system, because of a hiring freeze. Immediately after our field research concluded, the number of regular judges increased from thirteen to twenty, and the visiting judge program ended. In Chicago, the states attorney's office implemented a prosecutor screening program to examine cases at the station house during our research. In the midst of our observations, Cook County's voters rejected the incumbent state's attorney's reelection bid, precipitating a large-scale exodus of experienced personnel and several important changes in office policy. In Baltimore, the prosecutor's office tried to implement screening procedures analogous to Detroit's during our research. Recent changes in juror selection raised black representation on juries and increased the attractiveness of jury trials. Procedures for assigning district judges also changed; assignments were made for six months rather than one, thereby significantly increasing the probability of stable preliminary hearing organizations. Finally, just after our study, the incumbent black state's attorney lost his reelection bid after being denied renomination. Many of his administrative personnel, including those who sought to transplant many of Detroit's organizational features, left the office soon afterward.

Such change is normal. Social processes are always moving from past behavior and toward some future state. Every analysis, including ours, captures only a brief segment of that change. It is difficult to include such transitions in the analysis, but we must recognize their presence and their contribution to the complexity that marks the felony disposition process.

Two special features of felony disposition processes impede attempts to understand them. First, researchers often find it impossible to locate even the most basic statistics about a court system's output. In a nation known for the abundance and accuracy of its statistics, it is ironic that official records kept in felony disposition processes provide little or no help in unraveling and understanding their complexity. We have described the problems of court statistics and records elsewhere.[3] Here we need only note that courts frequently report outcomes for cases or charges rather than defendants, and that the accuracy of both court and prosecutor reports is all too often questionable. Thus would-be researchers must gather for themselves information that ought to be made available by public agencies. The time and energy this task requires compounds the difficulties of unraveling complexity. Second, it is extremely difficult to find informants who have an accurate picture of felony disposition processes. We repeatedly found confidently rendered description, by informants whom we felt ought to know how things were done, deficient in important respects. In retrospect, this finding should not have surprised us. The processes are complex and constantly changing. Most informants viewed the system's operation from only one perspective. Few internal reports existed to give informants the larger picture. The classic question "Does *anybody* know what's going on?" must be answered No.

Finally, those who wish to understand felony disposition processes must recognize the importance of organizations. Defendants are first apprehended by a bureaucratic agency, the police. They are then processed, we have shown, by courtroom workgroups, which are nonbureaucratic entities but organizations nevertheless. Although we have emphasized workgroup differences in each of the three cities, their common organizational structure is essential for understanding the felony disposition process. All the courtroom organizations seek to control uncertainty; they all claim to be pursuing the goals of justice and efficient disposition of cases. Each is influenced by the techniques at its disposal and each depends on sponsoring organizations. Each responds to a task environment that includes the police, prisons, appellate courts, local legislative bodies, and the media.

By examining the characteristics of courtroom workgroups and sponsoring organizations, we can understand much of what happens in felony disposition. The frequency of interaction among members affects the mutual dependence and mutual knowledge of behavior and intentions among participants. The strength of courtroom workgroups, relative to that of sponsoring organizations and competing organizations such as Detroit's pretrial conference, affects their operation. The relative importance of courtroom workgroups' goals also helps in understanding their behavior.

The need to evaluate sponsoring organizations' effect on courtroom workgroup members justifies adopting an organizational approach to the sponsoring bodies themselves. Thus, we find it useful to examine recruitment procedures, career patterns, internal organization, and the task environment of each organization that sponsored courtroom participants.

An approach that emphasizes organizations naturally leads to another useful analytical concept — incentive structures. Workgroup members respond to the incentives they encounter. These incentives have several sources: personal values and ambitions, sponsoring organizations, and courtroom workgroups themselves. We have described these incentives for judges, prosecutors, and defense attorneys in detail. Here we merely say that models that do not emphasize incentives are likely to produce misleading explanations. The duties of defense attorneys as enunciated in canons of ethics, appellate decisions, and statutes are not irrelevant. But the desire to earn a decent living is probably more important in explaining retained attorneys' actions.[4] Thus, reform proposals that do not both acknowledge the effect of incentives and seek to alter them are likely to fail.

Several of the variables traditionally used to explain outcomes (defendant characteristics, the charges, evidence strength, the method of disposition) affect some outcomes. When combined, they account for much of the variance of such outcomes as length of prison sentence. Often, however, they explain only between 10 and 20 percent of the variance in our measures of case outcomes. They improve our ability to classify defendants according to outcomes by between 30 and 50 percent.

These variables leave much unexplained. By placing their operation in an organizational context, we can enhance our understanding of felony disposition processes substantially. Such variables as defendant characteristics, evidence strength, and nature of the charges affect case outcomes in an organizational context. Judges, prosecutors, and defense attorneys do not view initial charges, for instance, as an ordinary citizen would. Rather, they perceive them as workgroup members; the way in which charges affect behavior depends on the nature of the workgroup that handles the case.

The organizational approach also clarifies the effect of a traditional variable — the identity of the judge. We have argued that differences between courtrooms cannot be attributed solely to differences among judges. Outputs in courtrooms result from the decisions of entire workgroups. Judges' contributions to these outcomes depend on a number of variables, including the workgroup's structure and goals.

We can also explain the operation of felony courts better by using concepts drawn from our organizational approach. Examining the stability of workgroups and sponsoring organizations allows us to clarify the choice among guilty plea, bench trial, and jury trial; traditional variables proved completely powerless to explain that choice. Prior explanations relied on the tradition in a city to account for heavy use of pleas or trials.[5] Likewise, when adversarial norms are weak and workgroup members negotiate with each other on the basis of mutual dependence and accommodation, the strength of evidence is unlikely to affect outcomes. Judges' attitudes and values are more likely to produce disparate outcomes when sponsoring organizations are weak, workgroups are unstable, familiarity among workgroup members is low, and differences in judges' backgrounds and attitudes are pronounced.

Finally, we can use organizational variables to help us understand differences in outcomes among cities. As noted earlier, few differences emerged when we compared charges, defendant characteristics, and nature of the evidence across the three cities. The origins of the significant differences in outcomes described in our study become evident only when we look at workgroups, sponsoring organizations, and environmental contexts.

EVALUATING FELONY DISPOSITION PROCESSES

Our approach provides no special formula for evaluating the performance of the felony courts in the three cities. Normative judgments about the fairness and justice of these courts rest on personal values that have little to do with the approach adopted. However, we believe we can describe, understand, and explain felony disposition processes fairly well. Given a set of personal preferences, we can ground value judgments on accurate conceptions of what really happens.

Are defendants treated fairly or justly by the processes we studied? No consensus exists on the meaning of fairness and justice.[6] But we believe that at least one important component of most people's conceptions of these terms is equality of treatment. Were defendants treated alike? Were the courtroom workgroups in these three cities blind to defendant's wealth, age, race, and other personal characteristics? Our study contains information on two aspects of the question of equal treatment: equality of treatment among cities; and equality of treatment within each city.

We found significant differences among the three cities on several important dimensions. In chapters 4, 5, and 6 we described sharp differences in the procedures used to process defendants. In chapters 8, 9, and 10 we documented the significant discrepancies in case outcomes. It is unlikely that these different outcomes are spurious, or that they resulted from differences in the characteristics of defendants, the evidence gathered against them, or the kinds of crimes they commit. Rather, differences in procedures and case outcomes result from the combined effects of structures and rules mandated by state law, local political and cultural values, the structure and policies of sponsoring organizations, and the characteristics of courtroom workgroups.

Consequently, defendants arrested for identical acts in different cities received different treatment. They were most likely to face conviction in Detroit, but when convicted in Baltimore faced the longest prison sentences. By contrast, they were least likely to be convicted in Chicago, and when convicted, their prison sentences were substantially shorter than those in Baltimore though longer than those in Detroit. Moreover, many defendants whose cases would have been dismissed in Chicago or Detroit because complaining witnesses failed to prosecute, the evidence seemed insufficient, or the incident seemed insufficiently important were convicted in Baltimore. Baltimore had the coarsest screen; few of its cases were dismissed in either the preliminary hearing or trial courtrooms.

Punishment meted out to unconvicted defendants also differed significantly from city to city. Baltimore imposed the highest bail costs, whereas Chicago kept defendants in jeopardy the longest while cases lingered on courtroom dockets.

Since our society delegates most law enforcement to the states, such discrepancies cannot be automatically labelled as gross injustices. Society may be willing to permit local values and procedures to produce widely divergent outcomes. However, those who argue that the United States has a single, unified social system and who prefer uniform responses to crime clearly cannot conclude that equal justice exists. Students of American criminal justice cannot ignore such striking differences, regardless of which view they adopt.

Less ambiguity clouds the argument that within a given city, defendants should be given equal treatment. Although we found some differences in defendants' treatment, the differences were less pronounced than prior research and popular belief led us to expect. There were too few women defendants to make statistically meaningful comparisons with men. But black defendants fared no worse than white defendants. The fact that some poorer defendants could not make bail and had to spend time in pretrial detention led to some discrepancies in treatment. Baltimore's poorer defendants more often felt this discrimination because of that city's higher bail levels, and because they waited longer before their case ended. However, some defendants in Detroit and Chicago spent time in pretrial detention only because they could not afford to pay the costs of bail. The very poor defendant's inability to make bail was the most significant instance of unequal treatment.

At the same time, we did not find massive discrimination against the very poor (keeping in mind that nearly all defendants we studied were either poor or near-poor) in aspects of case outcome other than pretrial detention. Baltimore trial courts did convict jailed defendants more often than bailed defendants, but no substantial relationship between trial-level conviction and bail status emerged in either of the other cities. Furthermore, on the reasonable assumption that Baltimore preliminary hearing defendants represented by public defenders can be classified as poor, they enjoyed a distinct advantage over other defendants. As reported in Chapter 8, only 28 percent of public defenders' clients passed on to the trial court, whereas private attorneys' clients were indicted 70 percent of the time. The time between arrest and disposition reflected these differences. Half the people represented by public defenders at the preliminary hearing in Baltimore waited less than 24 days for disposition compared to 186 days for all other defendants. In Chicago, bail status made no important difference in any outcome. In Detroit, bail status helped discriminate between those convicted defendants given probation and those imprisoned; jailed defendants were more often sent to prison. However, it did not affect dismissals, conviction, or the length of prison term.

We have already commented that most defendants were poor and black. It is also true, of course, that many victims of these offenders were poor and black. The predominance of black people as defendants and victims reflects the underlying reality of American politics. In evaluating the felony disposition process, we might ask whether it exacerbates these underlying inequalities, merely reflects them, or ameliorates them. The data suggest two observations. First, there appears to be almost no discrimination between those blacks and whites who become enmeshed in the felony process in these three cities. Second, although arrest affects defendants profoundly and results in at least pretrial punishment, it does not inevitably lead to conviction. Many defendants went free without being convicted. The failure to convict might be interpreted as an indication of leniency and fairness. But it can also be taken as a measure of discrimination on the part of arresting authorities or incompetence on the part of prosecutors. Felony disposition processes must dispose of all cases brought by the police, and cannot be held fully responsible for discrimination resulting from police practices. On the other hand, police behavior is not entirely unaffected by what happens to defendants and we cannot fully absolve the felony disposition process from responsibility for police conduct.

Regardless of which perspective is adopted, however, the felony disposition process at worst merely reflects injustice and inequality based on race and wealth. It does not, with the significant exception of bail, exacerbate inequality. It may even ameliorate it by refusing to convict many who are arrested and charged.

An analysis of justice should also consider how often courts convict innocent defendants. It is, however, impossible to answer that question precisely. The distinction made in Chapter 10 between factual and legal guilt provides a useful approach to this question. Legal guilt is more often in doubt. Although most defendants may have committed illegal acts, their conviction depends on the prosecutor's ability to prove it beyond a reasonable doubt while abiding by the procedural strictures of the law. Defense attorneys in all three cities mentioned the problem of police perjury in discussing this question. Police witnesses soon learn what to say to ensure conviction when it depends on their testimony. They also have incentives to see convictions. The real question (which no one can answer satisfactorily) is how often the police lie in court and how often that lie results in the conviction of truly innocent persons.

Do defendants get their rights? The answer depends heavily on what the questioner means. Defendants routinely waive many of their rights, including the rights to a jury trial, to confront witnesses, and to avoid self-incrimination. Whether they do so "knowingly" is difficult to judge. Their right to effective representation by counsel is also hard to evaluate. The mere fact that defendants enter guilty pleas rather than going to trial provides little reliable information about the effectiveness of representation. On the contrary, we believe Baltimore's tendency to convict its unscreened defendants at bench trials at about the same rate as the other cities convicted screened defendants provides evidence of ineffective representation. The easy assumption that defendants who go to a bench or jury trial receive effective representation is simply incorrect. Detroit, with its institutionalized plea bargaining and high guilty plea rate, had a vigorous adversarial defense bar, which often challenged the prosecution's case before obtaining a dismissal or entering a plea. Even dismissal rates do not always indicate vigorous representation. Chicago preliminary hearing courts dismissed charges against most defendants, but not because their attorneys fought brilliant legal battles. Most cases just petered out, and the court dismissed charges for lack of prosecution without the defendant being represented at all. Many defendants who did have attorneys at the preliminary hearing hired the regulars with unsavory reputations and minimal legal skills, who earned a living at the sufferance of clerks, bailiffs, and judges. Ironically, Chicago defendants received more effective representation at the trial level, where the dismissal rate was low and the guilty plea rate about equal to Detroit's. At the trial court the defense attorneys frequently used their status as workgroup members to win acceptable sentences for clients who pleaded guilty.

Finally, we can identify some of the complex interactions between competing interests and values imbedded in questions of fairness and justice. The lapse of time between arrest and disposition provides good support for the proposition that there are no easy answers. Conventional wisdom holds that the faster cases are disposed, the better, for "justice delayed is justice denied." Fast dispositions are "efficient," and efficiency is all too often accepted uncritically. Fast dispositions presumably protect society by punishing wrongdoers quickly and promptly releasing the innocent. Although there is some validity to these arguments, proponents of faster dispositions typically ignore other considerations. Prosecutors find it takes several weeks for many cases to jell. They regard quick dispositions as detrimental in serious cases. Retained defense attorneys typically struggle to collect their fee. They would hardly find swift dispositions desirable, and would not represent their clients without the fee. Moreover, delays may permit social "healing" and allow victims to cool off, be compensated, or be reconciled with the offender. The bail status of defendants also profoundly affects their calculations on disposition time. Jailed defendants typically face a dilemma. After several months, as their stay in jail continues, the prosecution's case decays. But the costs of staying in jail are very high. Whether staying in jail is preferable to pleading guilty depends on how much the chances of conviction decline and on what the punishment on conviction is likely to be. Clearly there are no easy answers to the question of whether justice delayed is really justice denied.

Other questions produce equally complex answers. Defendants were better off in Detroit and Chicago than in Baltimore. But it is not clear that the general public was better off in Baltimore because defendants were treated more harshly. The relationship between law enforcement patterns and crime is much clearer in the minds of partisans than empirical research has been able to demonstrate. Likewise, the effects of strict adherence to the adversarial ideal are not easily unraveled. Opponents of plea bargaining assume that all they need to do is demonstrate that it is detrimental to the adversary ideal and to defendants' rights to justify its abolition. But a sound judgment on the desirability of plea bargaining cannot ignore the effect its abolition would have on other interests and values. As noted, from the defendant's perspective plea bargaining may permit effective representation. Our evidence indicates that outcomes were not much different whether a person was convicted by plea or by trial. The benefits of reducing the number of pleas are therefore those that accrue from preventing the conviction of the innocent (although that may happen with trials too) and from the procedural rights that may exist at trial. On the other hand, since most defendants are poor, someone would have to pay for adversarial dispositions. Attorneys could be asked to assume substantial reductions in compensation, but many would refuse and leave criminal practice if the cuts were large, as they would probably have to be. Alternatively, taxes could be raised, but would the added expense be worth it to the general public? The answer is by no means clear. If the answer is no, we have to calculate the social costs connected with the reduction in the number of defendants who could be handled by the felony disposition process. Without a substantial increase in resources, more rigorous screening of cases would be required. Which defendants now convicted would be dismissed or convicted of a minor offense in misdemeanor courts? Would the inevitably allocative decisions of pruning be fair? What about the victims of crimes whose cases could no longer be accommodated?

THE QUESTION OF REFORM

Reform of the felony disposition process has been thrust to center stage by the emergence of crime and its treatment as one of the most visible and salient issues in American politics. A whole new bureaucracy — the Law Enforcement Assistance Administration — has been charged with developing reform programs and funding them. Its lifeblood has been federal money. The LEAA has played a key role in stimulating the growth of equivalent bureaucracies in the states and in setting priorities for the expenditure of these funds.

Several unchallenged assumptions underlie the elevation of

crime as a major political issue. Critics assume that something must be done. They also assume that something *can* be done to produce more desirable outcomes. Finally, and perhaps most basically, they believe that the criminal courts have *failed* to do what they could do.

Have the courts failed? The question cannot be answered unless we specify *what* they have failed to do. The widespread agreement on failure breaks down when this question is asked. Some critics argue that they fail to protect society and reduce crime. But this argument assumes that crime rates can be affected by outcomes of criminal cases. Many believe this is an unrealistic expectation. Others criticize the courts for failing to ameliorate the injustice and inequalities in our society with respect to the status of the poor and racial minorities. Again, we might ask whether it is realistic to expect the criminal courts to effect changes in the basic structure of society.

Critics of criminal justice who are sympathetic to the plight of defendants worry that the felony disposition process exacerbates the disadvantages faced by the poor and minorities in our society. As we suggested in the previous section, this sometimes occurs, particularly when jailed defendants are convicted more often as in Baltimore or imprisoned more often as in Detroit. But complete condemnation of the workgroups we studied is unjustified. They did not systematically disregard defendants' rights. Many defendants, including the poor and black, received effective representation. The courts did not convict large numbers of innocent defendants as far as we could tell. Substantial numbers of dangerous offenders received severe punishment, but some won acquittals because legal rules and rights operated effectively.

Other problems and faults emerged from our study. We believe the punishment of the unconvicted is morally inexcusable, even though it may be costly to avoid and pragmatically justifiable as punishment of factually guilty persons. The unequal treatment of defendants in different cities also offends our sense of equal justice. The frequency of apparently perjured testimony by the police troubles us. In an ideal world one might wish to see better lawyers dedicate themselves more fully to the tasks of prosecuting, defending, and judging.

These faults, significant as they are, do not lead us to condemn the felony disposition processes we studied. We approach the question of reform cautiously. It is neither realistic nor wise to advocate changing everything. We favor an approach that is pragmatic without being unprincipled. There is little point in analyzing reforms that have no chance of being implemented.[7] We might just as well recommend that everybody be law-abiding, thereby eliminating all crime and the necessity for a felony disposition process. At the same time, we recognize the dangers of being too pragmatic. It is easy to identify a sequence of obstacles to any reform proposal's implementation. To do so can readily lead one to discount the possibility of achieving any change. The result, however inadvertent, is support for the values and interests that dominate the status quo. Consequently, in considering reforms, we believe one must ask, Reform of what? To what end? And at what cost?

We are certain that we do not want to reduce crime regardless of the cost, or convict more defendants regardless of the techniques used. The strong negative reactions to methods used by the CIA, the FBI, and the Nixon administration show that the goal of reducing crime and convicting criminals must be balanced against competing goals that reflect other deeply held values, such as the supremacy of law, due process, limited government, and individual privacy. Any reform in the criminal justice system will favor some values and interests at the expense of others. There is no reform of the felony disposition process that will hurt no one; nor will any be favored by everyone.

Would-be reformers have not sufficiently understood the complexity of the felony disposition process. Well-intentioned tampering with an obvious defect nearly always produces far-reaching and often unanticipated changes. Reformers have not analyzed the effects of specific short-term changes on the criminal justice system's other components. It took a long time, for example, to realize that the massive infusion of resources into local law enforcement would create imbalances if additional support were not given to prosecution and defense and court personnel. Reforms that do not include attempts to predict and evaluate the consequences of change on other aspects of the system often surprise the reformers and produce adverse, counterproductive outcomes.

By the same token, complexity results in flexibility and adaptiveness among the courtroom organizations. As long as the incentives of courtroom organization members do not fundamentally change, those members will adapt their behaviors and absorb piecemeal efforts at reform. Thus, change must be far-reaching and coordinated.

Moreover, efforts to impose nationwide changes will fail. Our research indicates that differences among jurisdictions are so far-reaching that superficial introduction of similar procedures everywhere would produce very different results in different locations.

Reform will take a long time. Some characteristics of felony disposition processes are unlikely to change at all or to change only very slowly. Workgroups will continue to consist of a judge, a prosecutor, and a defense attorney. The procedures used — representation of defendants by counsel, notification of charges, bail, the need to establish probable cause at some point, the right to confront witnesses and cross-examine them, and the right to trial — reflect and embody a consensus that is unlikely to disappear. Public attitudes toward what behavior is criminal and what ought to be done about it are also likely to remain fairly stable.

Other things that affect the felony disposition process may change, but this change will not be subject to manipulation by would-be reformers. Patterns of crime help determine the felony work load, but it is not likely that the underlying social and economic causes of crime can be much affected by criminal justice reforms. Nor will reformers be able to change police practices or priorities significantly by themselves. Changes in the balance of political power among competing groups and interests in metropolitan areas will inevitably affect the operation of felony disposition processes, from the composition and predisposition of the personnel within it to the actual content of these decisions.

There remains a limited but nonetheless significant range of reforms that could be implemented. The approach we have taken throughout this book suggests their content. Reform proposals must at a minimum be evaluated in terms of their effect on courtroom workgroups, since they are primarily responsible for what happens. Proposals directly affecting courtroom workgroups have the best chance of success. If behavior is to be altered, the incentives and the distribution of influence in the courtroom must be altered.

There are several ways of doing this. The behavior of courtroom workgroup members is shaped by the stability of the organization and the knowledge they acquire of each others' values and probable behavior. Stability can be radically altered by tinkering with the techniques for assigning defendants to courtrooms, defense attorneys to defendants, and prosecutors to specific cases. Any action that increases the probability of the same set of participants disposing different cases increases stability and promotes nonadversarial dispositions. Any change that reduces uncertainty about which courtroom workgroup will ultimately dispose a case has the same effect. All of the following changes would enhance stability and promote plea bargains:

1. A central case assignment procedure that early in the proceedings designated the judge who had to dispose the case.
2. The longer assignment of judges hearing criminal cases.
3. Establishment of career positions in both public defenders' and prosecuting attorneys' offices.
4. Assignment of defenders and assistant prosecutors to a given courtroom for an extended period, with responsibility for all cases sent there by the central assignment procedure.
5. Assignment of as many cases as possible either to public defenders or to a small set of assigned counsel who specialize in trying cases within the courthouse.

Changes that had the opposite effect — increasing uncertainty and reducing the familiarity of major participants with one another — would create more transitory courtroom workgroups, which would rely on bench and jury trials. Such reforms would be far more likely to decrease plea bargaining than the naive blandishments profferred by the National Commission on Criminal Justice Standards and Goals.

Reform initiated by changing the nature of sponsoring organizations is also promising. The three cities used very different techniques to provide indigent defendants with counsel. The types of attorneys recruited, the number of cases they handle, and the method of paying them all varied, and these differences affected behavior directly. Detroit demonstrates the effects of encouraging the development of career assistant prosecutors by paying competitive salaries and protecting jobs when the prosecuting attorney changes.

Reform could also reduce disposition time. Any change that eases the private attorney's task of collecting his fee or enhances the incentive of assigned counsel to move cases will also shorten disposition time. Tying bail deposits to attorneys' fees and paying assigned counsel nearly the same amount for a quick disposition as for one that takes considerable time would also speed dispositions. Of course, such changes alone will not necessarily affect disposition in the intended direction. Their effects are indeterminate unless they are assessed in conjunction with the rest of the system's operating characteristics.

The task facing reformers remains formidable. Before plunging ahead, we would prefer to learn more about the manner in which courtroom workgroups operate under wider sets of circumstances than captured in our three cities. We need direct tests of the organizational hypotheses suggested by this study. We believe we have made a small beginning, but much remains to be learned.

NOTES

1. For exceptions see David W. Neubauer, *Criminal Justice in Middle America* (Morristown, N.J.: General Learning Press, 1974); George Cole (ed.), *Criminal Justice* (North Scituate, Mass.: Duxbury Press, 1972); Paul D. Wice, *Freedom for Sale: A National Study of Pre-trial Release* (Lexington, Mass.: Lexington Books, 1974); Jonathan D. Casper, *American Criminal Justice: The Defendant's Perspective* (Englewood Cliffs, N.J.: Prentice-Hall, 1972).

2. Cf. Martin A. Levin, "Urban Political Systems and Judicial Behavior: The Criminal Courts of Minneapolis and Pittsburgh," unpublished Ph.D. dissertation, Harvard University, January 1970; and Herbert Jacob, *Urban Justice* (Englewood Cliffs, N.J.: Prentice-Hall, 1973).

3. James Eisenstein and Herbert Jacob, "Measuring Outputs of Urban Criminal Courts," *Social Science Quarterly* 54 (1974): 712–724.

4. This argument was made earlier by Abraham Blumberg, *Criminal Justice* (Chicago: Quadrangle Books, 1967), pp. 110–113; and by Albert W.

Alschuler, "The Defense Attorney's Role in Plea Bargaining," *Yale Law Journal* 84 (May 1975): 1180 ff.

5. Donald M. McIntyre and David Lippman, "Prosecutors and Early Disposition of Felony Cases," *American Bar Association Journal* 56 (1970): 1157–1158.

6. Appellate courts, of course, have promulgated elaborate criteria for judging fairness by establishing such procedural safeguards as requiring warrants, mandating warnings to defendants about their rights, providing them legal counsel, demanding written records or proceedings, and the like. These criteria, however, beg the question of whether substantive fairness results, and it is substantive fairness to which we address ourselves.

7. The best example is the recommendation of the National Commission on Criminal Justice Standards and Goals that all plea bargaining be abolished. Note that the commission explicitly allowed prosecutors to continue to make recommendations at sentence! See National Advisory Commission on Criminal Justice Standards and Goals, *Courts* (Washington, D.C.: Government Printing Office, 1973), pp. 46–49.

Index

313